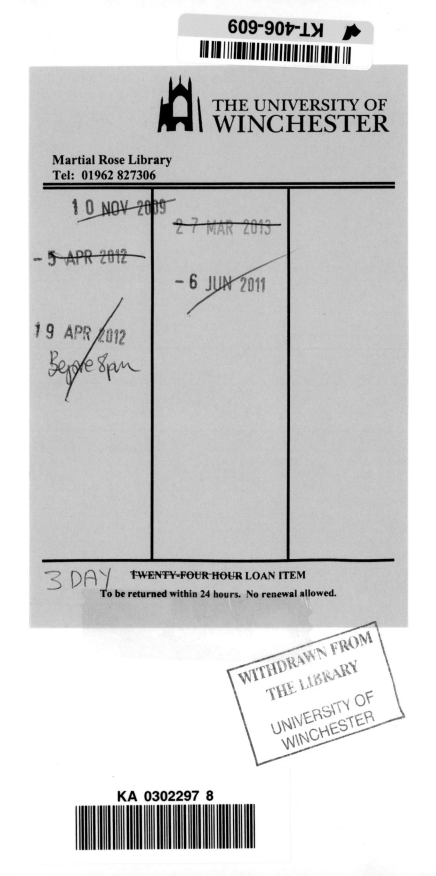

Consumer Culture, Identity and Well-Being

European Monographs in Social Psychology
Sponsored by the European Association of Experimental Psychology

Series Editor:

Professor Rupert Brown, Department of Psychology, University of Kent, Canterbury, Kent CT2 7NP

The aim of this series is to publish and promote the highest quality of writing in European social psychology. The editor and the editorial board encourage publications which approach social psychology from a wide range of theoretical perspectives and whose content may be applied, theoretical or empirical. The authors of books in this series should be affiliated to institutions that are located in countries which would qualify for membership of the Association. All books will be published in English, and translations from other European languages are welcomed. Please submit ideas and proposals for books in the series to Rupert Brown at the above address.

Published

The Quantitative Analysis of Social Representations
Willem Doise, Alain Clemence, and Fabio Lorenzi-Cioldi

A Radical Dissonance Theory
Jean-Léon Beauvois and Robert-Vincent Joule

The Social Psychology of Collective Action
Caroline Kelly and Sara Breinlinger

Social Context and Cognitive Performance
Jean-Marc Monteil and Pascal Huguet

Conflict and Decision-Making in Close Relationships
Erich Kirchler, Christa Rodler, Erik Hölzl, and Katja Meier

Stereotyping as Inductive Hypothesis Testing
Klaus Fiedler and Eva Walther

Intergroup Relations in States of the Former Soviet Union
Louk Hagendoorn, Hub Linssen, and Sergei Tumanov

The Social Psychology of Ethnic Identity
Maykel Verkuyten

Consumer Culture, Identity and Well-Being
Helga Dittmar

Forthcoming Title

The Passionate Intersection of Desire and Knowledge
Gregory Maio

Consumer Culture, Identity and Well-Being

The Search for the "Good Life" and the "Body Perfect"

Helga Dittmar

With contributions from Emma Halliwell, Robin Banerjee, Ragna Garðarsdóttir and Judita Janković

Ψ **Psychology Press**
Taylor & Francis Group
HOVE AND NEW YORK

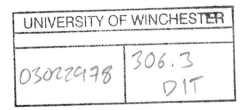
First published 2008 by Psychology Press
27 Church Road, Hove, East Sussex, BN3 2FA

Simultaneously published in the USA and Canada
by Psychology Press
270 Madison Avenue, New York, NY 10016

*Psychology Press is an imprint of the Taylor & Francis Group,
an Informa business*

© 2008 Psychology Press

Typeset in Times by
RefineCatch Limited, Bungay, Suffolk
Printed and bound in Great Britain by
MPG Books Ltd, Bodmin, Cornwall
Cover design by Design Deluxe

British Library Cataloguing in Publication Data
A catalogue record for this book is available from the British Library

Library of Congress Cataloging-in-Publication Data
Dittmar, Helga.
    Consumer culture, identity and well-being : the search for the 'good
life' and the 'body perfect' / Helga Dittmar ; with contributions from
Emma Halliwell . . . [et al.].
    p. cm.
    ISBN 978-1-84169-608-9 (hardcover)
    1. Consumption (Economics)—Psychological aspects.
2. Acquisitiveness.   3. Identity (Psychology).   4. Well-being.
5. Social values.   I. Title.
HC79.C6D58   2007
306.3—dc22   2007003275

ISBN: 978-1-84169-608-9

To the family who are closest to my heart, both young—Ben, Eric, Lars, Marius, Michelle, Molly, Patrick—and young at heart—Margot, Rod, and Steffi

Contents

Author and contributors

Helga Dittmar is Reader in Psychology at the University of Sussex. Her research (funded by ESRC, Department of Health, Office of Fair Trading) examines the impact of consumer society on individuals' identity and well-being. She was the first social psychologist in Europe to study the role of material goods in identity, and has since extended her work to include motives in conventional and online buying, dysfunctional buying behaviours, and media influences on body image and eating behaviours in children, adolescents and adults.

Emma Halliwell is Senior Lecturer in Social Psychology at the University of the West of England, and a member of the Centre for Appearance Research. Her ESRC-funded DPhil research focused on sociocultural influences on body image through the life span (supervised by Helga Dittmar and obtained in 2002), and her current research extends this work, focusing on social determinants of body satisfaction and eating behaviours.

Robin Banerjee is Senior Lecturer in Psychology at the University of Sussex. His research (funded by ESRC, British Academy, Ofsted, and several local educational authorities) addresses links between social behaviour, peer relations, cognition, and emotion in primary school children. He serves on the Advisory Committee for the Department for Education and Skills on the "Social, Emotional, and Behavioural Skills" project.

Ragna B. Garðarsdóttir is a senior researcher at the Social Science Research Institute of the University of Iceland in Reykjavík. In 2006, she obtained her DPhil at the University of Sussex (supervised by Helga Dittmar). Her research examines the relationship between materialistic values and subjective well-being, taking into account motives for making money, and income.

Judita Janković is a researcher working for a United Nations research department in Rome. Her research investigates the role of value conflict in the link between materialism and subjective well-being, specifically with family and community values. She was awarded her DPhil at the University of Sussex in England in 2006 (supervised by Helga Dittmar).

List of illustrations

Each chapter reporting primary research is introduced by an original illustration, drawn specifically for this book. The artist is Jessica Barlow, who was awarded a distinction for her Art Foundation course, completed in 2006 at the prestigious Central Saint Martins College of Art and Design in London. Jessica is now continuing her studies on the BA Graphic Design at the same college.

List of figures

List of tables

Acknowledgements

Like all books, this one would not have been possible without the support, inspiration, and expertise of a great many people. I would like to thank them all warmly, but here I can name only those to whom I am particularly grateful. First and foremost, I want to acknowledge the invaluable input of the contributors to this book—Emma Halliwell, Robin Banerjee, Ragna Garðarsdóttir and Judita Janković—who, each in their own way and to different degrees, have provided inspiration and stimulation, steep learning curves, and steady support. I love Jessica Barlow's imaginative illustrations, whose lively and ironic characters comment on the research reported in the book.

My thanks go to: Nick Anderson for his help with data collection for two studies reported in Chapter 5 and for being a friend; Daniel Hyndman and Tony Stubbens for their assistance with various technical aspects of the research reported; Catherine Aspinall, Susanne Friese, Suzie Ive, Rosie Meek, Mary Phillips, and Emma Stirling for being good research collaborators; Steven Heasman, Sean Scott, Michael Vleek, Lucy Waldeck, and Catherine Young for their help with data collection; Tim Kasser for his support and instructive discussions of materialism; Donna Jessop and Viv Vignoles for being constructive readers of articles and good colleagues.

And here are the people to whom I would like to express my special gratitude.

To Jane Beattie, who I still miss, for her help in getting me started on ESRC-funded research, her companionship, and her intellectual input to my thinking about impulsive and excessive buying behaviour. To April Benson, for the many transatlantic talks and thoughts about compulsive buying, body image, and materialism, and for her support and friendship. To Rod Bond, for being a critical reader of the whole book, a stickler for style, and for being the love of my life. To Rupert Brown, for suggesting that I write this book in the first place, for his enthusiasm and unflagging support as a colleague, and for being a really special person and friend. To Margot Dittmar, without whose staunch support I would have never started higher education, for keeping me in line when needed, and for being a wonderful mother. To Monica Greco, for being a critical reader of various chapters of this book, guiding me past sociological and philosophical pitfalls, and for her support, music, and sharing such a long chunk of my life. To Jim Maddux, for his confidence in me and his continuing support, particularly with respect to my body image research. To Karla Newell, for her ideas and help, which led to the illustrations for the book, and for being a good friend. To Eddi Piper, for her support when I most needed help. To Benjamin Stricker, for his diligent help in checking and compiling the bibliography, and for being the best godson ever. To Neil Stammers, for his political and philosophical challenges over many years, for support and music, and for being an invaluable critical reader of Chapters 1 and 9. To Stanjek (Zdenek) Kavan, for the thoughtful discussions about the framework and conclusions of the book, and for being a good friend. To Barbara Wilz, Michael Gollan, Gloria Muria, and Jutta Schildbach for always believing in me and being staunch friends.

1 Understanding the impact of consumer culture

Helga Dittmar

You only need to look at, and listen to, people around you, particularly children and adolescents, to appreciate that consumer culture has a powerful psychological impact. Celebrities, fashion models, media stars, even computer game heroes and toys, influence who they aspire to be and what they want to look like. Having the "right" things has become vital, not so much because of these material goods themselves but because of hoped for psychological benefits: popularity, identity, happiness. I have found this psychological impact so intriguing that I started to study it over 20 years ago, and have continued ever since. This book summarises my whole research programme.

Given the high visibility of consumer culture's impact on us, it comes as a surprise that, until recently, psychologists have been curiously reticent on this topic. This book therefore aims to help fill this gap, by outlining primary research that documents the consequences for our identity and well-being of the contemporary search for the material "good life" and the "body perfect". This chapter is not only an introduction to this research, it also offers a framework for understanding consumer culture from a social psychological perspective. It provides:

- An outline of the contents of the core research chapters.
- A discussion of the three core constructs: consumer culture, identity, well-being.
- A brief analysis of the material "good life" and "body perfect" as identity ideals that are central to consumer culture.
- A model of the psychological processes through which these ideals come to have a profound influence on our identity and well-being.

It is hard to overestimate the significance of consumer culture. Economic, socio-cultural, and psychological transformations, which have accelerated since the 1950s, have produced mass consumer societies characterised by mushrooming credit facilities, overwhelming consumer choice, and a central role for consumption in everyday life. Although Baudrillard's (1998) characterisation of contemporary life as "perpetual shopping" may still be exaggerated, leisure activities increasingly involve consuming, and shopping itself has become a leisure and lifestyle activity. Indeed, arguably, shopping malls have become centres of both socialising and socialisation (Underhill, 2004). At a deeper level, consumer goods have come to play a stronger psychological role for us: we value and buy them as means of regulating emotions and gaining social status, and as ways of acquiring or expressing identity and aspiring to an "ideal self" (Dittmar, 1992a, 2004a). This notion, that consumers can be thought of as identity-seekers, is central to this book. Research findings are presented which demonstrate that, although material goods can have positive functions for individuals in enhancing or maintaining their sense of who they are, there also is a "dark side" to consumer culture: it can be toxic for the identity and well-being of adults, adolescents, and children.

The link between material goods on the one hand, and identity and well-being on the other, is used a lot in advertising, a core component of consumer culture. Goods are marketed as bridges toward achieving the "body perfect" and the material "good life", as symbols of an "ideal self", with the message that we can—as if by magic—transform ourselves to be more like the glamorous models and celebrities who promote the products. Of course, consumers do not simply take these messages at face value, they are "interpretive agents, rather than passive dupes" (Arnould & Thompson, 2005, p. 875), but it is very hard—if not impossible—to remain untouched by the continuous exposure to the normative socio-cultural ideals portrayed in the mass media as "normal", desirable, and achievable. Idealised models in the mass media not only communicate that beauty and affluence should be central life goals for everybody, they also define what it means to be beautiful, successful, happy, and "cool". The sheer exposure to ads—on TV, radio, the internet, billboards, products, in cinemas, magazines, and shops—is staggering. Estimates suggest that exposure has hit an all-time high in developed consumer societies, such as those in Europe and North America, where individuals see as many as 3000 ads a day (Brower & Leon, 1999; Kalkbrenner, 2004). As we will see in this book, there is growing evidence that mass media exposure is linked in various ways to people internalising consumer culture ideals of beauty and affluence as personal values, no matter how unhealthy and unrealistic those ideals, and the pursuit of them, might be. Thus, there are psychological costs of consumer culture, and—at the extreme—they can manifest as mental and physical health pathologies, such as compulsive buying or extreme body-shaping behaviours. These two quotes capture some of these costs:

> Most of the world's population is now growing up in winner-take-all economies, where the main goal of individuals is to get whatever they can for themselves: to each according to his greed. Within this economic landscape, selfishness and materialism are no longer being seen as moral problems, but as cardinal goals of life. Vast numbers of us have been

seduced into believing that having more wealth and material possessions is essential to the good life. We have swallowed the idea that, to be well, one first has to be well-off. And many of us, consciously or unconsciously, have learned to evaluate our own well-being and accomplishment not by looking inward at our spirit or integrity, but by looking outward at what we have and what we can buy. Similarly, we have adopted a world view in which the worth and success of others is judged not by their apparent wisdom, kindness, or community contributions, but in terms of whether they possess the right clothes, the right car, and more generally, the right "stuff".

(Richard Ryan, foreword to Kasser (2002, pp. ix–x))

[In] our culture, . . . it takes less time for people to judge you for what they see you *have* than it takes for them to stop and ask you what you *do*. Much less than for them to ask you who you *are* . . . The danger, however, is that you yourself come to believe in these material signs of identity. You begin to confuse image (how other people see you) with self-image (how you see yourself). You begin to confuse self-image with self-worth. Ultimately, you may think you are only as good as the car you drive or your newest pair of shoes.

(Catalano & Sonnenberg, 1993, pp. 37–38, emphases in original)

OVERVIEW OF THE CORE RESEARCH CHAPTERS

This book cannot possibly give an exhaustive account of the many ways in which consumer culture impacts on individuals' identity and well-being—this would simply be an impossible undertaking—but what it does offer is a selective, but hopefully rich, review of research findings with two themes. The first is the role of having, buying, and desiring material goods, and the second focuses on how we respond to idealised media images of beauty. For both, the research documents consequences for individuals' identity and well-being, and considers vulnerability factors as well as underlying psychological processes.

Addressing the question "to have is to be?", Chapter 2 gives an overview of the social psychology of material possessions. It outlines different perspectives on the instrumental and symbolic functions of people's favourite possessions, offering an integrative model, but also demonstrates that constructing, expressing, and maintaining a sense of identity is central to why material possessions are so important to us. It reports research on identity-related differences in the functions of possessions, showing that life stage, culture, and gender all influence the relative emphasis people place on different psychological functions of their material possessions.

Owning material possessions is different from buying new consumer goods, but it stands to reason that psychological functions important in having material possessions, such as the desire to express or enhance identity, also play a role in motivating people to buy. Chapter 3 demonstrates that "consuming passions" are important drivers, where people buy goods in attempts to make themselves feel better and move closer to an ideal identity, which can crowd out "rational" concerns with how much the goods cost and whether they serve a practical purpose. This chapter also highlights the increasing significance of the internet as an alternative buying environment, and compares "clicks" with "bricks", i.e. buying motives online with buying motives in conventional shops and stores.

Psychological, rather than functional, buying motives are likely to be linked to an underlying value system that places a strong emphasis on money and material goods as a means to achieve important life goals, such as life satisfaction, success, and happiness. Yet, such a materialistic value orientation often leads to the disappointed question "is this as good as it gets?" Chapter 4 focuses on the link between materialistic values and individuals' well-being, where materialists are less satisfied, less happy, and have more psychological problems. The nature and strength of this negative link does vary, however, and some of the research reported identifies factors that influence the link between materialism and well-being: value conflict, money-making motives, and level of income.

Both identity seeking and materialistic values are vulnerability factors for compulsive buying, often called shopping addiction in the mass media, which manifests itself in uncontrolled, excessive buying with harmful psychological and financial consequences. Chapter 5 reviews the clinical perspectives used to understand this dysfunctional consumer behaviour, but then develops a new perspective on compulsive buying as identity seeking. This new perspective is supported through research findings in both conventional and online buying environments. Age trends suggest that compulsive buying is on the increase, which highlights the need for intervention aimed at questioning materialistic values and the associated "I shop therefore I am" ideology.

In addition to material ideals, the mass media also communicate norms and values related to appearance and the "body perfect". There is increasing concern about the negative impact of ultra-thin models, commonly used in the advertising and fashion industries, on women's body image. Yet, advertisers defend their use with the argument that these images "sell". Addressing the question "does size matter?", Chapter 6 reports a series of experimental exposure studies that provide direct evidence that ultra-thin models have a detrimental effect on many women's body image, whereas attractive models with a healthy body size, resembling that of the average UK woman, do not. In addition, these studies are also the first to examine, and challenge, the claim that thin models are needed for effective advertising.

If unrealistically thin models in advertising have a negative effect on many women, then it may well be the case that the muscular male models increasingly used in advertising have a similarly detrimental effect on young men. Thus, Chapter 7 extends experimental exposure studies to male body image, but it also examines the psychological mechanisms through which individuals come to feel bad about their bodies after seeing idealised media models. Drawing on Self-discrepancy Theory, it presents a process model whereby ideal models lead both women and men to think of their own identity in terms of ideal body shapes, leading to a "think ideal, feel bad" sequence. It is important to study such dissatisfaction because it is a precursor of unhealthy body-shaping behaviours (e.g. dieting, muscle-enhancing strategies).

What is, perhaps, most striking is how early children become aware of consumer culture's messages about "what is beautiful and who is 'cool' ". Given all the negative consequences of these consumer culture ideals documented by the research findings in this book, the question of how children come to internalise core values, such as material and bodily ideals, is both timely and crucial. Chapter 8 shows that exposure to the ultra-thin ideal—in the form of dolls such as Barbie—is a cause of body dissatisfaction in girls as young as 5 to 7 years, and that 8- to 11-year-old children endorse beliefs that having the "right" material goods will make them more popular with their peers, particularly if they already have problematic peer relations.

So, what is the price of consumer culture? This question is addressed in the concluding Chapter 9, which takes stock of the findings reported throughout the book and highlights the psychological costs of consumer culture ideals, delineating the processes through which negative effects and detrimental behaviours may occur, and who is most vulnerable to such negative effects. Developing a good understanding of why and when consumer culture exacts a high price can inform intervention and prevention. Yet change is not likely to be easy, either on a societal level—because there are profits to be made from the material "good life" and "body perfect" ideals—or on an individual level—because these consumer culture ideals can and do function as a "cage within".

CORE CONSTRUCTS: CONSUMER CULTURE, IDENTITY, AND WELL-BEING

Providing a comprehensive analysis of the three core constructs—consumer culture, identity, and well-being—is beyond the scope of this book. Instead, I will give a brief characterisation of each construct to give a sense of how each is understood and used from the social psychological perspective that informs the primary research reported in this book.

Consumer culture

Consumer culture is best seen as "the sociocultural, experiential, symbolic, and ideological aspects of consumption" that have been researched from a "family of theoretical perspectives that address the dynamic relationships between consumer actions, the marketplace, and cultural meanings" (Arnould & Thompson, 2005, p. 868). As such, it addresses exactly those dimensions of consumption that have been neglected in more traditional work on behavioural consumer decision-making, micro-economics, and consumer psychology. This has typically used "rational choice" models of how consumers supposedly maximise utility when they decide which products to purchase, or cognitive psychology, which maps the (often faulty) information-processing that happens during purchase. In contrast to these perspectives, the profound role of symbolic, experiential, and socio-cultural dimensions of consumption have been recognised for some time in diverse social science disciplines, including sociology, anthropology, human geography, history, communication, and media studies. Their main concerns have been with analysing links between consumer culture and broader social, cultural, and ideological structures (e.g. Appadurai, 1986; Douglas & Isherwood, 1979; Featherstone, 1991; Hochschild, 2003; McCracken, 1990; Slater, 1997). Notwithstanding the importance of this work, the main concern in this book is somewhat different: it is to understand the psychological impact of consumer culture ideals specifically on the identity and well-being of individual adults, adolescents, and children. Given this concern, relevant aspects of consumer culture theory and research are summarised here in terms of five interrelated themes.

The first theme concerns methods used when conducting research, where qualitative techniques of data collection and analysis have been central to consumer culture research, such as in-depth interviews with consumers (e.g. Belk, 1988; Dittmar & Drury, 2000; Mick & Bühl, 1992), or deconstructing popular culture "texts" as lifestyle and identity instructions to consumers, such as advertisements (e.g. Belk & Pollay, 1985) or comics (Belk, 1987). Yet consumer culture can, and should be, researched by a diversity of methods, including also quantitative methods, such as surveys or experiments. In the research described throughout this book, we have employed exactly such a multi-method approach. This is an important point to emphasise, because one of the book's unique contributions to a critical analysis of consumer culture is to document its impact on us through rigorous empirical research that offers a direct and precise assessment of psychological processes and outcomes. In particular, I would like to highlight some of the benefits of experimentation in this respect, because they may be less familiar to readers and researchers outside psychology. We use experiments because they allow us to demonstrate unambiguously that exposure to idealised media models actually *causes* dissatisfaction with our own bodies, through showing that those people who have seen such "body perfect" depictions feel significantly worse about their body than a comparison group of people who have not seen these depictions, but have been treated identically in all other respects (see also my address at the Frontiers in Research Conference at the University of Ottawa: http://www.research.uottawa.ca/frontiers/pdf/2006-dittmar.pdf).

Second, consumer culture's concern with the symbolic, experiential and socio-cultural meanings and functions of consumer goods is not limited to the purchase of products but spans the whole consumption cycle that includes acquisition, consumption, and possession. A related point is that consumer culture abounds with symbolic messages associated with material goods and "ideal" people. In brief, a symbol is an entity that stands for another entity, and—most importantly—it can have meaning only to the extent that it has a shared reality among people. Having a "fashion" designer briefcase can only be an effective symbol of being "trendy" if others (at least those in the owner's social reference group) share the belief that the briefcase is, indeed, fashionable. Our most obvious system of symbols is language, both written and spoken. However, there is increasing evidence that we can and do use material objects as a kind of quasi language, although there are limitations to this analogy (cf. Dittmar, 1992a).

Third, through the advertising and fashion industries, consumer culture presents individuals with images that contain "lifestyle and identity instructions that convey unadulterated marketplace ideologies (i.e. look like this, act like this, want these things, aspire to this kind of lifestyle)" (Arnould & Thompson, 2005, p. 875). The symbolism inherent in consumer goods can be defined as the images of "idealized people associated with [the good]" (Wright, Claiborne, & Sirgy, 1992), and the message is that buyers not only consume the actual good advertised, but also its symbolic meanings (successful, happy, attractive, glamorous), thus moving closer to the ideal identity portrayed by media models. Although there is diversity in the nuances of idealised imagery, they seem variations around prominent themes, with the "body perfect" and the material "good life" as central.

Fourth, given that global connections are expanding, predominantly through the mass media and the internet, it is important to consider increasing globalisation of consumer culture, which penetrates into, but also interacts with, local culture (e.g. Appadurai, 1990; Slater, 1997). This aspect of consumer culture is relevant to this book in two ways. First, the internet is offering a new buying environment that is fast becoming a serious alternative to shopping and browsing in conventional shops and stores. With limitless access 24 hours a day 7 days a week, a rapidly growing number of "[c]onsumers can shop the globe from the convenience of their homes" (Lyons & Henderson, 2000, p. 740). This book examines buying motives online (Chapter 3), and their relationship to dysfunctional, excessive buying behaviour on the internet (Chapter 5). Second, the psychological processes through which consumer culture has its impact on us are investigated here primarily in highly developed, long-standing mass consumer societies such as the UK, although we also study materialism in other European countries, one recently turned affluent, Iceland, and the other a former Eastern bloc country, Croatia (Chapter 4). However, these psychological processes are likely to generalise beyond already-established mass consumer societies, along with the rapid and florid spread of consumer culture to other, less developed and non-Western, countries. This issue of cross-cultural generalisability is addressed in Chapter 9, referring to India as a case example.

Fifth, as we shall see later in this chapter, consumer culture does not determine our thoughts, feelings, and behaviours in a direct way: there is no simple stimulus–response causal chain. Rather, the way in which consumer culture encourages, and makes more likely, certain patterns of interpretations, feelings, and behaviours penetrates to the very fabric of our experience and understanding of the world: "Much like a game where individuals improvise within the constraints of rules . . ., consumer culture—and the marketplace ideology it conveys—frames consumers' horizons of conceivable action, feeling, and thought" (Arnould & Thompson, 2005, p. 869). Thus, there is a powerful framing effect of consumer culture, alongside related developments, such as the construction of self as "entrepreneurial project", within neo-liberalism (e.g. Rose, 1996). Yet, through the ideal images, practices, and lifestyles that are associated with material goods, consumer culture simultaneously offers a set of symbolic resources individuals can draw on when defining their personal and social identities, using their symbolic dimensions to express, maintain, and transform aspects of their selves (e.g. Bourdieu, 1984). Some of these aspects concern more private and personal parts of identity, such as beliefs, values, and our personal history, whereas others refer to more public and social parts of identity, such as social status, or the groups and subcultures we belong to.

Identity

Thus, identity has both personal and social dimensions. There are related terms in psychology, "self", "self-concept", and "self-identity", but these have been given complex and sometimes inconsistent meanings. Identity can be defined as the subjective concept (or representation) that a person holds of him- or herself (Vignoles, Regalia, Manzi, Golledge, & Scabini, 2006). Two aspects of this definition need highlighting, because they are particularly important. First, "identity is located on the level of subjective psychological experience, rather than necessarily referring to an objective 'essence' " (p. 309). Second, identity defined in this way is inclusive, involving individual, relational, and group levels of self-representation (Sedikides & Brewer, 2001). This also means that identity is multi-faceted, and consists of diverse self-representations, "differentiated from each other, rather than integrated to form a unitary structure" (Donahue, Robins, Roberts, & John, 1993, p. 834). What this means is that each person has multiple identities, and this is consistent with research findings showing that people list very diverse qualities, and even material objects, when they are asked "Who are you?" (e.g. Gordon, 1968). A "material self" was identified early on in William James's *Principles of Psychology*, first published in 1890, where a person's identity is extended beyond the physical boundaries of the body to include material goods (Chapter 2). Furthermore, another identity domain that is receiving increasing research attention is body image (Dittmar, 2005c), which denotes thoughts and feelings about our physical body (Chapters 6 and 7). Although, traditionally, body image has not been seen as an identity domain, it makes sense to do so, given that it constitutes the subjective concept that a person holds of their body as part of their self-representation (Dittmar, Phillips, & Halliwell, 2007; Halliwell & Dittmar, 2006).

One central theme that runs through the entire book is the focus on two identity domains, material and bodily, which have been relatively neglected by social psychology. Yet each is central to people's psychological functioning (Cash & Pruzinsky, 2002; Dittmar, 1992a). Both are highly profiled in consumer culture. Advertising in particular abounds with images of two types of ideal identity: people with an affluent lifestyle leading the "good life" and people with the "body perfect". Both have associated values, concerning materialism and the ideal body, which individuals internalise—to different degrees—as part of their personal belief system. Most importantly, perhaps, the pursuits of the "good life" and the "body perfect" both have significant consequences for individuals' psychological and physical well-being.

Well-being

Psychology has traditionally been concerned with predictors of unhappiness and ill-health, whereas an explicit focus on factors that enhance individuals' well-being is a more recent development, termed "positive psychology" (e.g. Csikszentmihalyi & Csikszentmihalyi, 2006). An important aspect of well-being is the experience of happiness, which is highly subjective. Good and bad events influence happiness temporarily, but people can and do adjust. For instance, a famous study showed that both lottery winners and accident victims who ended up in wheelchairs, after an initial strong reaction to their good or bad fortune, returned to their previous level of happiness (Brickman, Coates, & Janoff-Bulman, 1978). Yet happiness is difficult to define or measure, and recent work has focused on the more precise construct of subjective well-being (e.g. Diener, Suh, Lucas, & Smith, 1999). This includes life satisfaction, a cognitive evaluation of our life over time, but also the frequent experience of positive emotions and the absence of negative emotions. Thus, evaluations of oneself, such as dissatisfaction with one's life or body, measures of positive affect, including self-esteem or body-esteem, and measures of negative affect, such as anxiety or depression, can all be used as indicators of well-being. Furthermore, related to material and bodily well-being, individuals can, and do, engage in behaviours that are detrimental to their psychological and physical health, such as disordered eating patterns or compulsive buying of consumer goods. The indicators of well-being that we have used in our research are: subjective well-being, negative self-perception, negative affect, and unhealthy behaviours.

In terms of theorising factors that are conducive or detrimental to well-being, Self-determination Theory (e.g. Ryan & Deci, 2000) proposes that human beings have an organismic self with intrinsic psychological needs whose fulfilment leads to well-being, social development, and the authentic, happy state of self-actualisation, thus taking a humanistic perspective. The fulfilment of our intrinsic needs for relatedness, competence, and autonomy is facilitated by pursuing intrinsic goals, such as close affiliation with others, self-development, and community involvement. In contrast, extrinsic motivation—the pursuit of goals because of external rewards rather than intrinsic interest and enjoyment—is seen as detrimental to psychological needs fulfilment, and thus to well-being. The pursuit of life goals such as wealth, fame, and image, i.e. values at the core of consumer culture, have been identified as undermining well-being, because their pursuit is unlikely to fulfil genuine psychological needs (see Chapter 4). Self-determination Theory has less to say about identity, but its theorising about well-being is potent because it offers a psychological account of goals and aspirations that can be healthy or toxic for well-being. This perspective would imply that consumer culture is inimical to well-being. Indeed, Self-determination proponents have set out to "demonstrate how the aims and practices that typify American corporate capitalism often conflict with pursuits such as caring about the broader world, having close relationships with others, and, for many people, feeling worthy and free" (Kasser, Cohn, Kanner, & Ryan, in press). These issues are discussed in more detail at the end of the book, where I analyse consumer culture as a "cage within".

MASS CONSUMER SOCIETY: ECONOMIC–STRUCTURAL, SOCIO-CULTURAL, AND PSYCHOLOGICAL TRANSFORMATIONS

The entire subject matter of this book has to be understood and placed within the context of societies characterised by mass consumption, an obsession with "to have is to be" (Fromm, 1978; Kasser & Kanner, 2004), and a cult of perfect beauty, however exacting (Grogan, 1999; Pope, Phillips, & Olivardia, 2000; Thompson, Heinberg, Altabe, & Tantleff-Dunn, 1999). Our thoughts, feelings, and behaviours as consumers have changed particularly dramatically over the past two or three decades. Linked economic–structural, socio-cultural, and psychological transformations have created a different climate in which individuals experience life as consumers.

Although continuing, or even growing, inequalities in wealth make it clear that poverty is by no means absent from developed mass-consumer societies, on average people now have more money to spend than ever in European and North-American countries. Figures from the UK and the US can be used to illustrate the main trends. Between the mid-1970s and early 1990s, personal disposable incomes in the UK increased by 75% in real terms, taking account of inflation (*Social Trends*, 1994). Between 1990 and 2000, the increase per person was 45% in the US and 27% in the UK. But even more important than greater disposable incomes are mushrooming credit facilities: it is now easier than ever to spend money that one does not, in fact, have. During that same time period of 10 years, the amount of outstanding consumer credit has roughly doubled in the US to a staggering $1561 billion, and the average amount of personal debt per UK resident in 2002—including man, woman, and child—was £11,380, or over $17,000. From 1970 to 1990, the number of credit cards in the UK multiplied more than fourfold (Rowlinson & Kempson, 1994). The average number of credit cards per family was 1½ in the US by 1998, and the UK figure for 2002 gives an average of just under 2½ credit cards per household. Statistics provided by Creditaction (2006) claim that Britain's personal debt is increasing by about £1 million every 4 minutes, and report that average consumer borrowing via credit cards, motor and retail finance deals, overdrafts, and unsecured personal loans rose to £4107 per UK adult at the end of March 2006, which represents an increase of 52% over 5 years.

Alongside growing opportunities for credit that outstrip individuals' ability to repay, consumption has come to play a central socio-cultural role, described as having "assumed an overwhelming significance in modern life" (Zukin & Maguire, 2004, p. 173). Shopping and consuming not only play a central role for adults and adolescents but, with respect to children, there is growing concern about the consequences of growing up in a consumer culture that is all pervading (see Chapter 8). The titles of three books published in the same year speak for themselves: *Brandchild* (Lindstrom, 2004), *Born to buy: The commercialized child and the new consumer culture* (Schor, 2004), and *Consuming kids: The hostile takeover of childhood* (Linn, 2004).

Research on the socio-cultural significance of consumption focuses on three aspects: the production of goods and the symbolic images associated with them, the ways in which individuals and groups respond to and use these products, and how this intersection between consumption, social structures, and cultural practices is the place where people define their individual and collective identities. For example, using the Sony Walkman as a case study, Du Gay, Hall, Janes, Mackay, and Negus (1997) develop a model of production and consumption as interacting, rather than dichotomous or sequential, processes, where material goods both reflect and transform consumers' experience in a "cultural circuit". Through analysing diverse sources, including Sony company documents and journalistic accounts, they illustrate Sony's intention to innovate and have global appeal, but also the company's sophistication in adapting the Walkman's production and marketing in response to consumer feedback. They analyse advertisements for the Walkman in terms of cultural representations of age and social class, organisational practices of the firm, and young people's social practices of self-expression, individuality, and sociality, as well as reflecting critically on the relative power of multinational corporations and individual consumers.

Parallel with these economic and sociocultural transformations is a stronger psychological role of consumer culture and consumer goods in people's lives. One reason for this greater psychological significance is that traditionally stable forms of identity construction—such as community, class, religion, family, or nationality—have become eroded, particularly in urban environments. Who somebody is and his or her social position are not necessarily fixed and inherited any longer. Instead of being *ascribed*, identity is increasingly *achieved* by the individual her- or himself. An important element of such achieved identity is the acquisition and consumption of material goods and wealth. Although this change in identity construction may entail greater freedom in some ways, it also means a loss of "ontological security" (e.g. Giddens, 2001).

> Identity shifts from a fixed set of characteristics determined by birth and ascription to a reflexive, ongoing, individual project shaped by appearance and performance. This freedom, however, comes at the cost of security; without fixed rules, the individual is constantly at risk of getting it wrong, and anxiety attends each choice.
>
> (Zukin & Maguire, 2004, pp. 180–181)

In other words, consumer culture and material goods have become modern means of acquiring, expressing, and attempting to enhance identity: they signify social status, express unique aspects of the person, and symbolise hoped for, better, more ideal identities (e.g. Benson, 2000, 2006; Dittmar, 2004a, 2004b). Given the prominent advertising strategy of associating goods with idealised images of people (e.g. Richins, 1991; Snyder & DeBono, 1985), it is not surprising that individuals are often motivated to "buy" such images, hoping to appropriate the symbolic meanings associated with goods in their attempt to move close to an ideal identity.

CONSUMER CULTURE IDEALS AND THEIR INDIRECT EFFECTS ON INDIVIDUALS

A significant aspect of the impact that consumer culture has on individuals is linked to the ideal identities that are portrayed and privileged in the mass media and advertising. Idealised media models and celebrities, heavily airbrushed and with digitally enhanced appearance and body shapes, do not just promote products, they also communicate lifestyle and identity instructions to consumers, providing cultural ideals of beauty, success, and happiness. Given that we cannot but fall short of the idealised images portrayed, the typical message, shown in Figure 1.1, is that we can move closer from how we are now (our actual identity) to how we would like to be (our ideal identity) through acquiring and consuming the symbolic meanings associated with the consumer goods through the idealised models promoting them.

People are not necessarily aware of the extent to which these ideals, over time, influence the way they think about themselves, and about others. Two

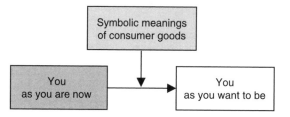

Figure 1.1 Diagram of the identity message given in advertising.

such ideal identities appear particularly pervasive in consumer culture, the "body perfect" and the affluent "good life". This book is the first to consider both at the same time, proposing that both have a profound and potentially detrimental impact on individuals' identity and well-being.

Ideal identities: the "body perfect" and the "good life"

Appearance, beauty, and the perfect body have long been central to the identity of many women and girls. They are socialised early into learning that their bodies should be used to attract others (e.g. Thompson et al., 1999), and they learn to see themselves as objects to be looked at and evaluated by appearance (Frederickson & Roberts, 1997). This pressure is constantly reinforced by a strong sociocultural ideal of female beauty, which has become synonymous with ultra-thinness (Wiseman, Gray, Mosimann, & Ahrens, 1992). The body size of glamorous models is often as much as 20% underweight and it becomes clear just how extremely ultra-thin this body size is when we consider that 15% underweight is one of the criteria used to diagnose anorexia (American Psychiatric Association, 2000). Typical media and fashion models, such as Kate Moss, have a body mass index (BMI, a measure of weight relative to height) that is as low as 14 or 15, thus falling substantially below the lowest figure signalling a biologically healthy weight, a BMI of 18.5. The "body perfect" for women is, indeed, very thin.

However, appearance is no longer a primarily female concern. Sociocultural emphasis on the ideal male body is growing, and concerns with appearance and bodily attractiveness have become more central for men, termed the "Adonis complex" (Pope et al., 2000). The ideal male body is well-toned, with a V-shaped, muscular upper torso. The media portrays an increasingly muscular ideal (Pope, Olivardia, Gruber, & Borowiecki, 1999) that is becoming as unattainable for the majority of men as the thin ideal is for women. Examples of advertising that uses male models typical of this muscular ideal abound. One pertinent example are advertisements for Calvin Klein underwear (see, for instance, http://www.soliscompany.com/cakladlibbypr.html).

Furthermore, these "body perfect" ideals are communicated early to children through dolls and toy action figures. For example, the ubiquitous Barbie doll, marketed at girls, is so thin that her waist is 39% smaller than that of anorexic patients (cf. Dittmar, Halliwell, & Ive, 2006), whereas boys are targeted with toy action figures whose muscularity has increased to such an extent that it often exceeds that of body builders (Pope et al., 1999). Examples of dolls and toys are shown in Figure 1.2.

It has to be emphasised that thinness for women and muscularity for men are not simply ideals of the perfect body; there is a halo effect (Nisbett & Wilson, 1977) around these appearance ideals, whereby they are connected— possibly unconsciously—with a whole host of desirable qualities that are not directly related to appearance. Research on body size stereotypes shows that the perfect body is associated not only with attractiveness but also with being in control, life satisfaction, happiness, career success, or having interesting and fulfilling personal relationships (e.g. Grogan, 1999). Adult's and children's psychological reactions to these consumer culture ideals are examined in Chapters 6, 7, and 8.

Yet, the "body perfect" is only one ideal identity; the other refers to the "good life", where an affluent lifestyle, studded with expensive consumer goods, possessions, and activities, is heralded as a material ideal (see Chapter 4). This material ideal is not new, of course, but it is profiled now more than ever by idealised models who are celebrities and who make it appear possible that "ordinary" people can actually achieve a super-affluent ideal. This ideal no longer needs to be presented directly in advertisements, it is sufficient that consumers know the celebrity's lifestyle, which is prominently displayed in

Barbie doll   Action toy figure

Figure 1.2 "Body perfect" ideals in children's dolls and toys. (*Note.* These images show photographs taken by the author.)

magazines, the internet, TV shows, and other forms of mass media. A typical example is David Beckham, known globally as an advertising model par excellence, promoting such diverse products as Police sunglasses, Vodafone, Gillette, and Pepsi. Similar to the "body perfect", there is a halo effect around the material "good life", whereby celebrity affluence is associated not only with success, control, and autonomy (e.g. Dittmar, 1992a), but also an interesting personal life, happiness, and intimate relationships. Thus, the problem with advertising is that it creates a "reality" that is not real; it provides a powerful, yet unrealistic, frame of norms of what it means to be beautiful and have an affluent material lifestyle.

Indirect effects

Advertising is geared toward promoting products and increasing sales, and therefore advertising effectiveness can be thought of as a direct effect. However, this book is mainly concerned with indirect effects, particularly with the role of consumer culture ideals in constructing norms and ideal identities, which then influence individuals' psychological functioning. The process through which advertising influences people is subtle. Of course, nobody believes that adverts are real in a literal sense, and nobody believes that they will transform into a supermodel or a celebrity if they buy product X. Rather, there is a more general process that is hard to escape over time, which can be illustrated by a research example. Indirect, but highly suggestive, evidence with respect to the material ideal discussed above comes from a US study that examined the role of television in the construction of consumer reality (O'Guinn & Shrum, 1997). TV life differs quite dramatically from social reality because expensive possessions, costly consumer behaviours, and wealth are heavily overrepresented. In a mail survey, American TV viewers were asked to estimate the percentages of adult Americans they thought (a) owned particular, expensive goods; (b) fell into high income brackets; and (c) regularly engaged in various consumer behaviours. The main finding was that the more television people watched, the more they tended to overestimate all of the above percentages. For example, hours of TV watching went hand in hand with the extent to which viewers overestimated the percentage of Americans who own expensive possessions, such as tennis courts, convertibles, and car telephones, and the extent to which they overestimated the percentage of Americans who are millionaires. Therefore, the mass media appears to play a significant role in how individuals construct their own versions of material norms, no matter whether they are asked about income distributions, consumer behaviours, or ownership of material goods.

Moreover, responses to advertising may not always be thoughtful and deliberate—on the contrary, there is some evidence that people react to ideal images quite automatically, i.e. regardless of whether or not they want to, and without necessarily being fully aware of the impact that advertisements can have on them. For example, exposure to advertisements with thin female models makes certain groups of women feel more anxious about their bodies, even when they see these images only fleetingly and do not pay much attention to them (Brown & Dittmar, 2005). In short, it seems that individuals cannot help engaging with unrealistic media ideals, and this is bound to have an effect over time.

This proposal, that consumer culture ideals have indirect, but powerful, effects on people's thoughts, feelings, and behaviours, raises two important questions: Who is most vulnerable to negative effects from consumer culture ideals? And what are the psychological processes through which these ideals come to impact on an individual's identity and well-being? When conceptualising how consumer culture ideals have an effect on individuals, there are two possible models, which were implied in earlier sections of this chapter. The first is a "cultural circuit" model, as discussed in the section on sociocultural transformations, and the second is a social psychological model, which takes individual vulnerability factors and psychological processes into account (see Figure 1.3).

These models are not in competition with each other in the sense that one might offer a more sophisticated or more accurate conceptualisation than the other. Instead, the issue of interest is which of the two models offers a better fit with the particular research questions that are being addressed. Thus, these models can be seen as describing two different lenses through which a researcher could examine the relationship between consumer culture ideals

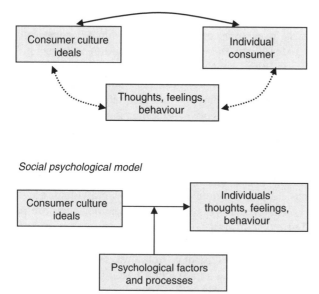

Figure 1.3 Models of consumer culture ideals' impact on individuals.

and individual consumers' thoughts, feelings, and behaviours. A central focus of the cultural circuit model is the recognition that consumer culture ideals do not have a unilinear, deterministic effect on individual consumers; rather the process is a reciprocal, circular one in which individuals are both the products and transformers of consumer culture. Ideals, norms, and practices pre-exist individuals who learn, re-appropriate and reproduce them throughout their lifetime. But, at the same time, by doing so they simultaneously transform these practices through active re-interpretation, innovation, or even rebellion. These simultaneous processes are bound up loosely with consumers' thoughts, feelings, and behaviours, but there is not a focal interest in specific self-thoughts that individuals have, or specific emotions, such as anxiety about their body or negative affect as part of well-being, or specific behaviours linked to consumer culture that are detrimental, such as compulsive buying or extreme body-shaping behaviours.

Social theorists and cultural researchers have been primarily interested in documenting and analysing the interface between consumer culture as a framework shaped by key social groups on the one hand, and individuals experiencing consumption as a project of forming and expressing identity on the other (e.g. Slater, 1997). Whereas this cultural circuit is important as a backdrop to this book, it is the second model that delineates the way in which the research reported here examines the impact of consumer culture ideals. Notwithstanding the fact there is no simple causal chain, the focus is on investigating how individuals perceive and respond to consumer culture ideals and, in this sense, these ideals are examined as direct predictors of specific thoughts, feelings, and behaviours of individuals linked to these ideals. Furthermore, the social psychological model that informs the whole book is also concerned with identifying psychological factors that make some people more vulnerable to negative effects from consumer culture, and with understanding the psychological processes through which these negative effects occur.

THE PSYCHOLOGICAL IMPACT OF CONSUMER CULTURE ON IDENTITY AND WELL-BEING

My account of how external consumer culture ideals become incorporated within individuals' internal beliefs to form part of their identity is informed by, but also goes beyond, Meadian symbolic interactionist principles. This broad analysis, or "meta-theory", is used here to understand how bodily and material ideals first come to be internalised during children's development of a sense of identity (cf. Dittmar, 1992a). I then draw on several, more specific, theories in social psychology to understand how people react to consumer culture ideals as adolescents and adults. Social Comparison Theory can be applied to how individuals compare themselves to consumer culture ideals, usually finding themselves wanting with respect to these unrealistic models. Value Theory is useful for understanding how internalised belief systems—such as ideal-body or materialistic values—make individuals more vulnerable to the influence of consumer culture ideals. Finally, Self-discrepancy Theory and Symbolic Self-completion Theory are used as a foundation for explaining why individuals are identity seekers and how identity deficits can lead to negative emotions and lower well-being.

Consumer culture "role models" and identity development

The body of thought outlined by George Herbert Mead (e.g. 1913, 1934) is now commonly referred to as *symbolic interactionism*. At the core of symbolic interactionism is the notion that developing a sense of identity stems from the human ability for self-reflexivity or, in Meadian terms, viewing oneself from the *perspective of the other*. This requires the capacity for self-reference and the development of role-taking abilities, both of which become possible only in the context of socially shared meaning systems, where self, others, and objects in the environment can be designated and represented symbolically. We "must [first] be others if we are to be ourselves" (Mead, 1913, p. 276), which means, put simply, that we start to develop our sense of identity by being able to imagine how we appear from the standpoint of others, thus seeing ourselves through the eyes of others.

However, material objects, or rather the symbolic meanings associated with them, can serve as imaginary points of view from which to see the self, too. The thought "My Rolex watch means that I am a successful person" could be an example. Within consumer culture, a Rolex watch is seen as a symbol of wealth and success, and by looking at myself on the basis of these symbolic meanings, I can view myself as a person who is wealthy and successful. This potential of a Meadian perspective for mapping the symbolic significance of material goods for identity (see Dittmar, 1992a) is applied here to consumer culture ideals more generally. Children's early interactions with material objects, such as toys or dolls, are intimately bound up with social interactions in which the symbolic meanings of these material objects are established and internalised. So, symbolic communication about material goods is involved in how children become aware of themselves and how they develop and maintain an identity.

The process of children developing an identity is a gradual one, progressing in stages. With respect to people, early on, a child can only adopt the perspective of a specific person with whom s/he interacts directly, and thus internalises the attitudes of that individual towards him or her as part of the self-concept. Subsequently, the child is able to adopt the perspective of several specific others simultaneously and thus comes to see her- or himself from the viewpoints of, for instance, her or his whole family or group of playmates all at once. Consequently, self-attitudes become more complex and integrated. But Mead speaks of a fully developed identity only when particular attitudes of specific others towards the individual are generalised into an internalised set of representations of larger social units and society as a whole. This process can be also applied to the link between material symbols and identity. Gradually, young children learn the symbolic meanings of material goods through observing and imaginatively taking part in others' interactions with objects, be it directly or via the mass media. For example, a mother might comment during a children's TV programme that the person who owns this beautiful, large house is very clever and successful. In this way, children are introduced to the idea that material objects provide symbolic information about the characteristics of the owner. But they will also experience that other people react to them in terms of the objects that they own, i.e. their toys. Thus, their toys can:

> act as essential models for certain roles in the socialization process. A model rocket, doll house or video game can signify to a child certain values of the culture that can be personified and internalized through fantasy and play activities.
>
> (Rochberg-Halton, 1984, p. 338)

To give a concrete example that is relevant to research presented in this book (see Chapter 8), we can consider how dolls influence girls' identity and body image. Dolls like Barbie can serve as an imaginary point of view from which young girls can see their own bodily self, where they come to understand the meaning of beauty and perfection through pretending to be their dolls. If dolls signify a socio-cultural ideal of the female body that equates beauty and thinness, such as Barbie, then the thin beauty ideal is gradually internalised through fantasy and play. Thus, the primary meaning of the term "role model" for Mead is a cultural representation that becomes internalised to form part of the child's emerging identity. This process involves different phases of play, where young children initially imitate, and identify with, "beautiful" Barbie in a direct, non-reflexive manner, but then—gradually—come to internalise thinness as a salient feature of what it means to be beautiful. Eventually, the internalised thin body can become a significant element of their ideal, if not easily actual, identity, and thus a guiding principle for their thoughts, emotions, and behaviours.

This brief account of how consumer culture ideals become internalised to form an integral part of how we conceive of ourselves and what ideal identities we strive towards lays a foundation for the book as a whole. This conceptualisation of identity as a social product, but in a non-deterministic way, accomplished through symbolic communication, forms a backdrop throughout. It is a meta-theoretical framework of identity development, whereas the theories used to interrogate the vulnerability factors and psychological processes that are significant when adolescents and adults encounter consumer culture ideals, after their identities have already formed, are more specific. These theories are outlined only in brief here, to give a summary of their central constructs with respect to the impact of consumer culture ideals on individuals' identity and well-being as a foundation for when they are revisited in some detail in various chapters of the book.

Social comparison and consumer discontent

Confrontation with consumer culture ideals is unavoidable. They are every-where—not only in advertising, but also TV, films, music videos, magazines, and the internet. The nub of Social Comparison Theory is that people have a need to evaluate themselves, that they often do so through comparing them-selves to others, and that these social comparisons have direct consequences for how they evaluate themselves (e.g. Festinger, 1954). Thus, advertising affects consumers "because they implicitly or explicitly compare themselves with the idealized images and life-styles portrayed in ads" (Richins, 1991, p. 72). Typically, comparing oneself to targets who are superior on relevant dimensions (upward comparison) leads to depressed affect and lower self-evaluations (Wood, 1989). This negative outcome is the result of contrast: individuals feel inferior to the target (Collins, 1996). Given that the great majority of individuals fall far short of the "body perfect" and material "good life" typically embodied by idealised media models, social compar-isons with such models should lead people to feel bad about themselves. Indeed, 71% of a sample of US college women agreed with the statement that "[w]hen I see models in clothing ads, I think about how badly I look compared to the models" (Richins, 1991). As we will see in Chapter 6, a whole host of experimental exposure studies show that many women feel worse about their body and themselves after seeing ultra-thin media models compared to other types of images (cf. Groesz, Levine, & Murnen, 2002).

However, not everybody engages in these detrimental upward comparisons all the time, and Social Comparison Theory has therefore been refined. The two main points of interest here can be illustrated with a recent set of studies concerned with social comparisons and women's body image (Trampe, Stapel, & Siero, 2007). Their findings confirm prior research demonstrating that social comparisons have self-evaluative consequences only when the comparison involves characteristics that are relevant and psy-chologically meaningful to the person concerned. Women evaluated them-selves negatively after seeing ultra-thin models only when they were already dissatisfied with their own bodies, i.e. when body size was already a salient concern to them. Furthermore, and this is novel, their findings suggest that, if a characteristic such as a thin body shape is of high personal import-ance, then even non-human, quite abstract stimuli can trigger negative self-evaluation. Trampe et al. exposed women to drawings of vases that had either a long, tall shape with a waist-like indentation or a wide, round shape like an apple, and found that body-dissatisfied women evaluated themselves and their appearance negatively after seeing long, tall vases, which seem to have activated a thinness schema in their thoughts. Thus, it appears that when particular qualities have high personal importance, such as having a thin body shape, then negative effects for self-evaluation become virtually unavoidable because all kinds of stimuli are perceived as related to thinness. However, research has shown that social comparisons do not always have an impact on how individuals evaluate themselves, and we now turn to an examination of the underlying belief systems that are likely to make them more vulnerable.

Ideal-body internalisation and materialistic values as vulnerability factors

Value Theory (e.g. Rokeach, 1973) proposes that people hold general, relatively enduring, value orientations that then give rise to specific motives and behaviours in particular domains, such as buying or eating. These underlying value orientations serve as guiding principles for how people think, feel, and act. They are general beliefs about desirable goals that transcend specific attitudes and behaviours, informing how people evaluate self and others, influencing their motives, and justifying opinions and conduct. It is proposed that the two consumer culture ideals examined in this book are internalised by individuals, so that they form a personal value system that guides how individuals construe themselves, how they respond to consumer culture stimuli, and what ideals they pursue in their behaviour. Of course, some individuals internalise these ideals more strongly than others, and thus endorse ideal-body and materialistic value systems to different degrees. It is precisely the extent to which individuals endorse ideal-body and materialistic values that makes them more vulnerable to detrimental consumer culture effects (see Chapters 5, 6, and 7).

With respect to ideal-body values, it is important to draw a distinction between individuals simply being aware of socio-cultural ideals of appearance and individuals internalising these ideals as their own personal goal. Ideal-body internalisation has been assessed in slightly different ways (e.g. Stice, 1994). We chose a measure for our research that has been used widely and is well validated: the *Sociocultural Attitudes Towards Appearance Questionnaire* (SATAQ; Heinberg, Thompson, & Stormer, 1995). The SATAQ consists of separate scales that measure awareness on the one hand and internalisation on the other. In the version for women, awareness of sociocultural ideals is assessed through the endorsement of statements such as "[i]n our society, fat people are regarded as unattractive". In contrast to simple awareness, internalisation is assessed using statements such as "I would like my body to look like the women who appear in TV shows and movies". Thus, this scale measures whether women have adopted appearance and the thin ideal as important personal goals, endorsing ideal-body values. Research demonstrates that thin-ideal internalisation presents a crucial risk factor in the development of body image concerns and eating disturbances in girls and women (Thompson & Stice, 2001), and that it is linked with a greater propensity to make social comparisons concerning appearance (Stormer &

Thompson, 1996). Thus, the endorsement of ideal-body values appears to be a significant vulnerability factor for body dissatisfaction and disordered eating, as well as for negative effects when exposed to consumer culture beauty ideals.

With respect to material ideals, there is a sizeable research literature on materialism as a value system. Materialistic values can be defined as "the importance ascribed to the ownership and acquisition of material goods in achieving major life goals" (Richins, 2004, p. 210). A person with highly materialistic values believes that the acquisition of material goods is a central life goal, prime indicator of success, and key to happiness and self-definition. Examples of statements typically endorsed by materialists include "I admire people who own expensive homes, cars, and clothes" or "[s]ome of the most important achievements in life include acquiring material possessions" (Richins, 2004). Such a materialistic value orientation is central to current consumer culture (Kasser & Kanner, 2004). Yet, as we will see in Chapter 4, materialism and the pursuit of affluence are often linked to lower well-being. This suggests that a materialistic value system is a vulnerability factor for negative effects with respect to the consumer culture material ideal, and this proposal is examined through research on compulsive buying (Chapter 5).

Identity deficits and identity seeking

So far, the argument has been that consumer culture's use of idealised images of people and lifestyles leads to consumer discontent because people typically find themselves lacking in comparison to these images, particularly those who endorse body and material ideals as personal value systems. To understand the psychological processes involved, we draw on Self-discrepancy Theory (e.g. Higgins, 1987), which postulates that negative emotions result when individuals experience discrepancies, or gaps, in their self-concept. In this book, we focus on discrepancies between how individuals are (actual identity) and how they would ideally like to be (ideal identity). Exposure to idealised models should give rise, there and then, to body-related self-discrepancies, because women's bodies are almost invariably much larger than those of thin female models, and men's bodies are almost invariably less muscular than those of male models (see Chapter 7). Thus, comparison with these models switches on an internal discrepancy where vulnerable people focus on the gap between their own body and the ideal body, making identity deficits like "I want to be thinner, I need to be thinner" or "I want to be more muscular, I need to be more muscular" central, leading to negative emotions.

Yet, there is a second prominent feature of advertising: it not only presents idealised images that are a "problem" for many people—producing self-doubt, identity deficits, and negative emotions—but it also presents the supposed "solution". The message is that consumers need only buy the consumer products promoted and this will help solve the "problem" because consumption will get them closer to these ideals. Buy and this will enhance your sense of self-worth; indeed, buy "because you are worth it"! Symbolic Self-completion Theory (Wicklund & Gollwitzer, 1982) offers an excellent starting point for an account of the process through which people engage in identity seeking through consumption (Chapters 2, 3, and 5). It proposes that, among diverse strategies, individuals can use material symbols to compensate for perceived shortcomings in their identity (e.g. Braun & Wicklund, 1989). Because material goods symbolise diverse qualities, individuals buy those goods in an attempt to "complete" their identity that symbolise aspects they feel they are lacking. For instance, people might buy a "glamorous" outfit to feel more glamorous and confident, and this might work, at least in the short-term. However, it is unlikely to provide a long-term solution for those who have chronic identity deficits of feeling unattractive.

These processes are integrated into an account of consumer culture ideals as a "cage within" (Chapter 9), after examining their operation in detail in the interlinked research projects summarised in the next seven chapters.

2 To have is to be? Psychological functions of material possessions

Helga Dittmar

Synopsis

The central proposal of this chapter is that material possessions are psychologically important because they are intimately bound up with our sense of identity. This is supported by evidence that documents that:

- Material possessions are experienced as parts of individuals' extended selves, reaching beyond the boundary of the physical body.
- The link between possessions and self is close, partly because possessions give people a sense of control and mastery but more importantly because they function as symbols of their personal and social identity.
- Differences in the psychological functions of possessions between cultures, as well as between women and men, reflect the ways in which they typically construe identity.

I am what I have

© Jessica Barlow

Imagine a list of personal qualities that describe a person—friendly, unique, assertive, self-reliant—and then ask yourself whether having each of these qualities is either intrinsic to a person or in any way related to material factors, such as what the person owns or how he or she dresses. Most people believe that these are all aspects of a person's identity that are independent of, and not influenced by, material context. But they are wrong. As we will see later in this chapter, material possessions systematically influence how we perceive the identity of other people. Yet material goods not only play a role in our perceiving others, people also use them to express who they are and to construct a sense of who they would like to be. Material goods fulfil a range of psychological functions, such as giving people control, independence, enjoyment, or emotional comfort. However, the main purpose here is to propose that the link between material goods and identity is of central psychological importance, thus arguing that, yes, in many ways, "to have is to be" in contemporary consumer culture.

Material possessions and consumer goods surround us in our everyday lives, they are common topics in our daily conversations and they feature prominently in the many hours of television and advertisements we watch. Perhaps because they are such an integral aspect of our existence, they might seem rather unremarkable at first sight. Many material goods are, of course, practical tools that make life easier, more controllable, and more convenient. A car, for example, serves as a means of transport and enables us to travel from A to B (traffic permitting). Yet rather than having mainly instrumental, pragmatic significance, there is growing evidence that possessions play a profound role for us because they fulfil a whole range of different psychological functions. Even a brief look at just one car advertisement (see Figure 2.1) illustrates a variety of symbolic and psychological messages to potential owners, which extend far beyond the car's immediate physical qualities and price. The headline states explicitly that the car and the owner's identity are fused into one: "I wouldn't be me without my Samurai" portrays the car as such an integral part of the male figure's identity that he would be incomplete without it. It appears that this message is visually echoed and reinforced through the alignment between man and car in terms of eyes–head-lamps and identical orientation to the right, whereby the car becomes a material reflection of the man and he in turn seems to personify the car. Indeed, the opening lines of "always on the move, great looking and full of fun" are ambiguous; they could just as easily refer to the man as to the car, but most likely are intended to convey that both have identical qualities. This car also functions as a symbol that the owner belongs to a particular group or subculture "with an active lifestyle". Imbedded in the descriptions of how and where you can drive the car is a declaration that it will make you visible and noticeable to other people, while you remain relaxed: "snug and warm cruising city streets". And, finally, the advert appeals to Western cultural values of what it means to be a person, to have identity: standing out from the crowd, being unique and highly individualised. The Samurai

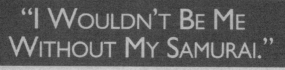

Figure 2.1 An example advertisement linking consumer goods and ideal identity. (*Note.* Part of advertising campaign run by Suzuki GB Cars, division of Heron Suzuki PLC, around 1994. Reproduced with kind permission of Suzuki GB PLC.)

offers you all this because it is—and therefore makes you—"anything but ordinary".

Such symbolic links between material goods and identity are used a lot in advertising, and there is a whole literature in consumer behaviour on product–self congruity, the match between the attributes of goods and consumers' self-concept (Sirgy, 1985; Sirgy et al., 1997; cf. Solomon, Bamossy, & Askegaard, 2002). Almost invariably, advertising implies that "you as you are now" falls short in some way of "you as you want to be", which is likely to fuel consumer discontent (Richins, 1991). As shown in Figure 1.1, the "solution" typically offered is that people can move closer to an "ideal self" by consuming not only the promoted product itself but the symbolic qualities associated with it. But is this strong emphasis on material goods symbolising ideal identities just something that characterises advertising and marketing? After all, nobody would be so naive as to take the magical, glittering promises of advertising at face value. Moreover, identity is seen as essentially located inside us and therefore quite independent from social context (e.g. Markus & Kitayama, 1991), such as the material possessions we own. At best, consumer goods are seen as a kind of "outer skin" of our identity, which we acquire to express the "inner self", but not as things that are intimately bound up with our psychological development and functioning. At odds with this common-sense belief, this chapter outlines evidence that material possessions are perceived as integral parts of the self and that their psychological importance is closely linked to their roles as symbols of the ways in which we construct our sense of identity (cf. Dittmar, 1992a).

PARTS OF THE SELF

The notion that, knowingly or unknowingly, people regard possessions as a part of the self is not new. For example, an interesting, classic social psychological study on property describes "magico-animistic" rituals of Amerindian tribes where owners' "life spirit" was thought to infuse their possessions (e.g. weapons, eating utensils), which were eventually buried with the owner so that the other tribe members would not become "contaminated" with their personality (Beaglehole, 1931). A close link between possessions and self is also proposed in this famous and oft-quoted passage from William James's *Principles of Psychology*, first published in 1890:

> it is clear that between what a man calls *me* and what he simply calls *mine* the line is difficult to draw . . . *a man's self is the sum total of what he CAN call his*, not only his body and his psychic powers, but his clothes and his house, . . . his reputation and works, his land and horses, and yacht and bank account . . . If they wax and prosper, he feels triumphant; if they dwindle and die away, he feels cast down.
>
> (1981/1890, pp. 279–280, emphases in original)

The speculations that possessions are viewed as part of the self and that they have implications for how people evaluate themselves are supported by research evidence. When adults rated over a hundred items in terms of whether or not they were "definitely a part of your own self" (Prelinger, 1959), possessions ranked about midway, slightly closer to self than not-self. Thus, material goods were perceived as parts of a more extended sense of self. Moreover, children, adolescents, and adults spontaneously name material objects as elements of their self when asked in an open-ended fashion to describe themselves (Dixon & Street, 1975; Gordon, 1968). In addition to these self-report findings, the association between self and possessions is also strong when measured by the Implicit Association Test (IAT), which was designed to identify individuals' preferences and beliefs, even when they are not conscious of them. Compared with objects they did not own, most respondents showed strong associations between their material possessions and their self-concept (Oyamot, 2004).

A whole range of material objects are self-extensions (Belk, 1988, 2000), with tools, musical instruments, books, houses, cars, bikes, clothes, and jewellery just a few examples. It seems clear that an absolute dividing line between an extended self through possessions on the one hand and a core self on the other cannot be drawn. A study addressing the question directly of "How is a possession 'me' or 'not me'?" found that "me-ness" was not uni-dimensional but was characterised by qualitatively distinct types of psychological significance: strong versus weak attachment to possessions, the extent to which they symbolised either close interpersonal relationships or autonomous identity, and what role they played for individuals' past, present, or future selves (Schultz-Kleine, Kleine, & Allen, 1995).

The mood people are in is reflected in their subjective evaluation of consumer goods they own or desire to own, such that they evaluate goods more positively when in a positive rather than negative mood, although this mood-congruent pattern is moderated by personality differences (Ciarrochi & Forgas, 2000). A further interesting illustration of the "psychological nearness" between an object and its owner is the "mere ownership effect": the simple fact that owning an object makes it more attractive to us. If the mere ownership effect occurs because of people's desire to maintain a positive self-image, where they enhance what they own in order to enhance themselves, then they should display a stronger mere ownership effect after receiving feedback that they have failed, rather than succeeded in, a particular task. Indeed, when people failed to solve an anagram they evaluated a drink cooler as more attractive when they owned it than when they did not (Beggan, 1992). If an object as trivial as a drink cooler can trigger the mere ownership effect, bolstering self-image through material possessions is bound to be more pronounced with goods of greater symbolic and personal significance.

If we use possessions for defining, extending, and evaluating the self, it would follow that their unintended loss should be experienced as a lessening of self. This would suggest that being a victim of a property crime might involve rather more psychological trauma than is often credited to the loss of "mere things". Among property crimes, residential burglary is most likely to have a strong impact because it involves an intrusion into the home of victims and is directed at the whole of their personal possessions. Home functions as an "identity shell": not only does it provide the physical location for social activities, personal interactions, and privacy, but the objects within it are also symbols of the self, reflecting our attitudes, values, and personal history (e.g. Dittmar, 2003; Doyle, 1992). The scant research on psychological reactions to burglary suggests that the ordeal people go through is related more to the perceived violation and shrinkage of self than to the financial value of possessions lost or stress associated with police and insurance procedures (cf. Van den Bogaard & Wiegman, 1991). The psychological distress and sense of violation experienced by burglary victims is comparable in kind with the traumas of rape or serious domestic violence, although it is less intense in degree (Wirtz & Harrell, 1987). Interviews with victims in Mexico also confirmed that burglary is experienced as a severe violation of intimate space, and psychological reactions might well include post-traumatic stress dysfunction (Caballero, Ramos, & Saltijeral, 2000).

The loss of the extended self also happens through losing possessions in natural disasters, where the loss of treasured objects, such as sentimental possessions, is linked systematically to psychological distress (Benight et al., 1999). A *Manual for Mental Health Advocates and Providers* published after the Tsunami in Sri Lanka on Boxing Day 2004 gives a list of the most important causes of trauma that can lead to stress, anxiety, grief, and bereavement. As well as threat to one's life or encountering the death of others, it also includes "loss of home, valued possessions, neighbourhood, or community" (South Asian Psychological Network Association, 2005). Empathy with people losing their home and possessions also comes across in this posted message in the World Peace Book of Prayers for Hurricane Katrina Victims (2006): "I pray for all those involved in the Katrina Hurricane—those who have suffered loss of homes, family, possessions, pets—it is unimaginable how they must feel". These powerful emotional reactions imply that these losses are central to individuals' sense of who they are, but there is also direct evidence that they are linked to identity. Students who had experienced an earthquake in either Japan or California reported that the most favourite of their possessions they had lost were those that were closest to their identity (Ikeuchi, Fujihara, & Dohi, 2000).

In conclusion, individuals perceive and experience material possessions as integral parts of their self, which shows that identity has boundaries that extend beyond the physical body. Psychological explanations of this close link between possessions and self fall into two broad camps. On the one hand, their instrumental functions are emphasised, particularly that they help people exert control over their environment and experience a sense of mastery. On the other hand, their symbolic functions are highlighted, where material objects can represent interpersonal relationships, emotional comfort, group belongingness, and a range of personal characteristics, values, and beliefs.

INSTRUMENTS OF CONTROL

An extensive cross-cultural and developmental research project used open-ended interview studies with children, adolescents, and adults from America, Israeli kibbutzim and Israeli cities to map the dimensions that constitute the meaning of, and reasons for, having possessions (Furby, 1978a, 1978b, 1980; see 1991 for a summary). These three cultures have different values with respect to possessions, with kibbutzim highly collective and non-materialistic in contrast to the individualist culture in US and Israeli cities. In considering the developmental origins of the possessions–self link, Furby proposes that infants reach for and handle objects because of "effectance motivation or the need for control" (Furby, 1978b, p. 60), which has been proposed as a universal motivation in humans (White, 1959). Such explorations are bound to come into conflict with the infant's social environment, particularly from the age of 1 year when physical mobility increases rapidly. Adults and older siblings have to prevent the child from touching and handling many objects in order to avoid damage. The result of these interactions is that children will gradually learn to identify with those objects that they can explore and control and come to view them as theirs, whereas objects that occasion restriction and interference will become defined as belonging to somebody else. In this way, possessions are used to draw a boundary between what is self and what is other. The distinction between self and not-self is thus closely linked to the infant's behavioural control over material objects. This developmental account is not only interesting, but also very plausible.

However, the proposal that the psychological significance of possessions resides mainly in the control they afford owners as quasi-physical extensions of the self becomes more problematic when Furby extrapolates it also to adolescents and adults. She singles out two related themes that: (1) possessions are important because they afford control over the physical and social environment; and (2) they are closely linked to self for precisely this reason:

> I propose that the central feature of possession—its *principal defining characteristic* . . . seems to lie in the very high degree of control it entails. The magnitude of control I exert over my possessions is of the same order as the control I exert over my body. Thus, possessions are included in one's concept of self . . . That over which I exercise . . . control becomes a part of my sense of self.
>
> (Furby, 1978a, pp. 322–323, emphasis added)

The first part of her claim, that possessions are psychologically important to people because they help them exercise control and experience a sense of mastery, is well supported by research. For example, an experimental study on self-completion, a process of compensating for aspects of self perceived as inadequate, examined the link between possessions and control motivation through manipulating people's sense of personal control and then collecting their judgements of the extent to which their possessions give them control and mastery (Beggan, 1991). Those who suffer control deprivation (being told that they had failed on an experimental task) should overemphasise the control their possessions give them, compared to those who experience control gain (being told that they had succeeded). The findings showed that this was indeed the case, but only for people who believe that, in general, they have control over their life (internal locus of control). A further intriguing example of research that can be interpreted as support for the mastery argument comes from the mortality salience literature, which shows that when people are confronted with the highly threatening inevitability of their own mortality (by writing a short essay about their own death), their focus on material possessions and resources is enhanced (Kasser & Sheldon, 2000; Sheldon, Greenberg, & Pyszczynski, 2004).

In contrast, the second part of Furby's claim, that the control and mastery function of possessions accounts primarily for their close link with people's sense of self, is more controversial. Even in her own interviews, the complexity of the functions that material objects fulfil for adolescents and adults clearly emerges: they symbolise social power and status, and are used as means of self-expression, individuation, and individuality.

A social psychological model linking attitudes, values, and possessions proposes a major dichotomy whereby material possessions fulfil instrumental purposes, such as providing control, entertainment, or activities, but also serve as symbolic expressions of aspects of self, such as personal and social identity (Prentice, 1987, 2004). Typical instrumental possessions include tools or means of transport. Symbolic possessions can be subdivided further into symbols of the historical continuity of self (e.g. photographs), expressions of artistic or intellectual interests (e.g. book collections), and signs of status or wealth (e.g. yacht). On the basis of this classification, respondents were divided into "symbolic" possessors and "instrumental" possessors, depending on the types of possessions they had listed as important to them. The main finding was a link between possessions, attitudes, and values in the sense that individuals showed a general outlook that was dominated by either a symbolic or an instrumental orientation. However, this leaves important questions unaddressed: Are people always either "instrumental" or "symbolic" possessors? Does their emphasis on one or the other change? Are there systematic differences between cultures or genders? But before I can address these questions, the symbolic dimensions of material possessions need more detailed examination.

SYMBOLS OF PERSONAL AND SOCIAL IDENTITY

Human beings use symbols when they relate to each other and the world at large. As already touched on in Chapter 1, a symbol is an entity that stands for another entity, which can have meaning only to the extent that there is a shared understanding among people that gives the symbol reality. Having "cool" sunglasses cannot be an effective symbol of being trendy unless a group of individuals, or a subculture or society, share the belief that the sunglasses are, indeed, trendy. In addition to spoken and written language, we can and do use material objects as a quasi-language (notwithstanding limitations to this analogy, cf. Dittmar, 1992a) when we draw on their symbolic dimensions to express, maintain, and transform aspects of our selves. Some of these aspects concern more private and personal parts of identity, such as beliefs, values, and our personal history, whereas others refer to more public and social parts of identity, such as social status, or the groups and subcultures we belong to.

Maintaining identity

Early evidence that possessions help people to maintain a general sense of identity and integrity can be found in Goffman's classic analyses of "self mortification" in prisons and mental hospitals (1961, 1968). He offers a vivid account of the identity-maintaining features of personal possessions by outlining how admission procedures where "inmates" are stripped of all personal belongings take away most of the previous basis of self-identification. Goffman argues that they are not only humiliating but also deprive inmates of their "identity-kit", which includes clothing, make-up, and other personal possessions, which function as *"embodiments* of self" (1968, p. 271, emphasis in original). Institutional practices have changed since, particularly in the psychiatric field, but the procedures of being stripped and issued with a uniform are still not uncommon. In this work, we find a clear statement that possessions are symbolic constituents of personal identity and are important for the maintenance of the owner's psychological integrity. From a different perspective, studies on de-individuation show that disguises that de-personalise people, such as hoods or masks, can play a role in overcoming barriers in hurting another person, an analysis that was recently applied to atrocities by guards perpetrated against Iraqi prisoners, such as in Abu Graib prison (Zimbardo, 2007).

Investigations concerned with elderly people stress the importance of taking treasured personal possessions into old people's homes or sheltered accommodation to counteract the trauma of relocation (Kalymum, 1985; McCracken, 1987), because they symbolise a person's life experiences and thus the historical continuity of self. A comparison of elderly women who lived at home, in sheltered apartments that they furnished themselves, or in a traditional nursing home, revealed differences related to their identity depending on the extent to which their possessions symbolised parts of their self, embodying memories of people, times, and places (Cram & Paton, 1993). Wapner, Demick, and Redondo (1990) investigated directly how well elderly people fared in different nursing homes in the US and found that those who kept their cherished possessions coped much better. They felt more in control, less helpless, more supported by staff, and were judged to be better able to resolve conflicts. This literature carries obvious implications for institutional policies, but also applies to other forms of relocation, such as emigrating to a different country (e.g. Mehta & Belk, 1991). This research highlights that symbolic aspects of possessions help people to maintain a general sense of identity, integrity, and self-continuity, providing a symbolic record of their personal history.

Symbolic self-completion

The notion that people use material symbols to bolster or enhance aspects of their identity is part of Symbolic Self-completion Theory, which proposes that people make use of material possessions, among other strategies, to compensate for perceived inadequacies in their self-concept (Wicklund & Gollwitzer, 1982). Because of their communicative power, material symbols have identity-creating and identity-enhancing features. Within limits, we can attempt to move closer to our ideal concept of ourselves by engaging in symbolic self-completion. For instance, by displaying a recognised masculine symbol, such as strutting around in a black leather motorbike suit, a young man can compensate for not feeling "masculine" enough by using the object to tell both himself and others that he is indeed "masculine". This compensatory symbolic function of material objects has obvious limitations—symbols have to fit in with a person's gender, age, or social roles—but it provides a potential bridge for closing perceived discrepancies between actual and ideal dimensions of self.

Business students who had a weak symbolic basis for a business career, in the sense that they lacked good qualifications, tended to display more relevant material symbols, such as an expensive watch, briefcase, or business suit, than students with better career prospects (Wicklund & Gollwitzer, 1982). A later series of studies examines the assumption that a compensatory relationship exists between increased use of material symbols of particular identity aspects and lack of experience, expertise, or competence in occupational, domestic, or ideological identity domains (Braun & Wicklund, 1989). Law students attached more importance to the outer manifestations of their professional identity (such as car or clothing) than practising attorneys, and first-year students reported buying more university-related clothes and accessories than students further advanced in their studies. Laying claim to relevant material symbols is explained for both junior groups by insecurity in their identities. However, symbolic self-completion presupposes that people have a personal commitment to particular identity domains and, when commitment was measured directly in four further studies, it was found that the compensatory relationship between recent entry into an identity and increased use of relevant material symbols held only for those people who were committed to that particular identity.

These studies are intriguing, but do not seem to substantiate fully the role of identity deficits implied by the theoretical framework of symbolic self-completion. They did not ascertain directly whether the respondents themselves (or their peers) actually felt that their identity was lacking in some respects. This makes it difficult to exclude the alternative explanation that the law or first-year students simply made more use of material symbols because of real or imagined peer pressure or because of their preconceived notions of how to display a certain identity, which later on they do not find substantiated. These explanations do not contradict a broad notion of self-completion, but they raise two as yet unresolved questions. The first concerns the extent to which the display of material symbols is based on an inner state of incompleteness rather than on social motivations to conform to the requirements of a particular identity. A second, related, question revolves around whether material symbols need to be displayed publicly, and appreciated by other people, for any self-completion to work. Surely, we can admire our new outfit in the mirror at home and feel better about ourselves by thinking and fantasising about the reactions of an imaginary audience. These ambiguities can be resolved, at least to some extent, if we conceive of self-completion as a process that dissolves an artificial public–private dichotomy, namely as a kind of psychological dialogue with both self and others (real or imagined) via the symbolic properties of material objects in terms of both personal and social identity.

Symbols of status, wealth, and group membership

Concentrating on social identities, clothes are perhaps the most obvious example of material possessions through which we can signify group affiliations and social standing, including sex-role identification, political orientation, or socio-economic status (e.g. Solomon, 1985). A more systematically researched expression of a person's standing are possessions that serve as status symbols, an area mainly investigated by sociologists. Inspired by Veblen's (1899) seminal essay on conspicuous and wasteful consumption of time and goods as a marker of high social status, later investigators have constructed reliable and valid measures for a family's socio-economic status and income based on inventories of their living-room interior and style (e.g. Laumann & House, 1970). Goffman (1951) offers a theoretical analysis of status symbols that distinguishes between their categorical significance, which identifies the social position of the owner, and their expressive significance for the owner's style of life and personal and cultural values.

As one would expect, status symbols change over time. Objects cease to serve as status symbols once they become shared too widely to denote exclusiveness.

Whereas "once a television was a symbol of affluence, now its near saturation makes its absence a sign of poverty" (Lunt & Livingstone, 1992, p. 62). With respect to the processes that might underlie changes in status symbols, there are both "trickle-down" and "trickle-up" effects (e.g. Blumberg, 1974; Frisby, 1984). Aspiring low-status groups imitate and adopt the status symbols of those groups slightly more affluent than they are, until higher-status groups discard these markers and adopt new ones to differentiate themselves. However, social groups are also engaged simultaneously in "upward" selection of new status symbols, some of which are drawn not from high-status groups but from rebellious subcultures (e.g. punk). Yet, it is important to recognise the power of an advertising-driven mass fashion that simultaneously informs, influences, and is adopted by social groups at many levels of the social–material hierarchy (Sproles, 1985). Yet, at an individual level, people also actively choose goods to be different from members of other social groups, selecting cultural tastes, including material possessions, that distinguish them from other groups and abandoning tastes when other social groups adopt them, all in order to both communicate identity and to avoid others making undesired identity inferences (Berger & Heath, 2007).

Moving on to a social psychological perspective on group membership, stereotypes of different social groups are typically examined through personal qualities ascribed to in-group and out-group members (e.g. Sedikides, Schopler, & Insko, 1998). However, for this chapter, the interesting question arises of whether stereotypes of different groups exist also in terms of material possession profiles. In the first study to examine this question empirically, I asked respondents from three different socio-economic groups (business employees, $n = 36$; students, $n = 40$; unemployed, $n = 50$) to list objects they thought of as favourite possessions, both for themselves and for members of the other two groups (Dittmar, 1994). When comparing the possessions group members listed for themselves with the possessions members of others groups had listed for them, two findings emerged that are typical features of stereotyping. First, members of other groups are perceived as being more similar to each other than they are, in that possessions listed for other groups were less diverse than those for one's own group. Second, differences between groups are perceived as greater than they actually are, given that goods related to the socio-economic differences between groups in terms of (relative) wealth and status were overemphasised. These are both examples of processes that are well documented in the stereotyping literature: outgroup homogeneity and between-group differentiation.

If people use material possession profiles to locate individuals in socio-economic terms and hold stereotypes associated with those profiles, it follows that first impressions of a person should differ, depending on whether that person is surrounded with material objects that denote a relatively higher, compared to lower, level of wealth. This hypothesis was examined in an experimental study (Dittmar, 1992b), disguised as research on first impressions of strangers, where I showed respondents a short video and asked them to describe the person they had seen. The respondents were 17- to 18-year-old adolescents ($n = 112$), attending different sixth-form colleges. The 4–5 minute video showed either a young man or young woman, coming home from work, making a cup of tea in his/her kitchen and flicking through the newspaper, putting some music on in the living room, and then leaving again, taking a sports bag to the car. These videos were carefully constructed to be as equivalent as possible in length and types of possessions shown, but the profile of actual material goods of the main character was chosen to denote either relative affluence (e.g. an expensive designer pine kitchen, state-of-the-art hi-fi equipment, high-status car), or a lack of affluence (e.g. basic kitchen and hi-fi equipment, small car). Video stills showing the man or woman in these two main experimental conditions are depicted in Figure 2.2. The levels of wealth shown in these two different video conditions were designed to convey affluent middle-class as compared to working-class material standing.

Affluent woman

Affluent man

Less affluent woman   *Less affluent man*

Figure 2.2 Video stills of the same individuals with affluent vs. less affluent material possession profiles. (*Note.* Reproduced from Dittmar (1992b), Perceived material wealth and first impressions, *British Journal of Social Psychology, 31*, p. 384, with kind permission of the British Psychological Society © 1992.)

The adolescent respondents themselves were either from an affluent middle-class or predominantly working-class background (operationalised by school catchment area) and, as expected, the middle-class adolescents described the affluent video as more similar to their family background, whereas the working-class adolescents saw the less affluent video as more similar. This material similarity between the video character and observer is important, because Social Identity Theory (Brown & Hewstone, 2005; Tajfel, 1984) leads to the expectation that people form more positive impressions of others who are members of the same in-group, in this case of the video character with a similar material background. Thus, impressions should differ depending on the inter-action between the video character's relative wealth and the socio-economic background of the observer. In contrast to this hypothesis based on Social Identity Theory, the wealth stereotypes prominent in consumer culture might be so pervasive and dominant that they are shared by both groups of adolescents, so that impressions would differ only on the basis of the material possession profile the video character was shown with. As argued in Chapter 1, the ideal of a "material good life" is pervasive in contemporary consumer culture, which leads to the prediction that the person shown in the video would be perceived much more positively by all when shown with expensive possessions.

It needs to be emphasised that the videos depicted the very same person, so that any differences in impressions are the sole consequence of the material possessions the person was shown with. The findings show that working- and middle-class adolescents agreed in their impressions, supporting the existence of widely shared wealth stereotypes. They perceived the person as significantly more intelligent, more assertive and forceful, and more in control when the possessions were expensive than when they were not. These are all attributes that are highly valued culturally. Yet impressions did not favour the more affluent person in all respects, because s/he was seen as less warm and expressive when affluent. Thus, the wealth stereotype combines less inter-personal warmth with a set of attributes that are overwhelmingly positive and important for success. These findings have been replicated consistently since (e.g. Christopher & Schlenker, 2000; Dittmar & Pepper, 1994).

Taken together, the research described in the earlier sections illustrates different ways in which material possessions are important to people because they constitute symbols for personal and social identity. They all stress the symbolic power of material possessions, almost to the exclusion of their functional utility or the control and mastery they afford. However, there is no reason to propose that recognition of the symbolic–communicational dimensions of possessions precludes an appreciation of their instrumental, control-related features.

An integrative model of the functions of material possessions

The psychological functions that material possessions fulfil for individuals have been examined mainly in qualitative research using the "favourite possessions paradigm", which asks respondents to choose their most treasured personal possessions and then explain in their own words why these objects are so important to them. I have used this paradigm in two of my own studies, which are detailed in the next section of this chapter (Dittmar, 1989, 1991). As in other research that has also used this paradigm, people's accounts are analysed to develop coding categories that summarise the reasons why possessions are important to individuals (e.g. Csikszentmihalyi & Rochberg-Halton, 1981; Kamptner, 1991; Richins, 1994). The resulting categories vary in number and detail, but tend to suggest a finely grained array of psychological functions. In contrast, a recent literature review that examines the construct of psychological ownership more broadly proposes just three main functions: efficacy and effectance, self-identity, and having a place to dwell, i.e. home (Pierce, Kostova, & Dirks, 2003). However, it could be argued that possessions providing people with a sense of home is not a distinct psychological function as such, but that "feeling at home" results from the diverse psychological functions that possessions can fulfil, such as providing emotional comfort, identity, and safety.

The integrative model in Figure 2.3 provides an analytical, hierarchically ordered map of the main types of psychological functions that material possessions fulfil, which we identified through content analyses of open-ended accounts (Dittmar, 1989, 1991), questionnaire studies (Dittmar, Beattie, & Friese, 1996), and in-depth interviews (Dittmar & Drury, 2000). This model first draws a distinction between the instrumental–functional uses of material objects on the one hand, such as making everyday activities more efficient

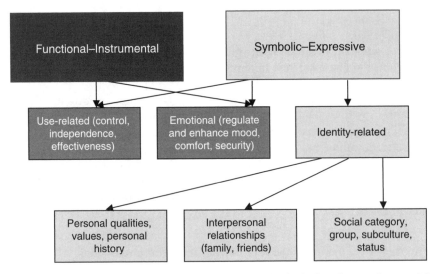

Figure 2.3 An integrative model of the psychological functions of material possessions.

and exerting control over the environment, and their symbolic functions as expressions of who we are on the other.

Moving one step down the hierarchy, possessions have use-related and emotional functions that draw on both instrumental and symbolic dimensions. If we take a car as an example, use-related meanings combine its functionality as a transport tool with it symbolising the owner's freedom and independence, and even sex appeal. This excerpt can serve as an example:

> [T]he Porsche ... roars and tugs to get moving. It accelerates even going uphill at 80 ... driving along Sunset at night in the 928 ... girls ... pulling up next to me ... and looking at me as if I were a cool guy.
>
> (Stein, 1985, p. 30)

Likewise, people use material goods for the purpose of making themselves feel better or enhancing their emotions, but the mood improvement and emotional comfort is usually tied not only to use-related features of these goods but also to their capacity for symbolising positive aspects of identity, such as a more ideal self, or being closely interrelated with significant others. An MP3 player is an example, where the great store of different songs enables people to fill their time, lift their mood, and feel belongingness with others who share the same musical taste.

The predominantly symbolic functions of possessions can be subdivided. First, as categorical symbols, signs of social identity, they enable individuals to express their social standing, wealth, and status, and they signify group membership, both in terms of broad social categories (e.g. social class) and smaller groups or subcultures (e.g. punks, travs). Second, possessions signify special relationships with specific individuals; gifts or heirlooms are prominent examples. These interpersonal relationships include romantic partners, friends, and family. Third, as self-expressive symbols, they function as signs of personal identity. They constitute a "snapshot" record of personal history and memories, giving individuals a sense of self-continuity. They can also represent a person's unique qualities, values, and attitudes. Recent work proposes that the desire to be differentiated from others, stand out from the crowd, and be unique is an important identity motive (Vignoles et al., 2006), which finds strong expression with respect to material goods (Tian, Bearden, & Hunter, 2001). These distinctions are analytical, rather than absolute, of course, and several psychological functions can be interwoven in a single material good. An expensive watch can function as a financial asset, as well as symbolise both social status and connectedness with one's family, if it is an heirloom.

IDENTITY-RELATED DIFFERENCES IN FUNCTIONS OF POSSESSIONS

Returning to the question of people's leanings toward being a "symbolic" or an "instrumental" possessor, we can now use this integrative model to review factors that influence the relative emphasis that individuals place on different psychological functions of their possessions. Socio-economic status (SES) is such an influence; high-SES, middle-class business managers are more concerned with their utility, leisure, and sentimental possessions as unique symbols of their personal history and development, whereas low-SES, working-class unemployed individuals focus more on the directly functional, active, and emotional uses of their leisure and utility objects, such as "switching off" or "escaping" (Dittmar, 1991). This was interpreted as reflecting a highly individualised, long-term perspective on self-development—more characteristic of a high social-material position—in contrast to a short-term, functional perspective more likely to be adopted by individuals from a low social-material position, at least in part arising from a constantly enforced concern with economic and emotional security. Generational differences are a further example, where individuals' views of their consumer goods constituting necessities or luxuries depends on the requirements associated with their life stage (e.g. young and single compared to older with family), but also on the extent to which they were socialised into contemporary consumer culture (Lunt & Livingstone, 1992). However, the main concern here is with differences in the psychological functions of possessions that are directly associated with identity construal.

Identity through the life-span

Changes in the psychological functions of possessions from infancy to old age have been documented consistently, where concerns with control, mastery, and independence are gradually overtaken by a focus on the symbolic functions of goods, first with respect to one's own identity and then increasingly with respect to close personal relationships with others, such as friends and family. This trajectory of change has been interpreted as reflecting different stages, or tasks, of identity development, which are thought to apply universally. Although this perspective is not without merit, the evidence on which it is based typically was collected in individualist, Western cultures. Challenging a universalist perspective, there is good evidence to support the viewpoint taken in this book that different orientations towards material possessions can be shaped at every stage of development: socio-cultural frameworks associated either with different cultures or with gender influence typical, or preferred, modes of identity construal, which in turn are reflected in the psychological functions that people emphasise.

Infants often establish a special relationship with just one or two material objects during the first 2 years of their lives, usually a cuddly toy or object (e.g. Passman, 1976), or "transitional object" (Winnicott, 1953), which has been argued to play a significant role in the child's development from total dependency towards autonomy by giving emotional comfort through symbolising the nurturing person when s/he is not physically present and—as the first "not me" possession—helping the child to draw a boundary between self and the external world. Yet, cross-cultural research suggests that socialisation practices influence object attachment, rather than cuddlies constituting a necessary, and therefore universal, step in infants' successful individuation and construction of self-identity. Young children in rural India and East-African Gabon had no special objects, but almost continuous body contact with the nurturer, whereas over 70% of (then West) German children needed such an object to be able to go to sleep (Stanjek, 1980). Similarly, figures of well over 50% of American children having cuddlies contrast with the much lower figure of 4% for Turkish children (Gulerce, 1991).

The findings from two extensive studies on older children, adolescents, and adults of different ages can be summarised briefly to illustrate the main findings reported. An ethnographic study that asked three generations—children, parents, and grandparents—in over 80 Chicago family homes which of the objects in the house were particularly important to them and why, found that the youngest generation described treasured possessions predominantly in terms of the active functions they fulfil for them in establishing independence and autonomy, whereas the oldest generation was concerned with the symbolic record that photographs and memorabilia provided of their lives and relationships with their loved ones (Csikszentmihalyi & Rochberg-Halton, 1981). A study with almost 600 South Californian respondents, which used five tightly defined age groups, reports a similar change (Kamptner, 1991). Older children (10–11 years) named sports equipment and toys most often, with two-thirds giving instrumental reasons, revolving around the enjoyment, freedom, and activities afforded by these objects and their physical properties. For adolescents (14–18 years), possessions were more varied, and, in addition to enjoyment and activity, peer-group ties associated with these objects and the aspects of identity they expressed emerged as the most common reasons. Young adults talked about both the interpersonal ties their cars, jewellery, photographs, and general memorabilia symbolised, as well as the enjoyment these items provided. In middle and late adulthood, photographs and jewellery take increasingly prominent places as favoured objects, with a growing emphasis on the social and family networks they signify, and the emotions and memories associated with them.

Kamptner (1991) draws on Erikson's (1980) model of identity development to explain these changes. Having developed a sense of trust and security in early infancy, the central task of childhood is to build a sense of competence, mastery, and independence, whereas the main task in adolescence is the development of an autonomous identity. Early adulthood is about finding intimate relationships, which is followed by establishing social links with different generations in middle adulthood through, for instance, building one's own family. Late adulthood is characterised by a retrospective life review process, where reminders of the past and relationships aid in the maintenance and assessment of one's lifelong sense of self.

Thus, developmental changes suggests a gradual shift of emphasis from instrumental to self-expressive and, finally, to the social, symbolic functions of material possessions, depending on the main identity tasks people are engaged in. However, this life span approach should not be taken to imply that there is a universal pattern for the links between identity and material possessions. Both sets of studies reported pronounced gender differences. And, as with the meanings of cuddlies in early childhood, there is evidence that culture influences these links.

Culture

The findings described previously are based exclusively on respondents in the US and the UK, but a growing literature in social psychology documents that identity construction differs cross-culturally. Individualist cultures, such as the US and UK, tend to privilege an independent form of self-construal, where identity is autonomous, separate from others, and defined by personal goals, whereas collectivist cultures emphasise interdependent self-construal, where identity is defined through connectedness with others and the importance of group goals (Markus & Kitayama, 1991; Smith, Bond, & Kagitcibasi, 2006). A study comparing favourite possessions and their meaning among US residents with those in a traditional, tribal community in Niger (Wallendorf & Arnould, 1988) found not only that the objects named were radically different, but also that the reasons why they were treasured focused predominantly on symbolising personal history in the US, in contrast to symbolising status within the community and commitment to shared values in Niger. Although this study was not designed to assess identity construction directly, its findings are consistent with the proposal that material possessions are likely to symbolise personal identity in an individualist culture, and social identity in a collectivist society.

We examined the hypothesis that the reasons why material possessions are important to individuals would reflect culturally prevalent modes of identity construction in a cross-cultural comparison of students from the US ($n = 139$), UK ($n = 158$), and Hong Kong ($n = 117$) (Bond, Dittmar, Singelis, Papadopoulou, & Chiu, 2002).[1] The US and the UK are highly individualist cultures, whereas Hong Kong is more collectivist; the country ranks are 1, 3, and 37 respectively on Hofstede's (1980) individualism–collectivism dimensions. We examined cultural differences in identity construction by asking respondents to give open-ended self-descriptions in response to the prompt "Who am I?", both in general terms but also in specific contexts such as at home or with friends. This procedure is an adaptation of the Twenty Statements Test (Kuhn & McPartland, 1954). Self-descriptions were coded as independent when they referred to qualities that centre on the individual only, such as "I am intelligent", and as group-based when they described group membership, such as "I am a student". As would be expected, a greater percentage of self-statements (across domains) showed independent self-construal in the US and UK than in Hong Kong (68%, 65%, and 51%, respectively), whereas the pattern was opposite for group-based self-statements (5%, 8%, and 14%, respectively). It has to be borne in mind that students are a fairly homogenous respondent group, and therefore less likely to show cultural differences than other populations. The findings showed that, in relative terms, identity construction was more individualist in the Western countries, and more collectivist in Hong Kong.

With respect to material possessions, respondents listed their three favourite possessions and evaluated their psychological functions on a number of six-point rating scales. For instance, they indicated the extent to which a possession was important to them because it "improves my mood, provides emotional outlet", "reminds me of my relationship with a particular person", or "expresses what is unique about me, different from others". It was expected that possessions are more likely to be valued in individualist cultures as markers of a unique and distinctive identity, and because they offer individuals the opportunity to regulate their mood and express their personal emotions.

The findings, shown in Figure 2.4, support the hypothesis that there is some match between cultural-level individualism and these two psychological functions of material possessions. Although there was little difference in the extent to which respondents from the three cultures valued material possessions because of their symbolised relationships with other people and associated personal memories, emotional functions focused on the individual were rated

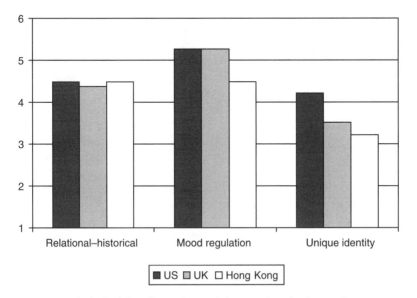

Figure 2.4 Psychological functions of material possessions in three cultures.

as more important in the US and UK than in Hong Kong. Similarly, possessions were valued as symbols of a unique identity most strongly in the US, followed by the UK, and least strongly in Hong Kong. Thus, there are systematic differences between cultures in identity-related and mood-regulation functions of material possessions that reflect culturally privileged forms of self-construal. Yet self-construal differences exist not only between, but also within, cultures.

Gender

All of the "favourite possessions" studies reviewed earlier confirm that women and men give rather different accounts. Men showed a preference for action-oriented goods, such as vehicles and leisure objects, and tended to refer more to the practical, control- and activity-related features of their possessions, as captured in this man's account of his motorbike: "Most valuable thing I own. Gives me a sense of independence and it's a means of transport. I feel it says something about me and I want to be different". By comparison, women are more likely to choose sentimental possessions, and their reasons refer more to the role of possessions as symbols of interpersonal relationships and their emotional significance. A typical example is this woman's account: "My necklace means a lot to me because it was given to me by my grandmother". These gender differences in the psychological functions of possessions can be understood as reflections of the ways in which women and men typically construct their identity. Men tend towards a more *in*dependent form of identity construction and expression (aimed at separateness from others, autonomy and being able to do things) in contrast to women's more *inter*dependent identity (concerned with embeddedness in close personal relationships). Of course, women and men can, and do, use both independent and interdependent forms of identity constructions, but gender differences have been demonstrated consistently in their typical preferences (Cross & Madson, 1997). These are reflected in the identity-related functions that individual women and men value most in their material possessions.

I analysed the reasons women and men gave when describing different types of favourite possession with a qualitative technique (correspondence analysis) that provides a graphic display of how closely associated reasons and possessions are, separately for women and men (Dittmar, 1989). As shown in Figure 2.5, instrumental reasons given by men are located in close proximity to transport vehicles, which means that they explained the personal importance of their cars or motorbikes strongly by referring to their functional, practical uses.

Correspondence analysis provides only a graphic display of the links between types of possessions and reasons given by women and men; its meaning needs to be interpreted. Overall, Figure 2.5 confirms that, independent of their preferences for different types of goods, women and men relate to their possessions in distinctive ways, consistent with the literature on gender

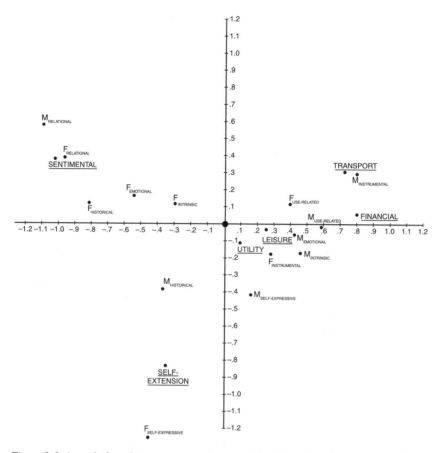

Figure 2.5 Associations between possessions and their functions in women and men. (*Note.* Reproduced from Dittmar (1989), Gender identity-related meanings of personal possessions, *British Journal of Social Psychology, 28*, p. 167, with kind permission of the British Psychological Society © 1989.)

identity. By comparison, women construe their relation to personal possessions in a relational and symbolic manner as compared to men's instrumental and self-oriented perspective. Women's responses tend to be located towards the left side, the location of symbolic concerns, whereas men's were located towards the right side, where practical and functional concerns were mapped. In addition, self-oriented concerns—toward the bottom end of the display—were more important for men's self-expression and personal history, whereas women had an other-oriented, symbolic focus as sources of personal history, relatedness to others, and emotions, mapped toward the top left of the display. Gender differences are relative, rather than absolute, of course, but it is interesting to note that they influence the psychological functions that people value in the material possessions they own.

CONCLUSION

The evidence is persuasive that material possessions are perceived as a part of the self, that they are related to how people evaluate themselves, and that their unintended loss can lead to painful disruptions of the possessions–self bond. Moreover, the research reviewed clearly supports the usefulness of a concept of extended self, i.e. a self that stretches beyond the boundaries of the physical body to include material objects.

Possessions clearly fulfil diverse psychological functions for individuals, as shown in the integrative model developed in this chapter. However, when it comes to understanding the nature of the close psychological bond between who a person is and what they have, it appears that symbolic and self-expressive dimensions of material objects are particularly important, over and above the control and mastery that they afford people. The psychological functions of material possessions can change throughout the life course, but rather than reflecting universally applicable developmental stages, these differences in the psychological functions that people emphasise can be viewed as reflections of identity construction. This chapter offered a social symbolic perspective on possessions as socially shared and constructed symbols of identity, and provided support for this proposal through studies that documented that the psychological functions of material objects reflect socio-culturally privileged form of identity construction, which differ not just between individualist and collectivist cultures, but also by gender.

This chapter suggests that material possessions can have positive psychological functions in maintaining or enhancing people's sense of who they are. However, identity seeking through material goods can have negative consequences for well-being when it becomes excessive, through a strong commitment to materialistic values (Chapter 4), or when people engage in compulsive buying (Chapter 5). Before I move on to report our research on these dark sides of consumer culture, we need to consider the role that psychological motives play when people buy new consumer goods.

3 Consuming passions?
Psychological motives for
buying consumer goods

Helga Dittmar

Synopsis

The close psychological bond between material goods and our identity documented in Chapter 2 is also evident when we buy new consumer goods. The very nature of shopping and buying has shifted away from functional toward psychological concerns, and this is examined in diverse ways:

- Managing our mood and enhancing our identity are significant buying motives in conventional shops ("bricks") and the new environment of the internet ("clicks").
- Buying motives are less gendered online than in conventional environments.
- Mood- and identity-related buying motives are important when people buy goods on impulse, and they are also linked to people's tendency to overspend.

Let's Go Shopping!

© Jessica Barlow

Having owned favourite material possessions for some time is clearly different from shopping for new material goods, but it stands to reason that psychological functions that are important in having material objects, such as the desire to express or enhance identity, also play a role in motivating people to buy. When we asked adults to tell us the thoughts that would go through their head when deciding whether or not to buy particular goods, the question "is it me?" emerged spontaneously as an important buying consideration (Dittmar & Beattie, 1998). It seems that the very nature of buying and shopping has become more psychological, with a stronger focus on hoped-for emotional and identity-related benefits. In popular culture, these developments are captured by such slogans as "retail therapy" and "I shop therefore I am". They make not only play a role for buying in conventional shops ("bricks"), but also for buying on the internet ("clicks"), which is showing exponential growth.

This focus on buying dimensions that entail psychological motives differs radically from traditional models of consumer behaviour, which take "rational" purchase decision-making as their normative framework. According to such utility maximisation or rational choice perspectives, consumers should make decisions based on elaborate information searches, detailed trade-offs between costs and benefits, and functional dimensions of goods, such as comparative value for money and practical purpose (cf. Dittmar & Beattie, 1998). For some time now, this framework has been criticised because it does not describe at all well how individuals do, in fact, buy goods (e.g. March, 1978). Later work is more radical in its criticism by proposing that rationality or irrationality should not be used as yardsticks against which to understand and evaluate consumer behaviour (e.g. Etzioni, 1988), although this position can be hard to defend when it comes to such dysfunctional behaviour as compulsive buying (see Chapter 5). The buying motives examined in this chapter span functional, emotional, social, and identity-related concerns. As we will see, buying in contemporary consumer culture is often about "hot" passions, not only mere "cold" deliberation.

FROM SHOPPER TYPOLOGIES TO BUYING MOTIVES

The first systematic approach to conceptualising orientations toward buying was the construction of diverse shopper types (e.g. Stone, 1954). A relatively recent example is a survey of UK respondents (Lunt & Livingstone, 1992), which identified five types: *routine shoppers*, who buy according to need rather than on impulse; *leisure shoppers*, who come close to the stereotype of "I shop therefore I am"; *thrifty shoppers*, who are economical; *careful shoppers*, who get some pleasure from buying; and *alternative shoppers*, who have an anti-consumerist stance and prefer second-hand outlets. These types vary on a host of economic, psychological, and socio-demographic factors. For instance, more women and younger people are leisure shoppers. Similar to the *leisure shopper*, Campbell (2000) recently added the *recreational shopper* to Stone's original US typology of *economic*, *personalising*, *ethical*, and *apathetic* shoppers.

These typologies clearly have merits: they provide an analytical map of possible buying dimensions and orientations. However, they are based on the assumption, at least implicitly, that an individual can be characterised sensibly in terms of a single, stable, and coherent buying orientation, which generalises across different buying situations. This inflexibility of buyer typologies might be one of the reasons why a number of researchers have focused instead on buying dimensions—motives and orientations toward buying—to analyse and understand consumer behaviour, such as utilitarian versus hedonic values (Babin, Darden, & Griffin, 1994), or leisure, economic, and social involvement in shopping (Bergadaa, Faure, & Perrien, 1995). As I will demonstrate in this chapter, there is good evidence for the usefulness of using buying motives to help us understand what drives people when they buy consumer goods in different buying environments, such as conventional shops compared to the internet.

Functional concerns on the one hand, such as usefulness or good value for money, and emotional–social factors on the other, such as fun and the benefits of social interactions during shopping, emerge as two major buying dimensions from previous studies. However, they neglect to include consumer concerns with identity construction, despite good evidence that consumers are motivated to buy goods as symbols of who they are or would like to be. Expressing identity and searching for a better self through consumer goods is proposed to be a core feature of modern consumption (Benson, 2000). Open-ended accounts of buying motives in women's shopping diaries we collected show that concerns with identity seeking were reported as frequently as concerns with whether goods are useful or good value for money (see Chapter 5 for more detail). In a set of UK studies, we used questionnaire scales to measure buying motives (Dittmar, 2000, 2001), where respondents rated how important different motives are for them personally for diverse types of consumer goods, so that each person gave multiple ratings for each buying motive. Here I report on the average importance accorded each motive across the different consumer goods. The first two items focused on functional concerns—"good value for money"; "useful and practical"—and the third assessed the extent to which people bought goods because "it puts me in a better mood", focusing on emotional benefit. The remaining three items measured identity-related concerns: the extent to which individuals buy goods to express who they are ("expresses what is unique about me"), to move closer to the kind of person they would ideally like to be ("makes me feel more like the person I want to be"), and to enhance their social image ("improves my social standing"). When we researched these buying motives, our sample included both ordinary buyers and individuals who had problems with compulsive buying. As the focus in this chapter is on ordinary buying, I report buying motives only for those individuals whose buying behaviour did not show any problematic or dysfunctional dimensions ($n = 236$, see Chapter 5 for comparisons between ordinary and compulsive buyers).

Functional motives were reported to be most important, receiving mean ratings of 4.1 for both usefulness and good value for money (on a six-point scale). This is not surprising, given that popular conceptions of what it means to be a "good" consumer centre on being able to get the best value for money and pick goods that are fit for their purpose. However, the buying motive to improve one's mood emerged almost as powerfully, with a mean rating of 3.7. Although identity-related buying motives were not quite as strong, they nevertheless emerged as concerns that were of importance. The motive to move closer to an ideal self was close to the scale mid-point, with a mean rating of 3.0, and the strongest of the identity-related concerns, as expected. This was followed by the motive for self-expression, with a mean rating of 2.9, whereas social status improvement was seen as less important (mean rating 2.0).

Thus, three main dimensions of buying motives can be identified. In addition to instrumental and economic motives, there are two main sets of non-functional buying dimensions, which have a motivational component: individuals engage in buying and shopping to obtain emotional and identity-related benefits. Knowing that psychological motives are significant when people buy consumer goods is important, of course, but there are the even more interesting questions concerning the type of person who is most strongly driven by these motives, as well as the type of context in which these motives become particularly salient. Here, we consider gender as an influence on buying motives, and type of good and impulsive buying as contexts of interest.

BUYING MOTIVES AND GENDER

Gender differences were noted in previous research, where women showed much stronger buying involvement than men (Bergadaa et al., 1995), particularly on the leisure and social dimensions, whereas men were particularly high on apathy. We document in an in-depth interview study that shopping seems to play a more psychologically and emotionally encompassing role for women than men, with respect to consumer goods other than routine household shopping (Dittmar & Drury, 2000). Campbell (2000) also reports that women have highly positive attitudes, associating buying with leisure, whereas men tend to have negative attitudes, seeing buying as work that they want to accomplish with minimum input of time and effort. In other words, women typically focus on the (often enjoyable) process of buying, whereas men focus on the outcome: obtaining the actual good with least fuss. Clearly, this general tendency might be less strong or even reversed for particular types of goods, such as tools or computer equipment, which are predominantly bought by male consumers. Notwithstanding such exceptions, it can be plausibly argued that, overall, buying consumer goods is more integral to the personal and social identity of women, at least in terms of traditional gender identity (see also Fischer & Gainer, 1991), and therefore plays a stronger emotional, psychological, and symbolic role for them compared to men, whose personal and social identity—traditionally at least—is less tied up with the processes of shopping and buying consumer goods. Of course, consumption is also important to men but they appear more concerned with having obtained the right, often expensive and rarely bought, goods, say a car that denotes high social status. Taking these arguments together, they lead to the expectation of gender differences in the relative importance of the three main sets of buying motives identified: functional issues should be more important to men, whereas emotional–social and identity-related motives should be stronger for women. It is important to emphasise that these predictions of gender differences should not be misunderstood as an essentialist account of differences between male and female consumers. Rather, buying is likely to remain gendered in the way described only as long as women and men continue to internalise sociocultural norms and socially shared representations that frame shopping and buying as differentially linked to women and men's social, personal, and gender identities.

In the survey already described, functional concerns were equally important to women and men, against expectation. Our expectations of gender differences in buying motives were supported with respect to mood regulation, where the importance of buying goods in order to cheer oneself up was significantly greater for women than men. Similar findings emerged for the identity-related motives, which were more strongly endorsed by women than men, and this difference is pronounced and significant with respect to buying consumer goods in order to express unique aspects of the self. In summary, then, gender differences in buying motives were evident, suggesting that women tend towards psychological buying motives more strongly than men. However, the strength of these motives is also affected by other factors, such as type of good, where some goods might lend themselves to psychologically driven, impulsive buying but others do not.

IMPULSE BUYING: WHEN PASSION TAKES OVER DELIBERATION

Impulsive purchasing has three main characteristics. It is "spur of the moment", typically done with little deliberation and prior planning; individuals' emotional and psychological involvement is high; and their desire for the good is so strong that they disregard financial constraints and consequences (Dittmar & Drury, 2000; Verplanken & Herabadi, 2001). Impulsive buying is extremely common, with 90% of people making such purchases at least occasionally (Hausmann, 2000). Yet, people often wish afterwards they had not done so. In studies of impulse buyers, 80% were found to refer to some negative consequences from their purchases (Rook, 1987) and 55% explicitly reported regret at least once in our purchase diary (Dittmar, 2001).

Impulse buying seems the prototypical consumption scenario where passion takes over deliberation. When we asked people ($n = 32$) during in-depth interviews about their experiences of planned buying as compared with impulsive purchasing (Dittmar & Drury, 2000), they described four main differences. Whereas planned buying involves deliberation, information search, and careful price and quality comparisons—"I'd actually hum and hah and look up the *Which* reports and all this type of thing before I bought" (p. 121)—impulse buying happens on the spur of the moment: "Just seeing something that I hadn't given any thought to. You know, wasn't in my mind to think about that item. Just buying it, quickly without going away and thinking about it, buying it straight away" (p. 123). Second, planned buying involves careful consideration of whether one can afford a good—"We consider our finance carefully, what we can afford and what we can't afford. In the end we will go for the best deal" (p. 125)—whereas financial constraints are ignored in impulse buying—"But impulse, you don't worry about whether you've got enough money in your budget or not. You just buy it and then you worry about it afterwards" (p. 125). Third, in contrast to planned purchases, impulse buying is driven by strong desire: "You see something and you think 'I've got to have that', and you buy it" (p. 125). Finally, it seems that psychological motives are important when buying on impulse. Emotional motives emerged, "if I'm really feeling pee'd off, I can go shopping and that will cheer me up" (p. 128), and, most significantly, identity-related concerns: "I probably wanted to make myself feel that I was something better than I was. And so, to do that, I bought expensive clothes, expensive make-up, expensive perfumes . . . I used to think 'Oh, the shop assistants probably think I've got loads of money and I'm this sort of person' . . . (*Interviewer: What kind of person?*) I think it was a kind of, sort of, a smartly dressed, young, trendy woman that you see around the places, can afford to wear designer labels and show them off, and have Chanel make-up and that kind of thing. The sort of image that they portray . . . in the make-up adverts" (p. 135).

If it is indeed the case that people are most likely to purchase those goods on impulse that symbolise ideal dimensions of their self-concept, then impulse buying should be highly selective. The experience of "I want it and I want it now" should depend on the type of consumer good, because the symbolic value of material possessions is shaped to a large extent by consumer culture, so that certain goods lend themselves more to projecting identity concerns than others (e.g. Dittmar, 1992a). For example, clothes should make more likely targets for consumer impulsivity than goods that have less symbolic potential. We asked a sample of adult employees ($n = 31$) how much they bought and valued four different types of consumer goods because they "express who you are, make you feel more like your ideal". The main finding was a strong effect for clothes having a much more powerful function of symbolising identity than other goods, such as basic body-care products or tools. In a series of experimental studies (Dittmar & Bond, 2007), we used a temporal discounting paradigm to study how difficult people find it to delay the immediate gratification of different types of consumer goods. Discount rates measure the subjective cost of delaying immediate gratification; respondents tell us how much money they would want as compensation for having to wait for a specified length of time.[2] The hypothesis that consumer impulsivity differs, depending on type of consumer good, was supported in three experiments, one with students ($n = 96$) and two with samples of adult consumers ($n = 57$; $n = 67$). Discount rates were significantly steeper for fashionable clothes than for basic body-care products in the first two experiments, and steeper for clothes than tools in the third. Thus, individuals were much more inclined toward impulsivity with respect to clothes, a type of good that lends itself particularly well to projecting identity, than with respect to body-care goods or tools, which offer little such identity-related potential.

In the survey described earlier, individuals rated the importance of buying motives with respect to clothes as well as body care products, when they buy these types of good on impulse, defined as "a 'spur of the moment' decision in the shop". The findings for psychological motives are shown in Figure 3.1. All psychological buying motives were much stronger for clothes as impulse buys than body-care products. The difference was most pronounced on the motives for self-expression and moving closer to an ideal self.

Considering the various findings reviewed, psychological motives for buying appear stronger when people buy goods on impulse, where there is little deliberation and a disregard for financial constraints. They also differ by type of good, such that they are much more salient for clothes, a typical impulse buy, than for items with little symbolic potential. In particular, motives related to expressing and enhancing identity seem particularly strong. However, the research discussed so far pertains to the emotional and psychological gratification of buying goods in conventional shops and stores. Yet this tells only part of the story of contemporary consumer culture, given the recent, exponential growth of buying in a radically different environment: the internet. It seems surprising that there is little research as yet that explicitly addresses buying motives in online buying.

THE INTERNET AS A CONTEMPORARY BUYING ENVIRONMENT

Nearly three out of four US adults now use the internet (73%), with the figure highest among young adults aged 18–29 years, where penetration hits an all-time high of 89% (Pew Internet & American Life, 2006). UK figures seem comparable, with surveys reporting between 68% and 75% of adults

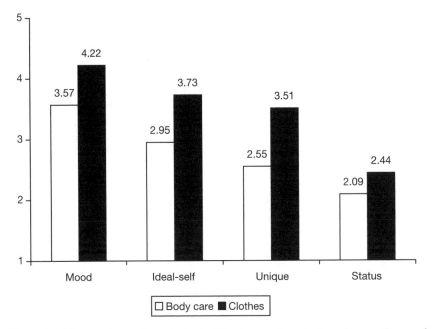

Figure 3.1 Mean ratings of psychological buying motives in impulse purchases of body-care products and clothes.

using the internet (Internet Statistics Compendium, 2006). The migration from conventional to internet buying is accelerating at an exponential rate (Interactive Media in Retail Group, 2004), and a considerable percentage of consumers, 21%, already prefer to purchase online rather than at conventional stores (Browne, Durrett, & Wetherbe, 2004). Internet buying prevalence is highest in the US, with estimates that between 65% (Pew Internet & American Life, 2004) and 93% (Business Software Association, 2002) of internet users buy online, but it is growing rapidly also in the UK: 50% of adults using the internet in the first 3 months of 2004 had ordered goods or services online (Office of National Statistics, 2004). Moreover, the demographic profile of internet users is changing: once dominated by affluent, professional men, the profile of typical internet users is fast coming to resemble that of the general population (UCLA Internet Report, 2003).

Although this is likely to be changing among children and adolescents now, the computer environment has traditionally been seen by adults as "masculine". This can make women feel disempowered, and possibly excluded, whereas men feel at home online (Woodfield, 2000). Indeed, gender gaps in internet use were pronounced until a few years ago, but appear to be closing. For instance, whereas UK users in 1998 were 85% men and 15% women (Moharan-Martin, 1998), women constituted half of the UK online population by November 2000 (Jupiter MMXI, 2000). This change mirrors US trends (e.g. Pew Internet & American Life, 2004). Yet notwithstanding this closure of the gender gap, women and men might still experience the internet differently. A stereotypically masculine culture around computer use is evident in the marketing of, and participation in, computer-based games, and such attitudes could still generalise to the internet, described as a "highly technological male domain" (Morahan-Martin, 1998). Skill and confidence in navigating internet sites have been identified as important antecedents of positive attitudes toward the internet as a shopping environment (Childers, Carr, Peck, & Carson, 2001). It might therefore be the case that, in contrast to conventional buying, women find buying online much less enjoyable, whereas the opposite may be true for men.

Online buying

Initially, research on internet buying focused on factors that predicted whether or not people buy online, particularly demographic profiles of internet buyers and non-buyers, rather than their psychological attributes. These studies focus on concerns about credit card security or internet fraud (e.g. UCLA Internet Report, 2003) and, when they address buying motives at all, they tend to be limited to the functional advantages of buying online. Of course, these are easy to identify: it facilitates price comparisons, and people can purchase from a single location at any time, 24 hours a day, 7 days a week. Understandably, convenience and efficiency emerged as consistent motives for internet purchasing, but findings are contradictory concerning price: whereas one survey found that internet shoppers were less price conscious than non-shoppers (Donthu & Garcia, 1999), another reported that 60% of shoppers claim to have saved money by buying online (Pew Internet & American Life, 2002).

Relatively few studies have considered the emotional or social factors associated with buying online. Such concerns have been demonstrated to be significant motives in conventional shopping, but it is not clear how such motives would extrapolate to the internet. For instance, people who derive pleasure from conventional buying might be deterred from e-commerce if they believe it to be less psychologically rewarding. However, those who believe that internet buying is (potentially) pleasurable should be more likely to make purchases in this way. Some online buying studies have investigated hedonic motives, but usually without specifying the environment in which the buying activity is carried out. Enjoyment of shopping (in general) as a recreational activity did not differentiate internet shoppers from non-shoppers (Donthu & Garcia, 1999), but a study that specifically examined buying motives online demonstrated that hedonic concerns are at least as important as utilitarian considerations when people purchase goods other than everyday groceries and household products (Childers et al., 2001). Social and experiential motives are less well facilitated online, despite the introduction of such internet retail website features as the ability to e-mail product information to a friend, or strong visual stimuli, including the opportunity to try clothes or make-up on digital "dummy" bodies or faces. Finally, the lack of direct contact with the goods being purchased has been examined, but whereas the need to see products before purchase was identified as important by 53% of non-e-buyers in one survey (Ernst and Young, 1999), it did not differentiate between e-buyers and non-e-buyers in another (Olivero, 2000). Indicative of likely future trends, Childers et al. (2001) showed that consumers' perception that the internet provides an acceptable substitute for direct product examination underlies positive attitudes toward online buying.

In summary, the internet is rapidly becoming a significant environment for buying consumer goods, yet little is known that can help build a foundation for a better psychological understanding of online buying. The majority of previous studies on internet buying are limited because they tend to focus on a narrow range of factors assumed to be of primary importance to internet buyers, such as convenience. Emotional and social buying motives online have been relatively neglected and there is no previous research at all on identity-related concerns. Yet these psychological buying motives are likely to be significant not only in conventional shops but also on the internet. Moreover, given gender differences in conventional buying motives, as well as with respect to using the internet, two interesting research questions arise: "How do buying motives in conventional shops relate to buying motives online" and "Do these relationships differ for male and female consumers?"

BUYING MOTIVE RESEARCH WITH YOUNG CONSUMERS IN THE UK

We carried out two studies (Dittmar, Long, & Meek, 2004) with the explicit aims of examining buying motives not only in conventional buying, but also in the alternative buying environment of the internet, while taking gender differences into account. Our concern with overcoming the limitations of previous research by identifying a comprehensive range of buying motives suggested a qualitative study as a first step. The findings can then be used in the development of a quantitative survey that uses finely grained, multi-item measures of the main buying motives that emerge.

For both studies, we chose students as respondents, because this population is particularly internet-literate, as well as making tests of gender hypotheses fairly stringent. They constitute a group of young consumers who all have internet access (through the university if not also at home), who use computers routinely, and who fall predominantly into the 18–25 age group, where internet use is highest. Internet use is encouraged in university settings and it has become almost a necessity for students when they search for information or communicate with tutors. It also seems that there is little difference between the online sites visited by college students and the general

US internet audience (ComScore Media Matrix, 2002). Although students are probably more limited in their capacity for spending money than young adults of a comparable age who are in full-time employment, this difference appears less important for an investigation of motives, as reported here, rather than for a survey of, say, purchase frequency. Moreover, students—compared to the general population—are more likely to have challenged or overcome traditional gender-role identifications.

Bricks versus clicks: Buying motives in conventional and online buying

In the first, qualitative, study, we used thematic analysis on respondents' written accounts ($n = 113$) to identify what they experience as advantages and disadvantages when they buy consumer goods, separately for conventional shops and the internet. They were specifically instructed to exclude grocery and household shopping, and to focus on personal consumer goods, a distinction supported by the finding of Childers et al. (2001) that, in comparison, everyday household purchases are more strongly driven by practical and economic motives. The analytic process was much the same as the one we used for transcribed interviews on impulsive buying (Dittmar & Drury, 2000). It involved coding of the text to identify recurring themes in responses, and then sorting these into a hierarchical order of predominant themes and associated subthemes. The content and relative prominence of primary themes and subthemes was identified across the sample as a whole, as well as in terms of comparisons between women and men, and between those who did and did not buy online, designated as e-buyers and non-e-buyers.

With respect to functional factors, convenience and efficiency emerged as motives in conventional buying, and men in particular referred to shopping with minimum effort and hassle: "[W]hen I go shopping for goods, I don't like spending much time doing it. Often I'll buy one of the first things I see" (Dittmar et al., 2004, p. 429). These functional aspects were emphasised by the majority of respondents more strongly in the context of the internet and, in addition, benefits of browsing and comparisons were highlighted, as well as increased access to goods and cheaper prices online. Three main findings emerged with respect to emotional, experiential, and social factors. Both women and men stated that an important advantage of conventional buying was the ability to have direct contact with the good (handle, try on), and women more strongly than men referred to the atmosphere in shops, as well as shopping being a social activity together with others (e.g. friends). In contrast, these social and experiential aspects were seen as comparatively lacking in internet buying by the majority of respondents, particularly non-e-buyers. Spontaneous descriptions of emotional involvement in conventional buying were given predominantly by women (75%), with three subthemes: "buzz" or thrill; excitement of an unexpected bargain or find; and mood regulation in the form of escapism, reward, or distraction. The majority of those respondents who described the internet as less emotionally engaging were also women.

Although not as prominent as the other two themes, buying motives related to identity did emerge as a distinct third dimension. The main focus was on self-expression, increasing self-esteem, and projecting a more ideal image to others and to oneself. This incorporates the ways in which purchases relate to the ideal self, the prestige of newly acquired goods, or how buying can make one feel better about oneself. Subthemes related to bringing new goods home or wearing new clothes when going out, and receiving compliments or feeling better about oneself because of the new goods. For example, respondents reported an additional thrill of wearing newly purchased clothes, in terms of a boost in self-image and self-esteem, as well as compliments they receive from others. This was found both for women—"I like shopping for clothes, to feel better about myself when wearing these new clothes"—and for men—"It is when I get to use the product that I enjoy the most, . . . wearing new clothes out, especially if I am complimented on them" (Dittmar et al., 2004, p. 432). Although identity-related motives were voiced explicitly only with respect to conventional buying, there is no reason why they should not also apply to online buying.

Three findings of our qualitative research are novel. First, three primary themes emerged and recurred: functional issues; emotional, experiential, and social factors; and identity-related concerns. These are consistent with the three main sets of buying motives postulated earlier. Second, functional motives seemed more prominent for internet than conventional buying, whereas online buying was seen as less psychologically involving because it is poorer with respect to social–experiential shopping dimensions and, particularly for women, emotional engagement. Finally, although expected gender differences emerged in conventional buying—women reported psychological involvement in the whole shopping and buying process, whereas men focused on efficiency and convenience in obtaining buying outcomes—gender differences were much less evident with respect to internet buying. Overall, there is an indication that the buying environment might play a more important role for women consumers, whose motives related to emotional involvement and social–experiential benefits might not easily translate to buying online. In contrast, men seem to be able to address their main concerns equally well in either environment.

This qualitative study is a useful foundation on which to build a quantitative assessment of the relative importance of buying motives in conventional and online buying. Questionnaire items to assess each type of motive were either adapted from previous research (e.g. Babin et al., 1994; Dittmar, 2000; Donthu & Garcia, 1999), or they were formulated on the basis of the qualitative findings. This quantitative study addresses gaps in the research literature. It covers a more comprehensive set of buying motives, particularly motives related to identity. Previous studies neglected to distinguish explicitly between the two different buying environments, conventional and internet, and thus could not offer a systematic comparison between them. Through developing scales that can be applied to both conventional and online buying, we are able to make a direct comparison between these two environments as experienced by the same individual.

The findings for four sets of hypotheses are presented in this chapter. First, building on gender differences in conventional buying, men were expected to place more emphasis on functional than emotional–experiential–social and identity-related buying motives, whereas women were expected to show either equally balanced or opposite preferences. Second, in terms of the impact of buying environment on motives, it was expected that functional motives would be more important for online than for conventional buying, whereas the psychological motives may be weaker online. The qualitative findings suggest that the impact of environment should be more powerful for women than for men, which suggests gender-specific patterns. Finally, our qualitative research also suggests that people find it easy to overspend on the internet, because they spontaneously talked about the buying transaction as particularly remote—a button click—and the quantitative study therefore also assesses perceptions of ease of spending money, both in conventional and online buying.

The study participants, 240 young consumers typically in their early twenties, completed a questionnaire that consisted of a set of statements about buying motives, designed to tap three main dimensions. The first concerned functional issues, which include: *economic concerns* about the "rational" benefits of goods (e.g. good value for money, price comparison, usefulness); *efficiency and convenience* (e.g. saving time, speed and efficiency, constant access); and *information acquisition and exploration*, which captures potentially important dimensions of internet buying, such as quick and easy access to consumer information. The second main dimension focuses on emotional and experiential–social factors. *Emotional involvement* in shopping refers to a pleasurable activity in which the actual purchase of goods can be of secondary or even little importance (e.g. leisure activity, enjoyment of browsing without buying), and as an activity that arouses emotions and can be used to regulate one's mood (e.g. fun, excitement, buzz, better mood). *Experiential–social* motives focus on the buying experience, contact, and social interaction. The final dimension of *identity-related concerns* includes both social and personal identity. On the one hand, consumers may want to buy consumer goods as a way of moving closer to an ideal self (e.g. feel more like the person they want to be) and, on the other, they can see goods as a means of improving social image and social standing (e.g. impress friends, gain prestige). Respondents were asked to rate the extent to which they agree or disagree with each statement, first with reference to conventional buying, and then with reference to buying online. After exclusion of a few items on the basis of exploratory factor analysis, confirmatory factor analyses (CFA) demonstrates that the same model with five factors provides a good fit for the data, both in the conventional and internet buying environments. We specified a stringent CFA in which each item was allowed to load only on its assigned factor. The items and factor loadings are shown in Table 3.1, confirming that these factors can be treated as separate scales, and can be classified into three main categories.

In support of the gender hypothesis in conventional buying, the relative importance of the three key concerns—functional, emotional–social, and identity-related—differed significantly for women compared to men. Identity-related, emotional, and social–experiential concerns were more important to women than to men, whereas the two functional factors were more important to men than to women. Further findings were that whereas identity was relatively less important to both genders than emotional and social–experiential concerns, this gap was larger for women than for men, which is partly a reflection of women's emotional involvement being particularly strong. Gender differences were least pronounced on identity-related motives. Scale means are shown in the top half of Figure 3.2. It is also interesting to note that, when gender is not taken into account, functional and psychological motivations are equally important overall, supporting the significance of "passions" when people buy consumer goods.

Next, the impact of the buying environment was examined for those respondents who had bought goods on the internet ($n = 110$). Women's and men's mean ratings for online buying motives are shown in the bottom part of Figure 3.2. A striking finding is just how similar their responses are: in contrast to "bricks", there is little by way of gender differences in buying motives for "clicks". An interesting way of making sense of these findings, given the pronounced gender differences in conventional buying motives and our expectation that the internet buying environment is likely to be experienced differently by women and men, is to compare online and conventional buying motives separately for women and men.

For men, buying environment did not have an impact overall on their buying motives, and the strong effect of functional motives being more important than psychological motives holds across both their conventional and online buying. However, a significant interaction showed that the impact of buying environment differs depending on the type of motives. Compared to conventional buying, motives relating to economic concerns and efficiency increased online, whereas psychological motives became less important. However, this decrease is uneven in strength. Compared to conventional buying, identity-related motives decreased less in importance online than the emotional–social–experiential factors taken together. Emotional involvement was not strongly affected by buying environment. In summary, then, the pattern of men's motives in conventional buying does not change qualitatively, but simply becomes more pronounced when buying online: functional concerns become more important and psychological motives somewhat less important, although this shift is comparatively less evident for identity-related motives and emotional involvement.

Table 3.1 Factors in conventional and online buying

Scale	Factor loadings		Scale item
	Conventional	*Online*	
Functional issues			
Economic	.74	.59	I like to compare prices carefully before I buy
	.59	.59	It is important to me that the goods I buy are value for money
	.58	.27	Goods I buy have to be useful and practical
Efficient	.82	.74	I want buying to be as fast and as efficient as possible
	.54	.57	Saving time while buying goods is very important to me
	.35	.51	It is important to me that I can buy things whenever I choose
	.22	.31	Buying things this way avoids hassles
Emotional involvement and social experience			
Social– Experiential	.76	.75	I need to see and touch consumer goods before I buy them
	.46	.47	The "feel" of the place I buy things is important to me
	.45	.43	It is important to me to have contact with people when I make purchases
	.42	.44	I wouldn't want to buy clothes without trying them on first
Emotional	.86	.76	Shopping is fun and exciting
	.83	.63	I get a real buzz from buying things
	.82	.61	I often buy things because it puts me in a better mood
	.78	.71	For me, shopping and buying things is an important leisure activity
	.74	.61	Compared to other things I could do, buying consumer goods is truly enjoyable
	.72	.63	Buying things arouses my emotions and feelings
	.70	.41	I like to shop, not because I have to but because I want to
	.56	.50	I enjoy browsing and looking at things, even when I do not intend to buy something
Identity			
	.83	.82	I like to buy things which impress other people
	.71	.84	I buy consumer goods because they give me "prestige"
	.57	.47	I want to buy things which make me feel more like the person I want to be

Adapted from Dittmar, Long, & Meek (2004), Buying on the internet: Gender differences in online and conventional buying motivations, *Sex Roles, 50,* p. 437 and p. 438, with kind permission of Kluwer.

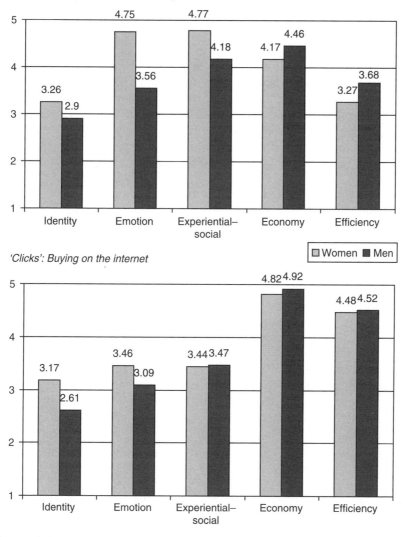

Figure 3.2 Young women's and men's conventional and online buying motives. (*Note.* Adapted from Dittmar, Long, & Meek (2004), Buying on the internet: Gender differences in online and conventional buying motivations, *Sex Roles, 50,* p. 437 and p. 438, with kind permission of Kluwer.)

In contrast to men, environment did have a significant effect on women's buying motives, such that there is a drop in importance, which suggests that buying online is less involving overall for them than conventional buying. However, this effect is produced by the strong decreases in emotional and experiential–social motives when women buy online, and therefore has to be understood in the context of the powerful interaction between motives and environment. For women, functional motives also increase online, whereas psychological motives decrease, but this shift is much stronger than for men. A closer examination reveals a further interesting finding for women. Although identity-related concerns were less important than emotional–social–experiential factors in conventional buying, the gap closes online, which suggests that the drop in emotional involvement and social experience has the effect that identity concerns become equally important. In summary, buying environment appears to have a stronger impact on women's than men's motives, with the possible exception of identity. Moreover, there is an interesting reversal of motivational priorities for women. Whereas emotional and social–experiential factors are more important than functional concerns in conventional buying, this order reverses when women buy on the internet.

Men are more functional in their buying orientation in conventional shops and stores than are women, whereas women stress social–experiential and identity-related concerns, and, in particular, emotional involvement. These findings confirm the hypothesised gender differences in conventional buying, which means they are still characteristic of young consumers, who should be less likely than general population samples to express gender-stereotypical motives. The environment in which buying takes place has a much stronger impact on women than on men. For men, functional motives become even more important online than in conventional buying, and psychological motives, especially social–experiential concerns, become less important. Further, men's emotional involvement in buying is hardly affected by environment, which suggests that men do not experience the online buying environment as dampening their hedonic enjoyment. Overall, their pattern of buying motives is amplified on the internet, rather than fundamentally altered. For women, there is an increase in the importance of functional concerns on the internet, and a strong decline in emotional and social–experiential motives, to the extent that their motivational priorities are reversed. Identity-related motives are affected less strongly. Thus, women's online buying motives are markedly more similar to men's online than they are in conventional buying. Once women engage in online buying, their motives resemble those of male internet buyers, with gender differences hardly in evidence. The shift from conventional to online buying entails greater change for women, which might explain why their overall involvement in shopping appears to be reduced on the internet.

So far, the reported findings predominantly describe buying motives, rather than focus on how different motives might influence consumer behaviour, particularly behaviours with negative consequences for consumers' well-being. The final section of this chapter starts to consider links between buying motives and potentially detrimental consumer behaviours, such as spending money inadvertently without realising just how much, which could easily lead people into paying out more than they can sensibly afford.

Buying motives and perceived ease of spending

In the qualitative study of young consumers' accounts of conventional and online buying a further theme emerged, additional to buying motives, concerning the nature of the purchasing transaction and the extent to which respondents felt in control of their spending. The following excerpt illustrates that internet buying can afford individuals greater control over spending money: "I do not waste so much money, because everything I buy is carefully thought out beforehand and, of course, I do not get intimidated to buy other things as I visit only the sites I'm interested in" (Dittmar et al., 2004, p. 429). This account is consistent with the widespread assumption in the wider social scientific literature, at least as expounded initially, that e-commerce should be associated with positive, healthy outcomes for individuals because it was thought to encourage "rational" buying (Donthu & Garcia, 1999; *Journal of Industrial Economics*, 2001). Possible reasons given were that buying online "avoids the marketing distractions of the conventional store" (Burke, 1997, p. 354), offers better information search facilities, price and product comparisons, increases convenience and freedom from time pressure, and should therefore lead to less emotional involvement and fewer impulsive purchases.

However, in contrast to this view, there are good reasons to propose, and some initial evidence, that the internet can be conducive to uncontrolled buying and spending (see Chapter 5). In the qualitative study, respondents expressed concern about the danger of over spending when buying online, because the nature of the online buying transaction is both easy and remote. After credit card details are submitted, usually with the option that they can be stored for future purchases, all that is required is just one "click" of a button. The remote, or "unreal", feel of online buying transactions is captured in this excerpt: "very easy to spend a lot . . . detaches you from a sense of actually spending money" (Dittmar et al., 2004, p. 429).

In the survey just described, respondents were asked to rate two statements as an indication of potential difficulties with uncontrolled spending: "I find it easy to spend money without realising what I am doing" and "It does not feel like spending real money when I buy goods". They rated them twice, once with respect to buying on the internet, and once with respect to conventional buying. The main finding of interest here is that young adults, independently of gender, report significantly greater ease of spending money inadvertently when buying online (mean rating 3.3 on a six-point scale) than in conventional buying environments (mean rating 2.9), because the internet facilitates the perception that the buying transaction is less real and people find it harder to be aware of actually spending money. This supports the concern that the internet is a source of uncontrolled spending, and hence consumer debt.

A particularly interesting question in the context of this chapter is whether ease of spending money inadvertently is linked to particular buying motives. As we saw in the discussion of impulse buying, a focus on psychological benefits of buying goods is linked to disregard for one's financial position and whether purchases are affordable or not, whereas concerns with price and good value for money should make it less likely that individuals part with their money easily. To examine these expectations, I carried out a regression analysis to determine whether buying motives predicted ease of spending money, after controlling for gender differences. Findings for conventional buying are summarised first.

Women and men do not differ in perceived ease of spending money in conventional shops and stores. Identity-related buying motives, when first entered, emerged as a significant predictor, such that stronger concerns with improving one's personal and social identity were significantly associated with greater ease of spending money ($\beta = .19$). The addition of emotional and social–experiential motives provide a further improvement in prediction, and emotional involvement is shown to increase ease of spending, although the effect is statistically marginal ($\beta = .24$). Finally, the addition of functional motives improves the predictive model still further, where concerns with price and usefulness emerge as a significant negative predictor, decreasing the ease of spending money ($\beta = -.37$). Identity-related motives and emotional involvement both increase ease of spending money when first entered into the analysis, supporting the expectation that these psychological motives are positively linked to uncontrolled spending. However, in the final model, functional concerns remain as the only significant and negative predictor, showing that a focus on price, value for money, and usefulness of goods is associated with reduced ease of spending money. This finding most likely reflects systematic relationships among buying motives, such that stronger identity-related and emotional motivations might well themselves be linked with decreased functional concerns.

In the context of the internet, the pattern of findings is somewhat different. Initially, gender differences are found, such that women report greater ease of spending money online than men ($\beta = .20$), but this effect disappears as soon as identity-related buying motives are taken into account, which means that this difference between women and men is due to, or mediated by, differences in this buying motive. Indeed, wanting to buy goods online in order to bolster identity significantly improves the predictive model and is associated with greater ease of spending money ($\beta = .25$). This finding is similar to the conventional buying environment. However, in contrast to conventional buying, the addition of emotional and social–experiential motives proves non-significant for the internet, which might be a reflection of the fact that emotional involvement, social interaction, and direct contact with goods are all reduced online. Finally, for functional motives, the findings are similar: their addition improves the predictive model and it is, again, the case that these concerns act as a negative predictor of perceived ease of spending money online ($\beta = -.25$). However, identity-related motives remain as an independent significant predictor ($\beta = .24$), demonstrating that the positive link between identity seeking and inadvertently spending money online is unaffected by economic concerns.

In summary, reported ease of spending money can be predicted successfully from buying motives for both young women and men. The less strongly individuals are motivated by concerns with value for money and usefulness of consumer goods, the more they report a propensity to spend money easily and without realising how much. This negative association emerges in both conventional environments and when buying on the internet. Identity-related motives and emotional involvement are associated with greater ease of spending money in conventional environments when considered by themselves, before functional motives are taken into account. For internet buying, identity seeking remains a significant independent predictor, even after all buying motives are taken into account, such that greater concerns with bolstering personal and social identity are associated with greater ease of spending money. This finding is consistent with the overarching proposal in this book that a strong concern with identity seeking through consumption is likely to have negative consequences for consumers.

CONCLUSION

The research on buying motives reported here lays an important foundation for work that examines potentially negative consequences of identity-related and emotional motives for consumer behaviour and well-being. It does so in three ways. First, the research summarised in this chapter offers good support for a more comprehensive conceptualisation and measurement of buying motives that includes identity-related concerns, as well as functional and emotional issues. Second, it highlights the importance of taking gender differences into account when studying the psychological impact of aspects of consumer culture on individuals, where emotional and identity-related buying motives continue to play a stronger role for women than men, at least as far as conventional buying is concerned. Yet, over and above such gender differences, we find that psychological motives are particularly strong when people buy on impulse, and for types of good that have greater potential for symbolising and enhancing identity. Third, this research highlights the increasing significance of the internet as a dimension of consumer culture that needs to be studied from a social psychological perspective. In doing so, it is important to assess buying motives with reference to this specific buying environment, given that motives differ systematically—for the same individual—depending on where he or she buys consumer goods.

The final section on buying motives as predictors of the propensity to spend money inadvertently, and thus overspend, provides suggestive evidence that a strong psychological orientation toward consumer goods might have negative consequences for individuals' well-being. Such links are examined further in the next two chapters. Identity seeking and regulation of one's emotions are motives that appear to play a strong role for compulsive buying, a dysfunctional consumer behaviour that manifests itself in uncontrolled and excessive buying with harmful psychological and financial consequences (see Chapter 5). But before doing so, the buying motives of seeking a better identity and positive emotions are considered as linked to an underlying belief structure that places a strong emphasis on money and material goods as a means to achieving important life goals, such as life satisfaction, happiness, and success. This belief structure is characteristic of a materialistic value orientation, which has increasingly become an integral component of consumer culture. Chapter 4 addresses the link between materialistic values and well-being.

4 Is this as good as it gets? Materialistic values and well-being

Ragna Garðarsdóttir,
Judita Janković & Helga Dittmar

Synopsis

Despite the strong belief that more money and material possessions would improve our lives considerably, it seems that those with a strong materialistic value orientation actually end up less satisfied, less happy, and with more psychological problems. However, this link is more complex than previously assumed, and we present new research from various European countries that extends what we know by showing that:

- Materialistic values are linked to lower well-being when there is conflict within a person's value system.
- The desire for wealth and goods is negative when it is driven by unrealistic money-making motives.
- People on lower incomes may be disproportionately more vulnerable to the negative impact of such money-making motives.

The Material Good Life?

© Jessica Barlow

The perceived importance of financial success has risen dramatically over the past three decades, as demonstrated by annual surveys of more than 200,000 US students (cf. Myers, 2000). The proportion of students who report that it is "very important or essential" that they become "very well off financially" almost doubled from 39% in 1970 to 74% in 1998. This growth in the desire for money and material possessions reflects the fact that the material ideal is now a central feature of current consumer culture. Yet, although material goods can give people the means of enhancing their well-being (e.g. increasing independence, maintaining identity, see Chapter 2), there is increasing evidence that a strong endorsement of materialistic values is associated with negative outcomes in adolescence and adulthood: Materialists are less satisfied, less happy, and have more psychological problems. In other words, materialists appear to have lower subjective well-being (SWB) than people who do not endorse materialistic values strongly. It is important to emphasise that materialism refers to the desire for, and pursuit of, affluence and possessions, not being affluent. It is what a person wants, rather than what he or she has.

This chapter focuses on research that examines the association between materialism and SWB. Previous studies, overall, provide consistent evidence for a negative link between materialism—having strong financial goals and material desires—and various measures of well-being. However, the strength of this negative link tends to be moderate and research has raised the question of whether it might hold only when materialism is in conflict with other, opposing values that a person holds (Burroughs & Rindfleisch, 2002), or with respect to particular motives for wanting money (Srivastava, Locke, & Bartol, 2001). Building on this work, we present new research in this chapter that examines three factors that can influence the link between materialism and well-being: value conflict, money-making motives, and level of income.

WELL-BEING AND SUBJECTIVE WELL-BEING

SWB, commonly referred to as happiness in daily discourse, has only recently caught the attention of psychologists and social scientists, so that there has been an upsurge of empirical work, making SWB a research area in its own right (for reviews see Diener & Oishi, 2005; Diener, Oishi, & Lucas, 2003; Diener et al., 1999). As outlined in Chapter 1, SWB as consists of three components over time: (1) satisfaction with one's life; (2) frequent experience of positive affect (e.g. happiness); and (3) the relative absence of negative affect, such as depression and anxiety (Diener, Emmons, Larson, & Griffin, 1985).

SWB is a good indicator of general and psychological health (Argyle, 2001), and that makes it an important variable to study. SWB has an inherent adaptive function, in that it buffers against negative health-related outcomes, such as depression, anxiety, or neuroticism, as indicated by research using a self-determination framework (e.g. Kasser & Ryan, 1996; Ryan, Chirkov, Little, Sheldon, Timoshina, & Deci, 1999). Evolutionary explanations for the existence of positive affect point to the adaptive advantages of being sociable and building social bonds, as well as health effects (Fredrickson, 1998). There are two major reasons why determinants of SWB need to be researched (Argyle, 2001). First, SWB enhances the happiness of both individuals and communities. Second, it complements objective indicators in quality-of-life research and policy decisions. Indeed, we agree with the proposal put forward recently that an indicator of SWB, *gross national happiness* (GNH), should be incorporated with existing economic indicators, such as gross domestic product (GDP) in national policies (Kahneman, Krueger, Schkade, Schwarz, & Stone, 2004).

WHAT IS MATERIALISM? DEFINITIONS AND MEASUREMENTS

In philosophy, materialism refers to a theoretical system where matter is seen as the only reality in the world, as opposed to spiritualism and idealism (Popkin & Stroll, 1993). Materialism, in the sense used here, is more precise, but has some connection to this viewpoint. It is a preoccupation with, desire for, and emphasis on, material goods and money to the neglect of other matters. Definitions of materialism often refer to the satisfaction or happiness people expect to gain from material goods. For instance, materialism has been defined as "an orientation emphasizing possessions and money for personal happiness and social progress" (Ward & Wackman, as cited in Fournier & Richins, 1991, p. 404). There is research on postmaterialist values, such as valuing free speech or involvement in politics, but the emphasis of this work is on political culture (Inglehart, 2006). Within psychology, the three most widely used approaches to defining and measuring materialism are outlined briefly below.

The materialistic personality

The earliest attempt to measure materialism within psychology was the development of the Belk Materialism Scale (BMS; Belk, 1984), which conceptualises materialism as a triad of personality traits, or stable internal properties that characterise an individual. Materialism is seen as a manifestation of three personality traits—possessiveness, non-generosity, and envy—which are so strongly associated with materialism that materialism itself can be operationalised and measured via these three traits. According to this approach, the more possessive, envious, and non-generous a person is, the more materialistic s/he is believed to be. Possessiveness is defined as "the inclination and tendency to retain control or ownership of one's possessions" (1984, p. 291). A possessive person should be worried about the possible loss of possessions, prefer to own rather than rent or borrow material objects, and be more inclined to save and retain possessions. The non-generous person is unwilling to share or give possessions to others. Envy is seen as a destructive trait, characterised by an attitude of displeasure and ill-will towards people who are seen as superior in "happiness, success, reputation or the possession of anything desirable" (Belk, 1984, p. 292), motivating negative, even criminal, behaviour.

This approach has been influential but it implies that materialistic personality traits are stable dispositions, whereas materialism might fluctuate during a person's life, such that they are more materialistic during some phases than others, or even choose a non-materialistic lifestyle, such as "voluntary simplicity" (Etzioni, 1998; Huneke, 2005). Furthermore, although it may well be the case that materialistic people are possessive, non-generous, and envious, this personality approach of defining materialism in terms of stable individual traits neglects some core elements of materialism that are held to be important in both scientific and common-sense understanding. These are: the use of material objects for status display, judgement of one's own and other people's success by wealth and possessions, and beliefs about the psychological benefits that material goods will bring, such as happiness or life satisfaction (Fournier & Richins, 1991). These elements are explicitly taken into account by an alternative approach, concerned with a materialistic value orientation.

Materialism as an individual value orientation

This approach defines materialism as a "set of centrally held beliefs about the importance of possessions in one's life" (Richins & Dawson, 1992, p. 308). Richins and Dawson, who developed the materialistic values approach, conceptualise materialism in terms of three key components, and validated a questionnaire, the Materialistic Values Scale (MVS), which is now the most widely used materialism instrument in consumer research (Wong, Rindfleisch, & Burroughs, 2003). The first component, *acquisition centrality*, is the belief that material possessions and money are a highly important life goal, indicated by agreement with statements such as "I would like a lot of luxury in my life". The second component, *success*, refers to the extent to which people see possessions and money as a good yardstick for evaluating their own achievements, as well as those of others. Example items are "The things I own say a lot about how well I'm doing in life" or "Some of the most important achievements in life include acquiring material possessions". Finally, the *happiness* component captures the conviction that goods and money are the major path to personal happiness, a better life, and a more positive identity, such as "I'd be happier if I could afford to buy more things" or "My life would be better if I owned certain things that I don't have". Thus, people with strong materialistic values not only focus on acquiring material goods and money but they also believe that consumer goods can provide important psychological benefits. Taken together, these components suggest that a materialistic value orientation indicates a conviction that material possessions can become sources of identity, to such an extent that they come to define who one is (Dittmar, 2005a). The MVS measures the intensity, or absolute strength, of individuals' materialistic values: the more they value material goods as a life goal, yardsticks of success, and means to happiness and identity, the more materialistic they are.

According to this approach, materialism is a socially constructed phenomenon, in the sense that its meanings are communicated within consumer culture and shared among a large number of individuals. In this way, materialistic values represent a committed relationship with material goods expressed by both individuals and society. The advantages of this theoretical approach are that it fully takes into account the influence of consumer culture and the shared meanings of materialism, and that it captures differences in the extent to which individuals endorse materialistic values. Thus, it measures the absolute importance of materialism in a person's life. However, its most obvious neglect is that it does not consider the relative importance of materialistic values with respect to other values a person may hold. Therefore, it does not distinguish between a person whose strong materialistic values reflect their only life goal, and a person with equally strong materialistic values, but who has satisfying personal relationships and community involvement as equally powerful life goals. Thus, it may be important to consider the relative importance individuals place on financial goals as compared to their other life goals.

The relative importance of financial goals

The most influential perspective on materialism within psychology was developed by Kasser and Ryan (1993, 1996), drawing on Self-determination Theory (e.g. Ryan & Deci, 2000). As outlined in Chapter 1, they draw a distinction between life goals or aspirations as either intrinsic or extrinsic based on their content and, to measure them, they designed the Aspirations Index (AI). The AI measures the importance a person places on intrinsic life goals (such as self-acceptance, affiliation, and community involvement) as well as extrinsic goals (financial success, fame, and image). The more a person rates the importance of financial goals as high compared to other (intrinsic) goals, the more materialistic s/he is. Self-determination Theory proposes that attaching high importance to an extrinsic life goal, such as financial success, is negatively associated with indicators of well-being, because extrinsically motivated goals are guided by external influences, such as coercion or approval from others, whereas intrinsically motivated goals are of interest in their own right, bringing pleasure and true fulfilment. "[E]xcessive concentration on external rewards can distract people from intrinsic endeavours and interfere with personal integration and actualisation" (Kasser & Ryan, 1993, p. 410). In short, seeking material rewards takes time and energy away from fulfilling basic psychological, intrinsically motivated needs, and therefore leads to lower well-being.

This relative-life-goals perspective captures an essential aspect of materialism but, given that it focuses predominantly on the desire for financial success, it neglects dimensions of materialism identified in the values approach, such as the beliefs about the psychological benefits expected from material goods, including enhancing happiness and satisfaction in life. Kasser's later publications, however, define a materialistic value orientation as involving both the relative financial goal perspective outlined here, as well as materialistic beliefs about status and a positive identity through material goods (2002; Kasser & Kanner, 2004).

THE DARK SIDE OF MATERIALISM

In fact, there is good evidence that "money can't buy happiness" (cf. Diener & Seligman, 2005), even if many of us want to believe otherwise. Commenting on recent research that failed to show increased happiness among 800 affluent US households, the *Los Angeles Times* is scathing: "Money can't buy happiness? That's rich" (Carlson, 2005). This strident reaction probably occurred because the findings run counter to the material good-life ideal in contemporary consumer culture, as well as the "American dream". Indeed, the beliefs that wealth and expensive material possessions lead to a happier and more successful life are core components of a materialistic outlook. Yet popular conceptions about materialism also hold that materialism is inherently bad, shallow, and unfulfilling, because of its associated indulgent behaviour and neglect of spirituality (Fournier & Richins, 1991). Humanistic theorists agree that materialism is bad for people because it takes energy away from more meaningful pursuits in life, i.e. activities that help satisfy the inherent psychological needs of human beings (e.g. Maslow, 1954; Fromm, 1978). Whereas opinions are divided and run high, a substantial body of empirical evidence does suggest that materialism has a negative impact on people's well-being.

Research on the link between materialism and well-being

With respect to the materialistic personality, a study with business school students found that scores on Belk's (1984) BMS scale were related negatively to life satisfaction and happiness. Belk concluded that materialistic people were not happy and that, particularly, non-generosity and envy were sources of human dissatisfaction. Ger and Belk (1996) gathered both qualitative and quantitative responses from residents in various countries, both Western (USA, New Zealand, West and North Europe) and non-Western (Thailand, India, Turkey, Israel, Ukraine, Romania). They found that levels of materialism were not dependent on the affluence of countries, and that materialism is not unique to Western capitalist countries. However, we need to be cautious about the link to lower well-being because envy and non-generosity are clearly negative emotional states, as well as being socially undesirable. It has been argued that people who are envious and non-generous may agree with statements in Belk's scale, not necessarily because they are materialistic but because of their negative emotional state. Indeed, the BMS was found to be linked to a general propensity toward negative emotions and neuroticism, which suggests that this particular measure of materialism might produce spurious links with SWB because it is already biased toward low well-being (Solberg, Diener, & Robinson, 2004).

Research on materialistic values, using Richins and Dawson's MVS, has consistently demonstrated a negative relationship with well-being measures (e.g. Burroughs & Rindfleisch, 2002; Kasser & Ahuvia, 2002; Mick, 1996; Richins & Dawson, 1992). For example, US adults who endorse materialistic values strongly were less satisfied with some important domains of life, such as satisfaction with family life and socialisation with friends, as well as reporting lower overall life satisfaction (Richins & Dawson, 1992). A negative link between materialism and well-being also emerged in a sample of both young and older adults in the US, where highly materialistic participants were less happy, less satisfied with their life, more depressed, more neurotic, more anxious, and reported greater psychological stress, as well as less religious, community, and family-oriented values (Burroughs & Rindfleisch, 2002). Business students in Singapore, a culture in which materialistic values are strongly held, completed three different established measures of a materialistic orientation, including the MVS, and it was found that students who had a strongly internalised materialistic orientation reported lowered self-actualisation, vitality, and happiness, as well as increased anxiety, physical symptoms of ill-health, and unhappiness (Kasser & Ahuvia, 2002). MVS scores were strongly correlated with the relative importance of financial goals, measured by the AI.

Two studies with US student populations showed that relative emphasis on financial goals (measured by the AI) was related to lower levels of self-actualisation and vitality, and higher levels of depression and anxiety (Kasser & Ryan, 1993). In a third study, respondents were "at risk" adolescents, whose well-being was assessed by clinical psychologists through a diagnostic interview (DICA; Herjanic & Reich, 1982, cited in Kasser & Ryan, 1993). The results showed that adolescents who place greater importance on financial goals than other goals have more behavioural disorders, lower global functioning, and lower social productivity. In two further studies, Kasser and Ryan (1996) examined the relationship between well-being and intrinsic and extrinsic goals, including fame and image in addition to financial success, one with adults and the other with students. Again, their findings show that the importance attached to extrinsic goals had a strong negative association with both self-actualisation and vitality and was positively related to physical symptoms of ill-health. The study with adults is important because it also assessed whether income played a role, but found no evidence. However, this may be due to the fact that financial goals were not examined specifically, but rather extrinsic goals in general. Surprisingly, there is virtually no other previous research on the link between materialism and income, as will be discussed later in this chapter.

Qualifying the link

Clearly, there is consistent evidence that supports both the popular notion and psychological theories claiming that there is a negative relationship between well-being and materialism. Moreover, a meta-analysis of studies examining this relationship reveals that there is an overall negative association between materialism and SWB (Wright & Larsen, 1993). The reason for this link is still unclear, notwithstanding that Self-determination Theory offers one possible account. Why should it be the case that being a materialistic person is bad for you?

If financial goals are inherently bad (the humanistic view), then they should be negatively associated with SWB, regardless of culture, the motives behind the goals, or whether or not the goals are achieved (financial success can be said to be achieved once people have acquired wealth). However, if financial goals are not essentially or necessarily bad in themselves, then the nature and strength of the link between materialism and well-being may vary. For instance, given that achieving one's goals usually has positive effects on well-being (cf. Dweck & Leggett, 1988), it could be the case that achieving one's financial goals also has a positive effect. In that case, it would be expected that materialism is worse for people on low incomes, but neutral or even positive for those with high incomes. Moreover, people can have very different reasons—or motives—for pursuing wealth and material goods, which raises the question of whether the materialism–well-being link would be the same for individuals who seek financial security for their family as compared to individuals who expect material goods to make them happier, more satisfied, and more ideal people. Finally, materialistic values may be particularly detrimental when they cause internal conflict, and hence stress, because individuals simultaneously endorse opposing values, such as a strong family orientation or community involvement. These issues are addressed in reverse order.

VALUE CONFLICT

Extensive cross-cultural research has shown that values (Schwartz, 1992) and goals (Grouzet et al., 2005) are structured in a circumplex fashion, which means that some are closely related, such as financial success and image, whereas others are opposite, such as financial success and community feeling. Building on Schwartz's finding that self-enhancement values (serving one's own interests) conflict with self-transcendence values (serving other people's interests), Burroughs and Rindfleisch (2002) proposed a value conflict approach to materialism. This approach holds that if the same person simultaneously and strongly endorses conflicting values, then s/he is likely to experience internal conflict and psychological stress, which in turn has a negative impact on his/her well-being. Burroughs and Rindfleisch's research found support for their model, showing that materialistic values had negative links with US respondents' well-being when they endorsed strong family values at the same time. They did not find the expected pattern with respect to materialism and community values, but this may be due to their study being carried out in the US, a culture where community commitment may be much lower than in European countries, particularly former socialist societies.

UK and Croatia as comparison countries

When conducting research on value conflict and materialism, the UK and Croatia are particularly interesting to compare because these two European countries differ in their cultural heritage, past and current socio-economic situation, and penetration of mass consumerism (Janković, 2006). Croatia's heritage as a former East European communist country is marked by traditional and collectivist values, placing particularly strong emphasis on the family and the collective (Radin, 2002). In terms of the overall socio-economic situation of Croatia, the transition from a socialist to free-market society was associated with great expectations of material prosperity but the process was, and still is, accompanied by economic hardship (Hayo & Seifert, 2003). For example, unemployment rates in Croatia were 23% (National Bureau of Statistics, 2003), when they were only 5% in the UK (National Statistics Online, 2003). Hence, economic instability is an important characteristic of Croatia, which contrasts with the long UK history of being a relatively stable and market-driven economy. Similarly, Croatia is lagging behind the UK in mass consumerism. For instance, average purchasing power in Croatia was US$5100 (in 1998), whereas the UK figures were more than four-fold higher with US$23,400 (in 2000) and US$24,700 (in 2001). We collected consumer indices for UK and Croatian students (Janković & Dittmar, 2006). The findings showed that, in both student populations, the great majority owned mobile phones (88% in the UK and 95% in Croatia) and computers (90% and 86%). In contrast, Croatian students lagged behind in owning credit cards (32% compared to 69% of UK students), debit cards (20% vs. 94%), and shopping online (6% vs. 39%). Thus, mass consumption penetration still appears lower in Croatia.

Research with students

We first conducted a study with students, examining whether individuals who endorse materialistic values strongly, as well as opposing family and community values, would show value conflict effects that were reflected in lower subjective well-being (Janković, 2006). Participants were recruited at the University of Sussex in the UK ($n = 100$) and the University of Zagreb in Croatia ($n = 100$). Their mean age was 20 and 24 years, respectively, and they completed a questionnaire that contained four core measures. The questionnaire was translated for the Croatian participants, and equivalence of meaning with the English version was checked through established back-translation procedures (Brislin, 1970). Richins and Dawson's MVS was used to measure materialistic values, and two scales assessed family and community values (from Burroughs & Rindfleisch, 2002). Community values assessed commitment to community involvement and willingness to contribute time, effort, or money to community improvement. Subjective well-being was assessed by the Satisfaction With Life Scale (Diener et al., 1985) and the Affect Balance Scale (Bradburn, 1969), which asks respondents to report the extent to which they experienced specific emotions during the previous year.

Value conflict was not measured directly in this study; rather, it was inferred when individuals endorsed both materialism strongly, as well as an opposing value, such as community commitment.[3] The impact of value conflict on SWB was examined in regression analyses, carried out separately for UK and Croatian respondents, where materialistic values were entered as a predictor of well-being, which was followed by adding community values, both by themselves and in interaction with materialism. Value conflict would be supported if the interaction between materialistic and community values proves a significant predictor of SWB, once both sets of values by themselves are taken into account. The findings are shown in Table 4.1.

For the UK students, stronger materialistic values were associated with lower SWB, as expected, but this negative relationship—although in the hypothesised direction—did not reach significance for the Croatian students. Thus, materialism seems less strongly linked to lower well-being in Croatia. Community values by themselves were unrelated to well-being. With respect to value conflict, the interaction between materialistic and community values predicted SWB among both groups of students, significantly among UK, but only marginally among Croatian, students.

To examine the exact nature of this value conflict further, respondents were categorised into those with strong and weak community values by splitting

Table 4.1 Materialistic and community values as predictors of subjective well-being

	UK		Croatia	
	ΔR^2	β	ΔR^2	β
Materialistic values (MV)	20%	−.37***	10%	−.13
Community values (CV)		−.04		.11
MV by CV (value conflict)		−.18(*)		−.22*

* $p < .05$; *** $p < .001$; age and gender were controlled in all steps.

the samples into the half scoring highest on the community scale and the half scoring lowest. It is hypothesised that the materialism–SWB link should be more negative for materialistic individuals who strongly endorse community values because they should experience value conflict, when compared to those who endorse community values to a lesser extent. This prediction was supported in the UK, where increasing materialistic values had a powerful negative impact on well-being among those participants high in community values ($\beta = -.53$) but did not have a significant impact among those who were low ($\beta = -.28$). For the Croatian participants, the same pattern emerged but the link among those high in community values was only marginally significant ($\beta = -.20$), whereas there was no link among those low in community values ($\beta = .01$). Thus, materialism had a stronger negative impact on well-being among UK than Croatian students, but there was evidence for conflict between strong materialistic and strong community values having a negative impact on SWB in both.

These findings are encouraging, but value conflict was inferred, rather than examined directly by asking respondents whether they experience conflict. Moreover, compared to students, the impact of value conflict between materialistic and other life goals on SWB may become stronger once people are older and in full-time employment, making it harder to balance work, family, and community life.

Value conflict, self-discrepancies, and well-being in employees

We therefore carried out a second study with adult employees in the UK and Croatia, which offers two further extensions of the student research, relating to the assessment of value conflict (Janković, 2006). First, value conflict was measured directly (see below for details), and second, the value conflict model based on Burroughs and Rindfleisch (2002) was extended by including value self-discrepancies (Figure 4.1). Value self-discrepancies are defined as the gap between a person's actual standing with respect to a set of values and their

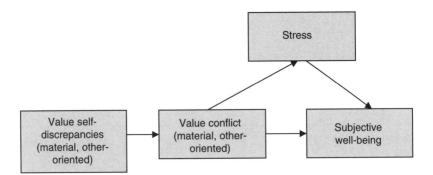

Figure 4.1 Extended value conflict model.

ideal standing. For example, an individual may want to be more family oriented than he or she is. If a person wants to be more oriented simultaneously towards material benefits as well as towards an other-oriented set of values, such as family values, then this should lead to value conflict. Value conflict, in turn, is expected to lead to lowered well-being, through producing psychological stress. Following Hobfoll (1998), psychological stress was defined and measured as a physically and emotionally draining reaction to tensions arising from either internal or external stressors, disrupting previously balanced states.

The overall sample of 327 full-time employees consisted of 158 UK adults and 169 Croatian adults. The mean age was 31 and 33 years, respectively. Again, English and Croatian versions of the questionnaire were used, presented as an online survey this time, which contained the same measures of materialistic and other-oriented values,[4] as well as SWB, as in the first study. In addition, value conflict regarding community was measured directly by asking participants to rate how easy or difficult they would find it to make a decision in a hypothetical scenario that described a dilemma between choosing a material benefit for oneself or choosing a benefit for one's community (spending a £5000 prize win on personal luxuries or agreeing to contribute it towards a community project). High scores indicate that participants found it hard to choose, which is likely to indicate underlying value conflict between the materialistic versus community-oriented choice. In addition, a psychological stress scale was used to assess specific states experienced over the last couple of weeks, such as finding it hard to relax or overreacting to situations (a shortened version taken from Burroughs & Rindfleisch, 2002). The relevant value self-discrepancy index was calculated from the multiplied ratings of the extent to which individuals would like to be more oriented than they currently are towards their community, and towards their materialistic goals.

To test directly how well our data fitted the extended value conflict model (see Figure 4.1) for UK and Croatian respondents, we used two-sample structural equation modelling (EQS 6.1; Bentler, 1995). The findings are presented in Figure 4.2.

Among UK employees, the model could explain 25% of the variability in respondents' SWB. The more individuals feel that they are falling short of both their material and community value ideal, the more they report value conflict in response to the material–community choice dilemma, as proposed. Value conflict then predicts increased psychological stress, which—in turn— is linked to lower well-being. Thus, the extended value conflict model finds good support in the UK. As we found for the student samples, the findings among Croatian employees also support the model, but not as strongly. Only 14% of the variability in SWB is explained, and the positive link between value conflict and stress—although in the predicted direction—fails to reach significance. However, the other hypothesised links are supported: Materialistic–community value self-discrepancies are linked to greater value conflict after the relevant choice dilemma, and stress predicts lower SWB.

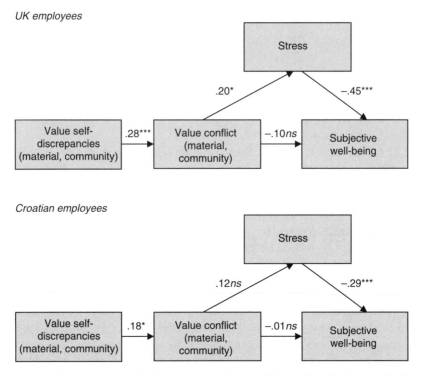

Figure 4.2 Structural equation model of value conflict and subjective well-being.
       $*p < .05; *** p < .001.$

Thus, the proposal that value conflict has a negative impact on SWB through increasing individuals' psychological stress is supported among UK, but not Croatian, employees.

One interpretation of these findings is that the relation of materialism to other-oriented values, specifically the extent to which materialism is inconsistent with community values, may differ between Western mass consumer societies and recently transformed, formerly socialist countries. The findings in the second study may suggest that materialism and community commitment are not necessarily perceived and experienced as conflictual to the same extent in Croatian society as they are in the UK. Notwithstanding this cultural difference, there is consistent evidence that the link between materialism and well-being is affected by conflict within an individual's value system. But this is not the only influence.

MONEY-MAKING MOTIVES AND INCOME

Financial goals can be pursued for a wide range of reasons or motives, where seeking financial security seems a rather different motive to wanting money to overcome self-doubt. Instead of assuming that financial goals are universally detrimental, recent studies have questioned whether aspiring to money and wealth is always detrimental for well-being, or whether there are some positive, as well as negative, links (cf. Garðarsdóttir, Dittmar, & Aspinall, 2007). Moreover, there are good reasons for expecting that the association between materialism and well-being will change depending on a person's actual wealth. We examined the implications of money-making motives and income for the link between materialism and SWB in two studies, comparing respondents from the UK and Iceland (Garðarsdóttir, 2006).

UK and Iceland as comparison countries

We selected the UK and Iceland as the two populations to compare, not because we expected that findings would differ much between these two European countries, but in order to assess whether the money-making model we developed (see below) would hold across both. Iceland is, however, a particularly suitable and interesting comparison country because its residents are likely to have particularly high levels of SWB. Iceland has repeatedly been found to have very high levels of life satisfaction and happiness in world-wide surveys (Diener, Diener, & Diener, 1995; Halman, 2001), as well as affluence. Using established back-translation procedures (Brislin, 1970), the questionnaire we used again has two versions, English and Icelandic.

Money-making motives and the materialism–SWB link

Research on the relationship between financial goals and SWB has been criticised for neglecting the many different reasons people may have for pursuing financial success other than seeking external approval and rewards as suggested by Self-determination Theory (Carver & Baird, 1998; Srivastava et al., 2001). In their studies, Srivastava et al. (2001) examined a wide range of motives, as well as financial goals and SWB. They reported a significant negative link between financial goal importance and SWB, consistent with previous research. However, their main finding was that this link was no longer significant once money motives were taken into account. Depending on how money motives were related to SWB, they categorised those linked to lower SWB as *negative money-making motives*, whereas *positive money-making motives* did not have a negative association with well-being. Negative money-making motives "reflect a lack of autonomous orientation wherein one wants to feel superior in social comparison or seeks to acquire power over others" (Srivastava et al., 2001, p. 963). In other words, people who want money to overcome self-doubt and to feel superior to other people are considered to have negative money-making motives. They therefore concluded that negative motives underlying the pursuit of money and possessions are more important than financial goals, which are problematic only when they are pursued for the wrong motives. In a response to these findings,

Self-determination researchers report three studies, which demonstrate that *both* goal content and motives behind the goals affect SWB independently (Sheldon, Ryan, Deci, & Kasser, 2004), which led to the argument that negative motives and extrinsic goal content, such as the pursuit of money, share significant features and are therefore both important when it comes to predicting SWB, but that the relationship with SWB is not reducible to one or the other predictor. Thus, motives are clearly important, regardless of whether or not financial goals also exert some influence.

This literature already raises important questions about the role of motives for the materialism–SWB association, but it neglects to address further, specific motives we believe are highly significant for the importance a person places on financial success. Pride and worth, self-doubt, and financial security were examined previously, but given that they were shown independently to have consequences for well-being (e.g. Chang & Arkin, 2002; Kasser & Sheldon, 2000; Watson, Clark, & Tellegen, 1988), they warrant further investigation. However, in addition, three further motives are likely to be significant: the motive for happiness through material goods and money, the motive for success, and the motive for a more positive identity. For example, research on buying motives and behaviours demonstrates that people want and buy material goods not so much for economic and utilitarian value but increasingly to gain hoped-for psychological benefits (Dittmar, 2004b; Kasser & Kanner, 2004). As shown in Chapters 2, 3, and 5, mood improvement, social standing, and identity seeking are all prominent motives for many people in having and buying material goods.

We therefore examined the effects of six money-making motives—overcoming self-doubt, financial security, worth and pride, happiness, success, and identity—on SWB in a study with 223 participants from the UK and 476 from Iceland, mainly employed adults (Garðarsdóttir, 2006). They completed a questionnaire (in English or Icelandic) that contained a shortened version of the AI, assessing the importance of financial as compared to other life goals, a measure of SWB, and six sets of scales assessing money-making motives, where they rate how important these motives are for them personally.

These six money-making motives differ in the extent to which they can be regarded as realistic and achievable. A judgement that some motives are more unrealistic than others is not an easy one to make, and the judgement presented here should be understood mainly as an aid in interpreting the effects of the motives. Financial security, success, and worth and pride can be achieved to a reasonable extent with money; through obtaining money individuals would be more secure financially, they are more likely to have more possessions that signal success and social standing, and—although this is less definitive—they may feel that they are receiving just compensation for their efforts, leading to a sense of worth and pride. Thus, these three motives are relatively realistic, or at least possible, outcomes of financial goals. We expect that these *realistic motives* have positive associations with SWB precisely because they are wants or needs that money is actually capable of fulfilling, at least to a reasonable extent, so that our investment of time and energy is likely to lead to positive outcomes.

In contrast, the other three motives can be classed as *unrealistic motives*: happiness, identity, and overcoming of self-doubt. These motives are expected to have negative associations with well-being, because it seems much less likely that they can find fulfilment through actually achieving financial goals. Therefore, the goal and the motives are incongruent. Research shows that greater wealth has surprisingly little impact on individuals' happiness and well-being beyond basic needs fulfilment (cf. Diener & Seligman, 2005; see also later). Thus, money does not make people happy. Happiness is more likely to be achieved by pursuing goals other than financial success. Supportive interpersonal relationships and a meaningful life (e.g. job satisfaction, spirituality, community involvement) have been identified as particularly strong predictors of well-being (Diener & Seligman, 2005). It is also unlikely that material goods would solve underlying self-doubts and identity-deficits, as shown in Chapter 5. The role of achieving a more positive identity is not as clearly unrealistic as the other two, because we saw in Chapter 2 that material possessions can make a contribution toward people feeling that their identity is stable and they are connected to others, although it is nevertheless questionable whether consumer goods can help people move toward a more ideal future identity. Based on these considerations, a money-making model was developed, shown in Figure 4.3.

Thus, we believe that these six money-making motives predict SWB positively or negatively, but we have no specific hypotheses about the relative

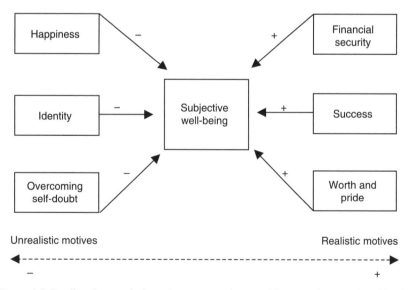

Figure 4.3 Predicted associations between money-making motives and subjective well-being.

strength of association. Overall, however, money-making motives are expected to predict SWB better than financial goal importance by itself (which should show a negative association with SWB). Furthermore, mediation should occur, such that the link between financial goal importance and SWB becomes weaker once money-making motives are taken into account, or possibly no longer in evidence at all. These hypotheses are tested in a regression analysis, where financial goal importance is entered first as a predictor (after controlling for age and gender), followed by money-making motives.

The findings show that, overall, the motives are indeed better predictors of SWB than financial goals alone, as expected. The findings are summarised in Table 4.2. Relative financial goal importance by itself showed the expected negative association with SWB in Iceland, but not the UK. As hypothesised, the addition of the money motives significantly improved the prediction of SWB, with an increase in explained variance of 12% in Iceland and 14% in the UK. In terms of specific motives, the most pronounced effects on SWB occurred for overcoming self-doubt, for happiness, and for success, both in the UK and in Iceland. In addition, the money-making motives for identity and for worth and pride also had significant impacts on SWB in Iceland.

The more emphasis a person places on feeling successful as a result of earning money, the higher that person's SWB is likely to be. The positive association of the success motive with SWB in professional employees is consistent with arguments that feeling competent and receiving recognition for achievements are psychologically intrinsically rewarding (Ryan & Deci, 2000). In contrast, wishing money to bring happiness and remove feelings of self-doubt had a negative association with SWB. The more a person wants happiness and self-assurance via money, the lower that person's SWB is likely to be. These findings are compatible with Self-determination Theory.

Table 4.2 Hierarchical regression predicting subjective well-being from relative financial goals and money-making motives in the UK and in Iceland

		UK		Iceland	
		ΔR^2	β	ΔR^2	β
Step 1	Relative financial goal importance	.00	−.05	.02	−.15**
Step 2	Relative financial goal importance	.14	.05	.12	−.09
	Success		.24*		.25***
	Financial security		.05		.01
	Worth and pride		.06		.13*
	Happiness		−.19*		−.25***
	Identity		−.12		−.16**
	Overcoming of self-doubt		−.33***		−.18**

$* p < .05; ** p < .01; *** p < .001$; age and gender were controlled in all steps.

Pursuing a happier, more confident self through an avenue that is unlikely to provide it—through money and possessions—probably means using up valuable time and energy that could otherwise be devoted to the development and maintenance of high-quality relationships, social support networks, self-development, and autonomy, all of which have been identified as crucial for well-being (e.g. Diener et al., 1999; Kasser & Kanner, 2004). The motive for financial security did not predict SWB, which can be explained by reference to previous findings (Richins & Dawson, 1992; Watson, 2003), which showed that materialism was unrelated to the amount of money people were willing to allocate to life necessities. In other words, financial security is likely to be a universal, basic, underlying reason for financial strivings and is therefore not deemed to be a materialistic motive, and—as such—unlikely to affect SWB.

The motive for identity was a moderate negative predictor of SWB, but the effect reached statistical significance only in Iceland. This finding can be interpreted once it is considered that actually gaining identity via financial success is likely to be relatively unrealistic, but not completely so. This may be the case because identity is socially created, socially inferred, and socially reinforced, as outlined in Chapter 1. Material possessions can serve as signs of identity and as symbolic self-completion for people whose sense of self is different from what they see as their ideal self. It is possible to argue that money can serve a similar purpose in the completion of identity (as a means of creating identity and decoding others' identity), both because money itself can take on different symbolic meanings and also because money can be exchanged for symbolic possessions. Placing importance on making money to attain an ideal self, or more sought-after identity, could therefore be successful to a limited extent, but because an ideal identity is more than just an accumulation of wealth and possessions, this motive still remains unlikely to be fulfilled. The motive for worth and pride did not have the expected positive association with SWB in the UK, but in Iceland it was a moderately strong positive predictor. Pride and worth are psychologically rewarding, with pride linked to positive affect (Watson et al., 1988) and worth linked to self-esteem (Rosenberg, 1965). Pride and self-worth can both be seen as reasonable outcomes of successful effort when they lead to financial achievement. Thus, a positive association with SWB seems more likely for affluent individuals. The extent to which this suggestion can explain the differences between the UK and Iceland warrants further investigation.

The influence of high and low income

As we have seen, materialism generally has a negative association with well-being, but this relationship is affected, at least in part, by money-making motives. However, there are good reasons for proposing that a person's income may be a further important influence. Negative associations between materialism and SWB are in line with what humanistic researchers would expect, such as proponents of Self-determination Theory. In contrast, cognitive theorists (e.g. Dweck & Leggett, 1988) claim that achieving one's goals is good for one's well-being, regardless of the nature of the goal. If this assumption is right, then having a high income should reduce the negative association between financial goal importance and SWB. A systematic comparison between high and low income groups is therefore vital when assessing the link between materialism and well-being.

Affluence has, indeed, been shown to relate to various positive outcomes. In their review of research on the link between income and SWB, Diener and Biswas-Diener (2002) provide a list of good outcomes for the wealthy, ranging from better physical and mental health through fewer stressful life events to getting lighter prison sentences than people of less wealth for the same crime. So, no wonder people think money brings happiness, because money can bring people out of the misery of poverty and buy them freedom. The actual relationship between SWB and income, however, is not that simple. Generally, research on a cultural level tends to show strong positive relationships between the wealth of a country [gross national product (GNP) or gross domestic product (GPD)] and its inhabitants' average SWB. On the level of individuals within the same country, however, findings from cross-sectional studies generally show that, although there is a significant positive link between income and well-being, the size of that link is rather small and mostly evident for lower levels of income (e.g. Diener & Biswas-Diener, 2002; Diener et al., 1995; Myers & Diener, 1995). On the cultural level, then, living in a richer nation makes people considerably happier than living in a poorer nation, but on the individual level, money can buy only slightly more happiness, if any at all.

As discussed, the beliefs that having wealth and expensive material possessions lead to a happier and more successful life are core components of a materialistic outlook. Despite this, actual income has largely been ignored in the research on the link between materialism and well-being. Prior to the research reported here, only one study measured this relationship directly (Nickerson, Schwarz, Diener, & Kahneman, 2003), and one is indirectly concerned with the topic through examining the match between goals and resources generally (Diener & Fujita, 1995). Diener and Fujita found that if there is a mismatch between people's goals and resources, then this is more likely to lead to diminished well-being. If, however, people's resources and goals match, their well-being should increase. Thus, if people lack the money to fulfil materialistic wants, this should cause lower SWB; conversely, if people have the means to support a materialistic lifestyle, their well-being should not be diminished because of their materialism. This argument was supported by one of the findings in the research by Nickerson et al. (2004), which showed that the negative link between financial goals and life satisfaction diminished as household income increased.

To assess whether the pattern of links between money-making motives and SWB is moderated by income levels, we re-analysed the data from the study described in the previous section, separately for high and low income groups (Garðarsdóttir, 2006). For the purpose of this analysis, any participant who was not employed at the time of data collection (e.g. student, retired) was removed from the dataset, leaving 187 participants in the UK and 416 from Iceland. This was done to assess only the answers of those participants receiving a regular income. The average annual income of UK participants was £29,700 (ranging from £5000 to £130,000), which is very similar to the national average in the UK of £29,400 in 2004 (*Social Trends*, 2004). The average income of the Icelandic sample was 300,800 kronur per month (ranging from 20,000 to 2,500,000 kronur), and the comparison with national statistics shows, as for the UK, that this sample is representative of the general population with respect to income (Statistics Iceland, 2005).[5]

Participants were divided into high and low income groups by median split for each country, i.e. into the highest and lowest 50% of earners. Associations between each of the six money-making motives and SWB were then assessed separately for high and low income groups in the UK and in Iceland, using two-sample structural equation modelling (EQS 6.1; Bentler, 1995). In the UK, the model explains 29% and 21% of the variance of SWB, for the high and low income groups respectively. In Iceland, the model explains 26% of the variance in SWB for the high income group and 19% for the low income group. The results from these analyses are summarised in Table 4.3, which also shows the outcomes of significance tests that compare the high and low income groups in terms of the strength of association between each money-making motive and SWB.[6]

For the *realistic motives*, the patterns of association are practically identical in both countries. Financial security was not associated significantly with

Table 4.3 Structural equation model paths and difference tests of the relationship between money-making motives and subjective well-being (SWB) for high and low income groups in the UK and Iceland

		UK			Iceland		
	Income	High	Low	$\Delta\chi^2$	High	Low	$\Delta\chi^2$
Realistic motives							
Success → SWB		−.02	.47**	*	−.02	.35***	*
Security → SWB		.09	.01		.10	.06	
Worth and Pride → SWB		.11	.17		.11	.07	
Unrealistic motives							
Happiness → SWB		−.03	−.35*	+	−.03	−.33***	*
Identity → SWB		.07	−.17		.07	−.11	
Overcoming self-doubt → SWB		−.46***	−.36*		−.48***	−.26**	

+ $p < .10$; * $p < .05$; ** $p < .01$; *** $p < .001$.

SWB, consistent with the findings in the first study. The association between the motive for worth and pride and SWB was not significant at either income level in either country. In contrast, the motive for success had a significantly different relationship with SWB, depending on level of income. For the low income groups, success had a significant positive association with SWB, whereas for the high income group there was no relationship between the two variables. This implies that, contrary to what we expect if the success motive is essentially achievable through money and possessions, if one earns less than the median amount of income, it is beneficial for one's well-being to place importance on earning money in order to feel successful. If, however, one earns more than the median amount, the importance of the success motive has no psychological consequence. This finding can be explained, however, by considering that people in the high income group may already have reaped the benefits of striving for success, in the sense that they may already appear successful in their society and their possessions may already signify their success. Striving to feel yet more successful may not add to their well-being, precisely because their success has already been established.

With respect to the *unrealistic motives*, striving for a better identity was not significantly related with well-being in any of the groups, which is consistent with the findings in the first study. The largest predictor of SWB in both the UK and Iceland was the motive for overcoming self-doubt. In both countries, this motive had a strong negative association with well-being for both the high and the low income groups. These findings suggest that materialists who strive for money in order to overcome feelings of self-doubt are striving in vain; having a higher income does not improve well-being or, most probably, feelings of self-doubt either. In contrast, for the happiness motive, association with SWB differed by income level. Happiness has a strong negative association with SWB for the low income group, but there is no association between SWB and the happiness motive for the higher income group. This was a rather unexpected finding because, although we had hypothesised that the impact of the happiness motive may well be stronger in the lower income groups, we had not expected that it would disappear altogether for the higher income groups. These findings suggest that people with a higher income experience no negative impact of the money-making motive for happiness. This implies the rather uneasy conclusion that money could possibly bring about some happiness.

CONCLUSION AND IMPLICATIONS

The first research programme described in this chapter, examining value conflict, showed that negative links between materialism and SWB may indeed be influenced by whether or not materialists endorse other-oriented values that are in opposition to, and thus likely to conflict with, materialism. For students, conflict between strong materialistic and community values was associated with lower well-being, but whereas this effect was pronounced in UK students, it was less strong in Croatian students. Similarly, whereas the negative impact of conflict between strong materialistic and family values on well-being was pronounced in UK adults, it was less strong in Croatian adults. These findings have two important implications. First, they suggest that value conflict, and associated self-discrepancies, needs to be taken into account in future research on the materialism–SWB link. Second, the findings suggest that there may be cultural differences in the meaning of materialism between Western and former socialist European countries. The weaker evidence for a negative well-being impact of simultaneously holding strong materialistic and other-oriented values in Croatia could suggest that, if materialism can be seen as serving collectivist goals (with benefits for community and family), then there is less opposition, and hence conflict, between these sets of values. Thus, sensitivity to the cultural context of materialism is important.

Moving on to the role of money-making motives, the main findings from the second research programme show support for five of the six motives proposed in the model. In particular, they confirm the importance of the motives for happiness, for identity, and for success as important indicators of SWB. They also provide a partial answer to the question of whether financial goals are essentially detrimental or whether there may be some positive reasons, or motives, for striving for money, whereas others are negative. Furthermore, they raise the interesting question of whether these findings might contribute toward a fourth way of conceptualising and defining materialism, in addition to the three approaches discussed at the beginning of the chapter. If materialism is the pursuit of money in order to be happier, to feel successful, to overcome ideas of self-doubt, to feel a sense of worth and pride in self, and to achieve a sought after identity, then, yes, it could be claimed that the money-making motives are assessing materialism. Building on definitions of materialism discussed earlier in the chapter, it can be argued that each of these five motives is associated with a materialistic outlook. For example, materialism has been described as the pursuit of money and possessions in order to gain psychological benefits, such as compensating for insecurities (Kasser, Ryan, Couchman, & Sheldon, 2004), or in order to be happier and feel successful (Fournier & Richins, 1991). Breaking materialism down into more and less realistic motives improves the understanding of what it is about materialism that has in past research had a consistently negative impact. The motives help to understand why materialism is detrimental to people's SWB and should therefore, arguably, be included in future research on the relationship between materialism and SWB.

The conclusion that can be drawn from the findings of the third study reported is that income does moderate the effect that money-making motives have on SWB, and that the resulting patterns are very similar in the UK and Iceland. In lower income groups, the motive for happiness had a strong negative impact on SWB in both countries, but for the high income groups, in both countries, this association disappeared. In fact, for people with a higher income, the only negative impact materialism had on their well-being was for overcoming self-doubt. It can be concluded that, to some extent, having a high income protects people from the negative impact of materialism. The findings for the happiness motive were especially intriguing. This motive was a negative predictor of SWB when income is not taken into account, leading to the conclusion that, paradoxically, wanting money to bring happiness leads to unhappiness. This was seen as a meaningful conclusion, given the lay wisdom that money cannot buy happiness, supported by research showing that wealth contributes little to individuals' happiness (e.g. Diener & Biswas-Diener, 2002). Our finding that striving for money with the intent to increase happiness does not lead to lowered SWB for people who earn well now places that former conclusion into question. Does money buy happiness for people who can afford it? In order to shed further light on this question, future studies could chart changes in income and SWB over time, in order to be able to see if the relationship between the motive for happiness and SWB really does disappear with increased income. Another implication for future research concerns the populations studied. Given the role of income, using student samples to assess the relationship between materialism and SWB might lead to conclusions that do not hold for other populations. This implies that researchers in this area need to be wary about generalising from student findings and should employ both non-student and student samples in future research on materialism.

Finally, having addressed the strengths and implications of the research reported in this chapter, one of its limitations needs to be considered. However, it has to be emphasised that this limitation is characteristic of the entire materialism–SWB research literature to date. The findings reported cannot address questions of cause and effect. Like all correlational studies, they can examine associations between materialism and well-being, but not the direction of the negative effect: they do not demonstrate that materialism causes people to be unhappy and unwell. Self-determination Theory does imply this causal direction, but it is also likely that people who are insecure in their identity and unhappy turn to materialistic pursuits in their attempt to find a solution to their problem. Thus, a bi-directional model is most likely (cf. Kasser & Kanner, 2004), and future research therefore needs to address the link between materialism and well-being over time.

One of the strongest findings is that the motive to remove self-doubt is a consistent predictor of negative SWB, regardless of income, which suggests that identity deficits cannot easily be addressed through buying new consumer goods. Thus, the idea that identity deficits and materialism may go hand in hand to produce lower well-being is interesting, and both factors are examined in the next chapter as predictors of detrimental consumer behaviour, leading to ill-being.

5 I shop therefore I am? Compulsive buying and identity seeking

Helga Dittmar

Synopsis

Compulsive buying, often called shopping addiction in the media, has serious negative consequences for individuals—causing debt, distress, and impairment—and the problem is growing. Yet, we are only starting to understand the underlying causes, and the research in this chapter makes three contributions:

- Excessive, uncontrolled buying of consumer goods can be understood as a form of identity seeking.
- Materialism and seeking to repair identity deficits make people vulnerable to compulsive buying.
- Compulsive buying affects an increasing number of young people, and it also occurs on the internet.

Shopaholics Anonymous   © Jessica Barlow

A growing number of people engage in uncontrolled, excessive buying of consumer goods that leads to psychological distress and has serious effects on their lives, such as substantial debt. This dysfunctional behaviour can come to dominate individuals' lives to such an extent that it has to be considered a clinical disorder, termed compulsive buying. The mass media has, of course, picked up on this problem, and the life stories, experiences, and confessions of "shopping addicts" and "shopaholics" abound.

As many as half a million people in the UK, one million in Germany, and 15 million in the US may be affected (Dittmar, 2004b; Koran, Faber, Boujaoude, Large, & Serpe, 2006). Yet, despite posing a substantial problem to consumer well-being, the underlying causes of compulsive buying are still poorly understood. The main approaches to date are clinical models, which tend to view compulsive buying as a manifestation of one or more underlying psychiatric disorders, but without agreement on the type of disorder (e.g. Black, 2006). However, this clinical approach does not offer explanations for why compulsive buying occurs only in developed mass consumer societies, why it shows a recent increase, or why some individuals are more vulnerable to it than others.

This chapter develops a new perspective on compulsive buying as identity-seeking behaviour. The central proposal is captured in the consumer slogan used as the title of a recent book *I Shop, Therefore I am: Compulsive Buying and the Search for Self* (Benson, 2000). The social psychological model proposed here views compulsive buying as an extreme form of identity seeking through material goods that lies on a continuum with everyday psychologically motivated buying. Building on the transformations of consumer culture over the last few decades (see Chapter 1), this model focuses on endorsement of materialistic values and identity deficits as vulnerability factors for compulsive buying, both in the "bricks" of conventional stores and "clicks" on the internet.

WHAT IS "COMPULSIVE BUYING"? MINORITY PATHOLOGY OR MASS PROBLEM?

In the current diagnostic manual DSM-IV-TR (American Psychiatric Association, 2000), compulsive buying is still included in the residual category "Disorders of Impulse Control Not Otherwise Specified". Although there is no agreed-upon specific definition, broad consensus exists on three core features of compulsive buying: the urge to buy is experienced as irresistible, individuals lose control over their buying behaviour, and they continue with excessive buying despite adverse consequences in their personal, social, or occupational lives, and financial debt (Dittmar, 2004b; Faber, 2004). These core features are consistent with proposed diagnostic criteria for compulsive buying, which emphasise a "maladaptive preoccupation with buying or shopping" impulses and behaviours that cause "marked distress, are time-consuming, significantly interfere with social or occupational functioning, or result in financial problems" (McElroy, Keck, Harrison, Pope, Smith, & Strakowski, 1994, p. 247).

Core features and a case example

"Nancy" took part in our interview study (Dittmar & Drury, 2000) when she was in the process of recovering from compulsive buying. Her experience provides a flavour of what is typical and common in compulsive buying:

> For Nancy, 35 years old, there is only impulse buying. If she sees something in a shop she likes, she must have it. She can't stop herself. It is always clothes and jewellery, smart clothes mainly, a size 12 which she desires to be . . . It does lift her up for a few hours. When home, she does not try on the clothes, but puts them away in the loft for fear her husband could find out. It is all her fault, she thinks. She feels guilty. She has ridden the family into debt. She says that she cannot tell her husband, because he would walk out on her. She started overspending after the birth of her daughter about 8 years ago. Since she did not have money of her own, she applied for credit cards. She complains that it is too easy to get them, and that credit limits are increased without consideration of whether the applicant can pay the money back. When she had about £9,000 ($13,500) of debt on her credit cards, she decided to go to a bank and take out a loan. She is paying back £266 ($399) per month, and now has two more years and £6,000 ($9,000) to go. With the interest, her repayments will add up to about £15,000 ($22,500).
>
> (Dittmar, 2004b, p. 412)

Research that focuses on compulsive buyers' own perspective refers to an "inability to control an overpowering impulse to buy" (O'Guinn & Faber, 1989), and this is echoed in Nancy's statement that, except for routine household shopping, all her buying is impulsive and experienced as irresistible: "she must have it". With irresistible impulses to buy a core feature of compulsive buying, the question of losing control over one's behaviour arises. Indeed, Nancy "can't stop herself", and the common subjective experience of shopping coming to dominate self and everyday life is the second core feature of compulsive buying (e.g. Faber, 2004). The third core feature, also reported by Nancy, is that individuals carry on with their behaviour in the face of harmful consequences. The most obvious adverse effect is financial. In addition to credit and store cards, there are diverse unsecured personal loans, all with extendable limits, and, in the UK virtually no lender policies exist to check or ensure that individuals are financially capable of making repayments. Debts can accumulate so frighteningly fast and steeply that, at the extreme, they result in financial ruin. A recent UK interview study with 36 households in severe debt found that 20% showed a compulsive buying profile (Elliott,

2005). Money is by no means the only problem, however. Time is another resource most people can ill afford to manage badly (Kasser & Sheldon, 2006), and the preoccupation with buying can become surprisingly time-consuming, both in terms of thinking and fantasising about goods, and in time spent shopping or browsing. A further consequence is neglect of commitments to work, friends, and family, resulting in impaired occupational, social, and personal functioning. Individuals end up becoming distressed psychologically, experiencing self-blame, guilt, and disordered mood states, most commonly anxiety and depression (Black, 2006; Lejoyeux, Adés, Tassian, & Solomon, 1996).

The interview excerpt with Nancy stresses a further feature, which is not commonly discussed when defining compulsive buying. This feature concerns the central argument of this chapter: An additional characteristic of compulsive buyers is that they seek to move closer to their ideal identity through buying identity-relevant consumer goods. In the case study here the identity sought is the attractive, thin self central to the socio-cultural ideal for women: "it is always clothes . . ., smart clothes mainly, a size 12 which she desires to be". This is consistent with reports in clinical research that compulsive buyers are highly selective in their purchases—usually clothes, shoes, appearance-related goods, and accessories (Dittmar, 2004b).

Measurement of compulsive buying

The diagnosis of a fully blown clinical disorder is warranted only when the extent of impairment is significant, an assessment that requires a personal interview by a clinician. However, as we will see, there is unlikely to be a radical dichotomy between ordinary buyers on the one hand and those who are clinically dysfunctional on the other. The perspective taken here therefore conceptualises compulsive buying as constituting the extreme "abnormal" end of a continuum that has at its other end the kind of ordinary buying where individuals buy goods because they seek psychological benefits, such as a better self, social image, or improved mood, rather than practical, utilitarian value. Between these two extremes is a large middle ground, which is characterised by increasing degrees of excessive, uncontrolled buying that has dysfunctional elements, but is subclinical in nature.

The relative strength of a person's tendencies toward compulsive buying can be measured by questionnaire-based scales that assess the core features of compulsive buying and have been validated on clinical samples. Such measurement is therefore well-suited to the main purpose of the research presented in this chapter: predicting individuals' tendency, and thus vulnerability, toward compulsive buying. The two most widely used scales were developed by Faber and O'Guinn (1992) and by Valence, d'Astous, and Fortier (1988). Dysfunctional cut-off points have been published for both and, although these cannot be used for the purposes of diagnosis, they provide a tool for identifying individuals whose compulsive buying symptoms are severe enough to indicate dysfunctional dimensions. The Faber and O'Guinn screener has been employed predominantly in US research, whereas the Valence scale, or a later modification (d'Astous, Maltais, & Roberge, 1990), has been used in Canadian and European studies, as well as in the UK (e.g. Elliott, 1994); we therefore chose this scale for our research. The following example items illustrate how each of the three core features of compulsive buying is addressed: irresistible urges, "As soon as I enter a shopping centre, I want to go in a shop and buy something"; loss of control, "I sometimes feel that something inside pushes me to go shopping"; and continuing despite aversive consequences, "I have often bought a product that I did not need even when I knew I had very little money left".

Prevalence of dysfunctional buying

Estimates by clinicians suggest that 2–5% of adults in the US are compulsive shoppers (e.g. Black, 1996), but percentages derived from screener cut-off points in general population surveys are higher, ranging from an estimate of 8% (Faber & O'Guinn, 1992) to figures as high as 12% (Hassay & Smith, 1996) or even 16% among younger samples (Magee, 1994). Yet these studies used samples that are either small or unrepresentative. For the US, we now have a firmer base for estimating prevalence, through a large-scale household telephone survey with a nationally representative sample of over 2500 adults aged 18 years and over (Koran et al., 2006). Using the screener by Faber and O'Guinn (1992), they report an estimated prevalence of 5.8%. However, this figure represents the average across the full range of age cohorts, including people in their twenties to their eighties and above. Indeed, the authors report that age is a significant predictor, demonstrating that the prevalence of compulsive buying is higher among younger people.

The figures from our four UK surveys are higher (Dittmar, 2005a, 2005b), but they focus on younger respondents and used the Valence scale, whose cut-off point may be less stringent. Among an adult sample ($n = 236$) that excluded respondents who either had been in contact with a self-help organisation or responded to appeals concerning shopping problems, 13% scored above the cut-off point. Among students ($n = 126$) it was 20%, rising to 28% among consumer research panellists for a multinational corporation ($n = 250$), who are likely to be particularly strongly involved with consumer culture, given that payment for participation is often in kind (i.e. consumer goods). Finally, for 16- to 18-year-old adolescents ($n = 195$), 44% scored beyond the dysfunctional cut-off point. Although this should be interpreted with some caution, given that their spending power is limited and that adolescence is a developmental stage marked by extreme behaviours in various consumption domains (e.g. drinking alcohol), it does suggest that potentially problematic shopping and spending habits are extremely widespread among adolescents, whose reported attitudes and habits are consistent with early indications of compulsive buying symptoms.

Although "oniomania" (buying mania) was first described as early as 1915, these UK findings are consistent with the proposal that dysfunctional buying is fast emerging as a widespread phenomenon, and one that is on the increase. Published research studies on compulsive buying started to appear only from 1986, first in North America, then also in Europe, showing a steady increase in number over time (Dittmar, 2004b). Mass media attention and self-help literature are proliferating (cf. Benson, 2000, 2006). This growing concern can, of course, not be equated with prevalence, but it does suggest that increasing numbers of individuals are experiencing problems with their buying behaviour, and thus a detriment to their well-being. A recent study on two nationally representative samples in Germany 10 years apart provides the first direct evidence for an increase, finding that compulsive buying scores are significantly higher in 2001 compared to 1991 (Neuner, Raab, & Reisch, 2005).

PSYCHIATRIC DISORDER OR IDENTITY SEEKING?

When it comes to explaining the causes of compulsive buying, psychiatric and clinical perspectives are the main approaches to date, which tend to treat it as a specific manifestation of underlying psychiatric disorders. However, there is good evidence to support a social psychological model of compulsive buying (e.g. Dittmar, 2001, 2002, 2004b, 2005a, 2005b), which is intended to extend and complement received clinical wisdom.

Clinical perspectives

Clinical perspectives view compulsive buying as a manifestation of, or as caused by, other underlying psychiatric disorders. The focus has been on four main types: impulse control disorder (ICD; e.g. Christenson, Faber, De Zwaan, & Raymond, 1994), obsessive-compulsive disorder (OCD; e.g. Hollander, 1993), addiction (e.g. Scherhorn, 1990), and mood disorders, particularly depression (e.g. Lejoyeux, Tassian, Solomon, & Adés, 1997). Yet, there is little support for one type of disorder over another (Black, 2006). Moreover, the main form of evidence used as support is co-morbidity, or co-occurrence, between compulsive buying and these disorders. Co-morbidity rates found in samples of psychiatric patients (whose compulsive buying was often diagnosed during treatment for some other disorder) are usually much higher than co-morbidity rates reported in studies that identified compulsive buyers in general population samples through a questionnaire (cf. Dittmar, 2004b). This raises the possibility that the evidence for co-morbidity of compulsive buying with other psychiatric disorders may be less compelling than assumed, or that it applies to a specific subpopulation of individuals who have generalised psychiatric problems, including dysfunctional buying.

The clinical perspectives tend to assume a radical disjuncture between the pathological behaviour of compulsive buyers on the one hand and ordinary consumer behaviour on the other. This disjuncture may be one of the reasons why the mainstream psychiatric approach has two "blind spots". First, it does not offer an account for why compulsive buying is highly selective, rather than indiscriminate. As already mentioned, it is commonly reported that only certain types of consumer goods, such as fashionable clothes, are typically bought by compulsive buyers, whereas others are not, such as basic kitchen equipment. Second, the clinical approaches do not provide models of underlying psychological processes that may be evident in both ordinary psychologically motivated buying and compulsive buying, albeit to different degrees.

Mood enhancement, managing negative affect, and escape from painful feelings are seen as the main psychological drivers of compulsive buying in the clinical literature. For example, Lejoyeux et al. (1997) view compulsive buying as caused directly by depression, where sufferers use the hedonic aspects of shopping as self-medication to alleviate their depressive symptoms. Other perspectives focus on the relief or escape from anxiety that compulsive buyers gain momentarily through the thrill of the shopping experience and spending money (cf. Black, 2006). Indeed, there is direct evidence that compulsive buyers report more intense negative and positive emotions than ordinary buyers, and that they experience more mood change from before to just after purchase (Faber & Christenson, 1996). However, we have already seen that emotional buying motives are also common in ordinary buying (see Chapter 3). A study in which ordinary and compulsive buyers kept a detailed shopping diary for a month (Dittmar, 2005a) reports findings that are consistent with greater mood changes in compulsive buyers, but suggests that these are a matter of degree, rather than disjuncture. Moreover, the diaries also demonstrate that identity seeking is an important concern in compulsive buying, thus offering support for the significance of identity concerns for consumer well-being.

Social psychological model of compulsive buying as identity seeking

Over a 4-week period, respondents recorded psychologically motivated purchases of personal consumer goods (excluding routine household shopping) in a shopping diary. The diary focused on three different phases of the buying process: just before the purchase, just after, and after getting home. Of central interest here are individuals' open-ended accounts of their thoughts and feelings during each of these buying phases, which they wrote down as soon as possible after each purchase. We chose this unstructured format, rather than prompting respondents with specific questions, because we believe that this approach makes it more likely that participants record those concerns most salient to them. A coding system was developed that recorded four types of buying motive just before purchase, as well as consequences experienced after purchase: good value for money, usefulness, mood change, and identity seeking. Examples of identity seeking are "something that fits 'me' " or "just how I want to look". Buying goods in order to change one's mood was reported less often, with an average of 7% across all purchases, than the other three motives, all of which were reported with equal frequency for just under 20% of purchases: buying because the good is useful (18%), because it is good value (18%), and because it improves identity (17%). Thus, even when respondents were not prompted by researcher-generated constructs, they stated buying motives related to identity seeking spontaneously and more often than motives related to mood change.

Statements about perceived benefits after purchase were also coded, thus providing "timelines" for mood change and identity seeking: motivation before purchase and benefits reported just after purchase and after getting home. Although mood change was hardly mentioned as a motive, positive mood change was often apparent after purchase (48% just after and 54% after getting home), but this pattern differed between ordinary and compulsive buyers (classified on the basis of their score on the Valence scale). Compared to ordinary buyers, compulsive buyers reported a greater change from more negative feelings just before purchase to more positive feelings just after, but their mood gain peaked just after purchase and was short-lived because they felt worse by the time they got home with their purchases.

However, psychologically motivated buying may be as much about wanting to feel better about *oneself*, as about simply wanting to feel better. This argument that mood is tightly interwoven with how individuals see and evaluate themselves is supported by the similarity in pattern found for the identity-seeking timeline. Ordinary and compulsive buyers were very similar in reported identity-seeking concerns before and just after the purchase, but they differed after getting home. Whereas ordinary buyers reported increased identity benefits from goods, compulsive buyers reported less. For ordinary buyers, the mean percentages of purchases where they explicitly state identity seeking or identity gains were 18% just before purchase, 17% just after purchase, and 30% after getting home. In comparison, the figures for compulsive buyers were 17% just before and 17% just after, but only 11% after getting home. In summary, then, there are similarities between ordinary, psychologically motivated buying, and the dysfunctional behaviour of compulsive buyers, where the attempt to move closer to a more ideal identity through acquiring relevant material goods seems a significant concern.

The conceptual starting point of my two-factor model of compulsive buying is Symbolic Self-completion Theory (Wicklund & Gollwitzer, 1982), which argues that the perception of shortcomings in one's self-concept produces a motivation to compensate. As we saw in Chapter 2, this can involve acquiring and using material goods that symbolise those aspects of self felt to be lacking. Yet identity deficits are inferred in self-completion research, rather than measured directly. Identity deficits, in particular gaps between how a person sees her-/himself (actual self) and how s/he would ideally like to be (ideal self), are theorised explicitly in Self-discrepancy

Theory (e.g. Higgins, 1987), as outlined in Chapter 1. Identity deficits are therefore the first of the two factors central to our model; the second factor concerns the likelihood that individuals would choose the acquisition of material goods, rather than some other compensation strategy, in their pursuit of a more ideal identity.

The first factor in the model, identity deficits, concerns self-concept dynamics that lessen or intensify people's motivation to strive for an ideal self. The greater the discrepancies between how individuals see themselves and how they would like to be, the more likely it should be that they engage in behaviour intended to compensate for these deficits. Originally, Self-discrepancy Theory focused on negative affective outcomes of actual–ideal discrepancies in the form of dejection, which is consistent with the earlier proposal that identity deficits are interwoven with negative mood. However, "possible selves", that represent people's ideas of who they would like to become, can function as incentives for future behaviour (Markus & Nurius, 1986), and more recent self-discrepancy research has started to focus also on behavioural outcomes, such as disordered eating (Strauman, Vookles, Berenstein, Chaiken, & Higgins, 1991) or alcohol consumption (Wolfe & Maisto, 2000), but not compulsive buying. We propose that individuals with a particular commitment to buying consumer goods as an identity-repair strategy (see below) are likely to engage in identity-seeking buying behaviour when their self-discrepancies are high or salient. It is likely that compulsive buyers have chronically high self-discrepancies, and this was confirmed empirically (Dittmar, 2001). High self-discrepancies are also consistent with previous reports of low self-esteem, as well as an "empty self" (Dittmar, 2004b).

The second factor in the model identifies the type of person likely to use buying goods as an identity-seeking strategy, rather than other strategies, such as engaging in body-shaping behaviours intended to achieve a more ideal bodily self (see Chapters 6 and 7). Consumption-oriented individuals hold strong materialistic values and, as outlined in Chapter 4, believe that the acquisition of material goods is a central life goal, prime indicator of success, and key to happiness and self-definition (Richins, 2004). In that sense, strongly held materialistic values indicate a commitment to identity construction through material goods. Materialistic values are a necessary factor in the model because they constitute a belief system that channels an individual toward consumption as a strategy to deal with perceived identity deficits. Identity deficits, measured directly through self-reported self-discrepancies, are likely to function as a second, but additional, predictor of compulsive buying. Self-discrepancies should amplify identity seeking in materialistic individuals when they are particularly strong or salient. Self-discrepancies may also be a stronger predictor for women than men, given the pre-existing socio-cultural link between psychologically motivated buying of consumer goods and traditional gender identity (see Chapter 3). Thus, before going on to examine the role of self-discrepancies, materialistic values are investigated first by themselves as a vulnerability factor for compulsive buying.

MATERIALISM AND COMPULSIVE BUYING

An examination of materialistic value endorsement as a factor that makes individuals more vulnerable to compulsive buying needs to take age into account, given that compulsive buying is negatively correlated with age (e.g. d'Astous, 1990; Magee, 1994) and there are findings that young people are becoming increasingly more materialistic (cf. Myers, 2000). Gender is also examined, given the disproportionate prevalence estimates of compulsive buying among women reported in many previous studies (see reviews by Black, 2006; Faber, 2004), although not the recent US survey by Koran et al. (2006). Therefore, the series of UK studies summarised below (Dittmar, 2005a) all examine these three factors as predictors of compulsive buying tendency.

Gender, age, and materialistic value endorsement

Over 30 previous research studies on compulsive buying report that women are disproportionately affected, constituting around 90% of sufferers (e.g. Black, Repertinger, Gaffney, & Gabel, 1998), and typically scoring significantly higher on screener scales than men (e.g. Scherhorn, Reisch, & Raab, 1990). However, there are two reasons why we should be cautious in taking this at face value. First, many studies have sampled people in such a way that women are more likely to participate (e.g. appeals for people with shopping problems in women's magazines or TV programmes aimed at women), and the focus has been predominantly on high-street shopping, rather than on buying goods at auctions, or collecting goods, which are activities in which men engage more prominently than women. Thus, men may have been systematically underrepresented among compulsive buyers (cf. Dittmar, 2004b). Second, there may be changes over time, such that men have become more affected, as consumption and buying have started to assume a greater role with respect to their identity and everyday lives. Indeed, gender differences in compulsive buying scores were mild in young adults (Magee, 1994) and a study on adolescents failed to find any (Roberts & Tanner, 2000); the largest general population survey of its kind recently reported that women and men are equally strongly affected (Koran et al., 2006). Thus, it is unclear whether we should still expect gender to be a vulnerability factor for compulsive buying in our UK studies, although we found that shopping typically still plays a stronger psychological and symbolic role for women than men (see Chapter 3).

Younger individuals appear more strongly affected than older people, at least in the US (Koran et al., 2006). Furthermore, the majority of studies that compare compulsive buyers with ordinary buyers report that the average age of compulsive buyers is lower by between 8 and 11 years. This was found in studies conducted in France (Lejoyeux et al., 1997), Germany (Scherhorn et al., 1990), and the US (Hanley & Wilhelm, 1992; O'Guinn & Faber, 1989), although some studies found small (Lejoyeux et al., 1999) or no age differences (Black et al., 1998; DeSarbo & Edwards, 1996). Studies that correlate age with scores on compulsive buying scales consistently report negative links, ranging from $r = -.19$ (d'Astous et al., 1990) to $r = -.33$ (Magee, 1994) or $r = -.34$ (d'Astous, 1990). Furthermore, a recent European Union project identified 46% of Scottish 16- to 18-year-olds as showing possible early tendencies toward uncontrolled buying because they reported a lack of control over their spending habits, being unable to resist advertising stimuli (Garcés Prieto, 2002).

It is, of course, possible that such trends are short-lived in adolescents' lives, because they could reflect developmental needs to explore consumer activities or to establish an independent, adult identity by whatever expressive means available, including material goods. However, they might also reflect cohort effects, suggesting instead that socialisation into consumer culture values plays an important role. Indirect support comes from bringing together research that shows links between overspending and compulsive buying on the one hand, and increasing debt levels in younger people on the other. Although overspending has a multitude of causes, there are parallel increases in both overspending and compulsive buying during the last two decades (Lee & Mysyk, 2004). At the same time, younger people have stronger pro-debt attitudes (e.g. Lea & Webley, 1995; Lunt & Livingstone, 1992) as well as higher levels of debt. In the UK, over 60% of insolvency cases involve young people aged under 30 (Creditaction, 2006) and, similarly, US bankruptcy judges state that overwhelming credit card debt often afflicts young consumers (Newsletter of the Federal Courts, 2004). For our UK research, we therefore predicted that younger respondents would show stronger compulsive buying tendencies than older respondents, making it important to include adolescents in our sample. However, it is not clear whether these expected age differences can be linked to the increasingly more materialistic value orientation that characterises both North America and Europe.

If compulsive buying can be understood as compensatory behaviour aimed at mood repair and identity improvement, an association between materialism and compulsive buying seems highly probable. One reason to expect such an association is that both are linked to similar factors. When materialistic values are strongly held and override other values, they have detrimental correlates: low self-esteem, dissatisfaction with one's life, low subjective well-being (SWB) and poor psycho-social adjustment (see Chapter 4). Compulsive buying, too, has been consistently linked with low self-esteem (e.g. d'Astous, 1990; DeSarbo & Edwards, 1996; Elliott, 1994; Faber & O'Guinn, 1992; Hanley & Wilhelm, 1992), as well as negative affect (a core component of low SWB) and psychiatric symptomatology, such as ICD, OCD, or substance abuse (e.g. Black, 2006; Christenson et al., 1994; McElroy et al., 1994; Schlosser, Black, Repertinger, & Freet, 1994). More direct evidence comes from an early study that showed a link between compulsive buying and materialistic personality traits (Faber & O'Guinn, 1992). Such a link was also found in young adults whose parents were separated (Rindfleisch, Burroughs, & Denton, 1997; Roberts, Manolis, & Tanner, 2003), and has been interpreted as the outcome of their attempt to deal with insecurity through a focus on material goods.

In research that aimed to identify different pathways into compulsive buying, materialistic values emerged as a significant predictor for compulsive buyers who were externally motivated and less extreme in their behaviour (DeSarbo & Edwards, 1996). A link between compulsive buying and compulsive hoarding is also documented, and the acquisition and psychological functions of possessions are described as central aspects of compulsive buying (Frost, Steketee, & Williams, 2002). Compulsive buyers show a stronger commitment to money as symbolic of power and image (Hanley & Wilhelm, 1992), particularly if they are heavy credit card users (Roberts & Jones, 2001). Highly materialistic people are more likely to have favourable attitudes towards borrowing money and to overspend (Watson, 2003). Finally, compulsive buyers believe that they can deal with negative mood and low self-esteem by buying goods (Kyrios, Frost, & Steketee, 2004). Thus, it seems likely that the intensity of individuals' endorsement of materialistic values emerges as a strong predictor of their compulsive buying tendencies.

Moreover, it may be that materialism can account for age differences in compulsive buying. As reported in Chapter 4, annual surveys of US students demonstrate a dramatic increase in the importance attached to financial goals, an important component of materialism (cf. Myers, 2000). A recent US survey identified a heightened focus on materialism in 9- to 14-year-olds (Goldberg, Gorn, Peracchio, & Bamossy, 2003), and three books that were published simultaneously a year later were all concerned with growing commercialisation among children and adolescents (Lindstrom, 2004; Linn, 2004; Schor, 2004). If it is accepted that consumer culture socialisation can lead younger people to be more materialistic (see also Chapter 8), then this value endorsement could be a psychological mediator of age differences in compulsive buying tendency.

Surveys with UK adults and adolescents

To examine these predictions, I carried out three questionnaire studies (Dittmar, 2005a). The first was a postal survey ($n = 330$), with two different groups of adults as respondents: those who are likely to have experienced buying problems (having contacted a London-based compulsive buying self-help organisation or responded to appeals) and comparison respondents whose addresses were selected so that they residentially matched, by town and street, those of the buying problem group. In the second study, younger adults ($n = 250$) completed a questionnaire during their normal consumer panel duties for a large multinational manufacturer of consumer goods, and in the third, 16- to 18-year-old adolescents ($n = 195$) attending sixth-form colleges in north-west England completed questionnaires during class time. All three studies recorded gender and age (and other relevant demographic information) and used the same two core measures: the Materialistic Values Scale already introduced in Chapter 4 (Richins, 2004) and the revised Compulsive Buying Scale (CBS; d'Astous et al., 1990). It was ensured, through exploratory and confirmatory factor analyses, that these two scales measure distinct constructs.[7]

A series of analyses assessed how well the three factors of interest—gender, age, and materialism—predicted individuals' compulsive buying tendency (i.e. their scores on the CBS scale). The important feature of the type of hierarchical regression analysis used is that it determines, at each step, the additional predictive power of a factor once other factors have already been taken into account. To provide a stringent test of materialistic value endorsement as a vulnerability factor for compulsive buying, other predictors were entered first, one by one.

To control for their influence, indicators of socio-economic status (for the adult respondents) and financial standing (personal income and/or monthly personal spending money) are assessed first of all, but they do not emerge as significant predictors of compulsive buying tendencies in any of the samples. For the adolescents, compulsive buying tendencies are linked initially to more personal spending money per month, but this effect disappears once materialism is taken into account. This suggests that materialistic adolescents are those who have more money to spend on themselves each month, and although the causal connection can only be speculated about, it stands to reason that materialistic adolescents make active efforts to obtain greater sums of money, either by persuading or pressurising parents, or findings ways of earning some money themselves. In summary, however, the findings show that compulsive buying is not systematically associated with spending power as such, but that it affects people independently of their level of income.

Next, the influence of gender is assessed. Among the UK adults, women's compulsive buying tendencies are found to be significantly stronger than men's, and this finding remains constant and unaffected when age and materialism are also taken into account. Thus, a gender difference emerges as an independent effect in the first survey, with women's average score close to the midpoint of the six-point CBS scale (3.43) and higher than men's (2.67). However, the gender effect ($\beta = .26$) is small, explaining only an added 6% of the variability in CBS scores. Among the consumer panellists, who were 5 years younger on average, gender effects are even smaller ($\beta = .19$), although still statistically significant. In contrast, no gender differences are found in adolescents. Thus, compulsive buying tendencies are more pronounced among adult women than men in the UK, although gender differences are less evident in younger samples, where gender role identities are likely to be less traditional and an emphasis on shopping and buying among men is more common.

The hypothesis that compulsive buying tendencies would show systematic age differences is well supported by the findings. In the first sample, the addition of age (with gender already controlled) improves the prediction by adding 7% to the explained variability in CBS scores. The relationship is negative ($\beta = -.27$), demonstrating that younger respondents report higher scores. For adults aged 35 years or over, the CBS mean score is 3.0, whereas it is almost half a scale point higher for those younger than 35 (3.5). However, once materialism is taken into account, the strength of the relationship with age is reduced ($\beta = -.20$), suggesting that age differences in compulsive buying tendency may be due, at least in part, to differences in materialistic values. Among the consumer panellists, adults under 35 years also report significantly stronger compulsive buying tendencies than their older counterparts ($\beta = -.13$). In contrast, though, the age effect in this sample disappears altogether once differences in materialistic value endorsement are taken into account, which suggests that the observed age differences are due to younger respondents holding stronger materialistic values. Among adolescents, compulsive buying scores are significantly higher than those of the under 35 consumer panellists, thus lending further support to systematic age differences. Adjusted CBS mean scores[8] across these samples are 3.2 for the over-35 consumer panellists, 3.5 for those aged between 19 and 34 years, and 3.7 for the adolescents. The adolescents' score thus falls above the mid-point of the CBS scale.

The impact of materialistic value endorsement is examined last. This is a conservative test, given that all other factors are already allowed to act as predictors of compulsive buying tendency. Nevertheless, it proves a powerful additional predictor. In Study 1, materialistic value endorsement produces a substantial improvement in prediction, explaining an additional 15% of variability in CBS scores. Thus, materialistic values prove to be the strongest predictor of compulsive buying ($\beta = .39$), outstripping gender and age. This finding is replicated in Study 2, where materialistic value endorsement emerges among consumer panellists as an even more powerful vulnerability factor for compulsive buying ($\beta = .52$), adding a substantial 26% to the explained CBS variability. Finally, among the adolescents, materialism again emerges as a strong, and this time the only, predictor of compulsive buying tendency ($\beta = .29$), although the additional variability explained (8%) is much more modest and most likely due to greater homogeneity in materialism among 16- to 18-year-olds. In summary, what stands out as the major finding across all three studies is the powerful link between an individual's endorsement of materialism as a personal value system and his or her proclivities toward compulsive buying, confirming the expectation that a materialistic value system guides people toward psychologically motivated buying that can take on compulsive dimensions.

Finally, age-related differences in compulsive buying were significantly mediated by stronger materialistic value endorsement among younger consumers. Detailed analyses can be found in Dittmar (2005b), but to illustrate this second central finding, simplified summaries of two regressions are presented here, separately for UK adults (Study 1), consumer panellists (Study 2), and adolescents combined with consumer panellists (given that age differences cannot be assessed sensibly within the 2-year span from 16 to 18 years). The left-hand column of Table 5.1 shows gender and age as predictors of compulsive buying when materialistic values have not yet been taken into account; the right-hand column shows the findings after materialistic values are entered in addition to gender and age. By comparing the strength and significance of gender and age as predictors in these two analyses it becomes possible to assess the extent to which their links with compulsive buying are independent of, or affected by, materialistic value endorsement. The unchanged effects for gender indicate that women's somewhat stronger compulsive buying tendencies are independent of their endorsement of materialistic values. This gender effect is likely to reflect the remainders of the traditional socio-cultural link between shopping and women's identity, as well as the home-maker and child-carer roles, that may entail fewer opportunities for other psychological compensation strategies. Yet gender was a comparatively minor vulnerability factor. With respect to age differences, the predictive strength is reduced consistently after materialistic value endorsement is taken into account. Indeed, younger people held significantly stronger materialistic values, and formal tests of mediation were significant across the three data sets. These findings are important because they demonstrate that younger people's stronger compulsive buying tendencies are due, at least in part, to their greater endorsement of materialistic values.

Table 5.1 Summary from two sets of regression analyses of gender, age, and materialistic values as predictors of compulsive buying tendency

Predictors	*Without materialism*[a]	*With materialism*[b]
UK adults (Study 1)		
Gender	.25***	.26***
Age	−.27***	−.20***
Materialistic values		.39***
Consumer panelists (Study 2)		
Gender	.16*	.19**
Age	−.13*	.05ns
Materialistic values		.52***
Adolescents and panelists (Studies 3 and 2)		
Gender	.09*	.10*
Age	−.21***	−.15**
Materialistic values		.41***

[a]Adjusted R^2 in the three studies respectively was .11, .03, and .04; [b]adjusted R^2 respectively was .26, .39, and .21. * $p < .05$; ** $p < .01$; *** $p < .001$; ns, not significant. Adapted from Dittmar (2005b), Compulsive buying behaviour – a growing concern? An empirical exploration of the role of gender, age, and materialism, *British Journal of Psychology, 96*, p. 479 and p. 486, with kind permission of the British Psychological Society © 2005.

Thus, the internalisation of materialistic value endorsement appears to be an important underlying psychological mechanism that constitutes a powerful vulnerability factor with respect to compulsive buying. Having found strong support for the first factor in the proposed two-factor model, the next programme of research examines the additional role of identity deficits, the second factor in the model.

THE QUEST FOR A MORE IDEAL SELF

As part of the postal survey with UK adults, respondents indicated how true for them personally six different buying motives are: good value for money, usefulness, mood improvement, self-expression, social status improvement, and ideal self (see Chapter 3 for a more detailed description). The ideal-self motive assesses the importance of buying because "it makes me feel more like the person I want to be". A statistical comparison of buying motives endorsed by women classified as ordinary ($n = 165$) and compulsive buyers ($n = 74$) shows that compulsive buyers are less concerned with economic–rational buying motives (value, use), but that all psychological buying motives are much stronger for them (Dittmar, 2005b). The difference is greatest with respect to the ideal-self buying motive, which is higher among compulsive buyers, thus supporting the identity-seeking perspective on compulsive buying.

Individual differences in the ideal-self buying motive should be related to both materialistic values, as well as to identity deficits. The greater the gap between a materialistic person's actual self and his or her ideal identity, the more the individual should be motivated to buy goods because she or he believes that they help to move him or her closer to the person she or he ideally wants to be. It is expected that both materialistic values and self-discrepancies jointly predict compulsive buying tendencies, at least for women, for whom there is a stronger socio-cultural link between shopping and identity deficits, although possibly not for men. In addition, individual differences in ideal-self buying motivation should mediate, at least in part, the association between materialistic values and self-discrepancies on the one hand, and compulsive buying tendency on the other. In other words, materialism and self-discrepancies should strengthen the ideal-self buying motive which, in turn, should be linked to stronger compulsive buying tendencies.

Evidence from two UK questionnaire studies

The first study used respondents from the same postal questionnaire sample already introduced ($n = 330$), which also included measurements of self-discrepancies and ideal-self buying motivation. As outlined in Chapter 7, self-discrepancies were measured directly with the Self-discrepancy Index (SDI), which we developed specifically for this research programme (Dittmar

et al., 1996), for which respondents complete sentences of the format "I am
. . . . . ., but I would like to be . . . . . .", and then rate each statement they
generate in terms of the magnitude and psychological importance of the gap.
The second study, reported in Dittmar (2005b) and using similar measures,
sampled young consumers in their early 20s ($n = 126$), for two reasons. First,
they should show relatively strong compulsive buying tendencies, given the
finding that compulsive buying is more prevalent in younger, rather than
older, consumers. Second, given that gender differences seem less strong in
younger consumers, this sample should offer a particularly good opportunity
to test whether the two-factor model applies equally well to men.

We use structural equation modelling (SEM; EQS 6.1, Bentler, 1995) to
test these hypotheses, because it can assess directly how well the two-factor
model fits the data, and whether it applies equally well to different groups of
people (in our case women and men). In the first set of analyses, we used a
two-sample test to assess whether self-discrepancies and materialistic values,
jointly, predict individual women's and men's compulsive buying tendency.
These analyses were carried out both for older and younger adults.[9] Materialistic values were allowed to co-vary with self-discrepancies, given previously
reported links between materialism and low self-esteem.

For women, both materialistic values and self-discrepancies were significant, independent predictors of compulsive buying, as expected. There was
also a positive link between materialism and self-discrepancies. Among the
older UK women, the associations with compulsive buying were comparable
in strength for the two predictors ($\beta = .33$ and $\beta = .36$), whereas the association was stronger with materialistic values than with self-discrepancies for
the younger women ($\beta = .58$ and $\beta = .23$). It appears that materialistic values
play an even stronger role for young women than women in mid-adulthood.
Thus, the two-factor model is supported in two different samples of women,
representing older and younger adults.

In contrast, the findings for men are different in several respects. First, the
two-factor model held less strongly for men, because it explained less of the
variability in their CBS score, although the percentage was higher among
younger than older men. The direct influence of materialistic values on compulsive buying tendencies is as strong for men as it is for women; this aspect
of the model is thus similar for both genders, where the influence among
young adults is even greater than among middle-aged adults ($\beta = .53$ and
$\beta = .37$). Where the findings for men differ qualitatively from women is with
respect to the predictive role of self-discrepancies: they are not a direct,
independent predictor of compulsive buying tendency, neither for men
in mid-adulthood ($\beta = .02$), nor for younger men ($\beta = -.00$), for whom they
are not even associated with materialistic values. This evidence of gender
differences implies that, for men, only materialistic values predict compulsive
buying tendency, but not self-discrepancies.

The finding that the two-factor model fits women better than men, particularly with respect to self-discrepancies, supports the notion of a stronger

cultural link between female gender identity and identity repair through shopping. It is worth considering, though, that, whereas there is an identity–*shopping* link for women, there may be links between identity repair and other forms of dysfunctional consumer behaviour for men who are materialistic and high in self-discrepancies. There is some evidence that pathological collectors of expensive items are predominantly men (e.g. Belk, 1995), and excessive participation in auctions—both conventional and online (e.g. e-Bay)—seems a male activity, too. Therefore, it may be limiting to equate compulsive buying of material goods only with *shopping* as a particular consumer activity, given that there are also other potential forms of compulsive buying, collecting and auctioning, which may be common among men, and linked to their self-discrepancies. This issue deserves attention in future research.

Next, we turn to the hypothesis that materialistic values and self-discrepancies increase compulsive buying tendency through heightening the motivation to achieve the ideal self by purchasing goods, which means that the ideal-self buying motive should function as a mediating psychological process in the two-factor model. Predictive paths from self-discrepancies and materialistic values were modelled both directly to compulsive buying tendency, as well as indirectly through the ideal-self buying motive. The findings from this second set of analyses are shown in Figure 5.1 as standardised path coefficients, which indicate the strength of association, separately for middle-aged and younger adults.

The main findings are best considered by gender. For men, the two-factor model holds only partially, with respect to materialistic value endorsement. For the older men, materialistic values remain a direct, significant predictor of compulsive buying tendency. The ideal-self motive is also predictive, as hypothesised, but it is not significantly associated with materialism. In contrast, the mediation model is supported for younger men with respect to one of the two factors in the model: materialistic values. They are significantly associated with the ideal-self buying motive, which, in turn, predicts compulsive buying tendency. In addition, materialism also remains a direct predictor. With respect to women, the two-factor model is well supported, and the outstanding finding is that their compulsive buying tendency is predicted independently by identity deficits, in addition to materialistic value endorsement. Greater self-discrepancies and materialistic values lead to stronger ideal-self buying motivation in both samples of women, and the ideal-self buying motive is a significant, direct predictor of increased compulsive buying tendency. For women in mid-adulthood, mediation through ideal-self buying motivation is partial—the direct paths from self-discrepancies and materialistic values to compulsive buying are reduced in strength, but nevertheless remain significant. Mediation is stronger among the younger women, in the sense that ideal-self buying motivation predicts compulsive buying tendency more strongly and, in particular, that the direct path from self-discrepancies to compulsive buying is fully mediated, becoming non-significant (and is therefore not shown in Figure 5.1). This finding

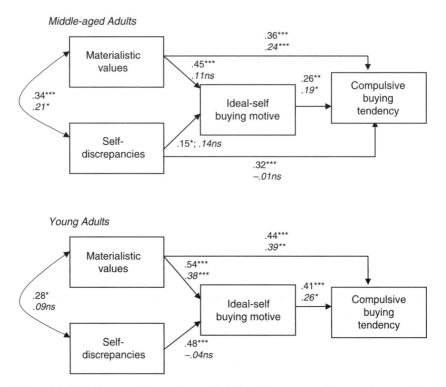

Figure 5.1 Self-discrepancies and materialistic values as predictors of compulsive buying tendency in middle-aged and young adults (findings for men in italics). *$p < .05$; **$p < 0.1$; ***$p < .001$; *ns*, not significant. (*Note.* Adapted from Dittmar (2005a), A new look at "compulsive buying": Self-discrepancies and materialistic values as perdictors of compulsive buying tendency, *Journal of Social and Clinical Psychology, 24*, p. 848 and p. 852, with kind permission of Guilford Publications.)

suggests that the ideal-self buying motive may constitute a stronger motivation among younger women, a motivation that is more closely linked to their self-discrepancies, which could reflect stronger consumer culture socialisation and/or a sense of identity that is not yet stable.

In summary, materialistic value commitment was a strong, direct predictor of compulsive buying tendency, both for women and men of different ages. Materialistic values also predicted the relative strength of ideal-self seeking as a buying motive, except in older men. In contrast, self-discrepancies were an additional, independent predictor only for women, where they lead to both stronger ideal-self buying motivation and stronger compulsive buying tendency. This suggests that perceived identity deficits, in addition to materialistic value endorsement, are a significant factor that makes women more vulnerable to compulsive buying.

COMPULSIVE BUYING TENDENCY ON THE INTERNET

Compulsive buying does not only take place in the "bricks" of conventional shops and stores, but also through television shopping networks, such as QVC (Ridgway & Kukar-Kinney, 2005). In our UK adult sample, individuals' CBS score significantly predicted the extent to which they used QVC or other TV channels for shopping ($\beta = .23$). Yet, as we saw in Chapter 3, the internet is fast becoming a serious alternative to conventional buying, and there is some preliminary evidence that compulsive buying does occur online. This raises the interesting question of whether underlying factors and consequent buying motives for conventional compulsive buying tendency may also be applicable to the internet. Perspectives are mixed when it comes to the nature and likely consequences of buying online. As discussed at the end of Chapter 3, there was an initial assumption that internet buying should have primarily positive consequences for individuals, because it protects them from the emotional and experiential features of conventional buying, designed to increase unplanned buying, and affords them the time and good information search facilities needed for well-considered decision-making. In contrast to this view, there are good reasons to propose that compulsive buying is likely to occur on the internet. As indicated in Chapter 1, consumers can shop world-wide online, with limitless access 24 hours a day, 7 days a week. Over one-fifth of respondents in a US survey agreed that they spend more online than they intend (UCLA Internet Report, 2003), which is consistent with the findings of the qualitative study summarised in Chapter 3 that young, computer-literate adults were concerned about overspending when buying online, and a content analysis showed that popular retail websites include a number of features that could stimulate uncontrolled buying (LaRose, 2001).

Although the internet is fast becoming a significant buying environment, research on compulsive buying online is only just starting to emerge. Lyons and Henderson (2000) make a theoretical case for compulsive buying emerging on the internet as an "old problem in a new marketplace" (p. 739), and an exploratory survey with 355 Korean consumers (Lee & Lee, 2003, personal communication) identified 17% of internet shoppers as having compulsive buying tendencies, using a screener for conventional compulsive buying (Faber & O'Guinn, 1992). A survey on US students identified the alleviation of negative mood as a significant predictor of unregulated online buying (LaRose & Eastin, 2002). These studies identify the extent to which individuals have a "wired lifestyle" as an important predictor of compulsive buying, which means that they use the internet frequently for other activities besides buying, such as diverse leisure and work purposes. However, it is likely that general internet use becomes a less discriminating correlate of online buying with greater internet penetration. Given that young adults use the internet with high frequency, there is likely to be a "ceiling effect" so that psychological variables become more predictive of compulsive buying tendencies online than simply a wired lifestyle. However, psychological factors associated with compulsive buying online have hardly been studied.

Our research (Dittmar, Long, & Bond, 2007) is the first to relate individual differences in compulsive buying tendencies online to materialistic value endorsement and to psychological online buying motives. The model tested in this research constitutes a further development of the two sets of vulnerability factors identified in conventional buying, because we integrate and extend them into a general social psychological model that predicts compulsive buying tendency. A further innovation is that this model is tested in the new buying environment of the internet. The first vulnerability factor concerns individuals' underlying value systems with respect to consumer culture, which functions as a general guide for more specific motives and behaviours. The extent to which individuals endorse materialistic values should be linked to their compulsive buying tendency online. The second set of vulnerability factors comprises specific buying motives, and we already saw that individuals seeking to move closer to an "ideal self" through buying consumer goods have stronger compulsive buying tendencies. Yet, individuals' self-concept, how they see and evaluate themselves, is likely to be linked to affect (e.g. Higgins, 1987), and emotional regulation and mood enhancement have been described in the clinical literature as important aspects of compulsive buying (e.g. Black, 2006; Faber, 2004). In the research reported here, we therefore examine both emotional and identity-related buying motives as predictors of individuals' compulsive buying tendencies, proposing that these motives, in turn, are a reflection of materialistic value endorsement.

Materialistic values as underlying beliefs should manifest themselves in emotional and identity-related buying motives. The more individuals believe that the acquisition of material goods will bring them happiness—improved emotions and mood—the more they should be motivated to buy goods online to obtain these emotional benefits. The same should hold for beliefs that material goods bring them social status and self-definition: the more individuals endorse such materialistic beliefs, the more they should seek social and personal identity gains when they buy goods online. The proposed model thus conceptualises endorsement of materialistic values as a more distal, or general, predictor of compulsive buying tendency, exerting its impact through the more proximal, or direct, predictors of emotional and identity-related buying motives (Figure 5.2)

In a preliminary survey of 110 young online buyers, we demonstrate that there are two distinct psychological motives in online buying, over and above instrumental concerns with economic benefits and efficiency, commonly shown for online buying. The first is identity seeking, consisting of wanting to move closer to an ideal self, to gain prestige, and to impress other people. The second is emotional enhancement and mood regulation, such as seeking pleasure in browsing and shopping, getting a buzz, and improving their mood. This is an important foundation for the main survey, where we use these two motives as specific predictors of compulsive buying tendencies

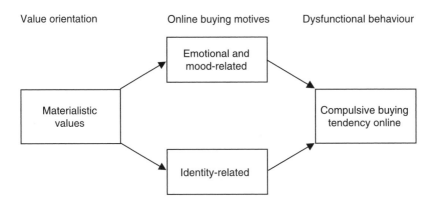

Figure 5.2 Model of associations between materialistic values, online buying motives, and compulsive buying tendency online. (*Note.* Reproduced from Dittmar, Long, & Bond (2007), When a better self is only a button click away: Associations between materialistic value endorsement, emotional and identity-related buying motives, and compulsive buying tendency online, *Journal of Social and Clinical Psychology, 26*, p. 342, with kind permission of Guilford Publications.)

online, as well as potential mediators of the proposed link between materialistic values and compulsive buying.

The main survey was carried out with a further sample of young online buyers of both sexes ($n = 126$). To be able to measure compulsive buying tendencies online, we adapted the CBS used in the studies reported earlier by rephrasing a number of items so that they refer to the internet specifically, while preserving their meaning as closely as possible. For example, the item "As soon as I enter a shopping centre, I want to go to a shop and buy something" becomes "As soon as I log onto the internet, I want to go to a retail site and buy something". Given that general internet use had been identified as a likely predictor of compulsive buying online, we also measured how often respondents used the internet per week, for any purpose, including e-mail or information searches. Greater internet use was indeed associated with higher CBS-online scores, but this association was no longer significant when online buying motives were taken into account. This supports the view that psychological factors make better predictors of compulsive buying on-line than simple internet use, at least among young, highly computer-literate people who routinely use the internet. There were no sex differences in CBS-online scores, which is consistent with the finding reported in Chapter 3 that the internet provides an environment where psychological engagement with buying is similar for women and men.

As before, structural equation modelling was used to test the proposed model, and the initial analysis showed, as expected, that materialistic values were a powerful predictor of compulsive buying tendency online, explaining 29% of CBS variability (see top half of Figure 5.3). Thus, just as in

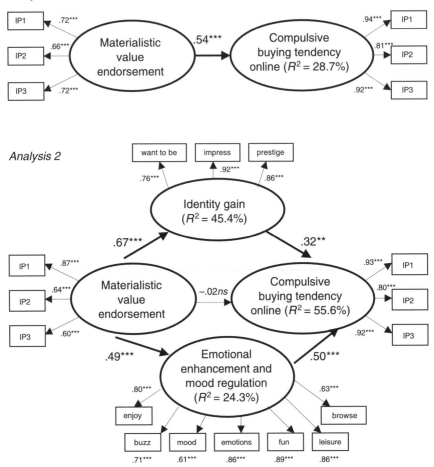

Figure 5.3 Structural equation models of relationships between materialistic values and compulsive buying tendencies online, with and without buying motives as mediators. (*Note*: **p<.01; ***p<.001; *ns*, not significant; IP, item parcel. Error terms are omitted for visual clarity. Reproduced from Dittmar, Long, & Bond (2007), When a better self is only a button click away: Associations between materialistic value endorsement, emotional and identity-related buying motives, and compulsive buying tendency online, *Journal of Social and Clinical Psychology*, *26*, p. 353, with kind permission of Guilford Publications.)

conventional buying environments, the more individuals endorse materialistic values, the stronger their compulsive buying tendencies online.

Yet when emotional and identity-seeking buying motives are added to the model as mediators, the direct link between materialism and compulsive buying tendency online drops to near zero ($\beta = -.02$), supporting full mediation.

This final analysis is shown in the bottom half of Figure 5.3, demonstrating that individuals' endorsement of materialistic values predicts emotional buying motives and, even more strongly, identity-related motives. In turn, these two motives are both direct, and unique, predictors of compulsive buying online, emotional motives even more strongly than identity seeking. As would be expected, the motives of mood regulation and identity seeking are closely related ($r = .50$). Direct assessments of the extent to which these online buying motives mediate the materialism–compulsive buying link prove highly significant for both. Moreover, the explanatory power of the model is substantially increased through including online buying motives: 56% of CBS-online variability.

Thus, in summary, the proposal that a materialistic value orientation is associated with individuals' seeking emotional benefits and identity gains when buying online found strong support, as well as the proposition that these emotional and identity-related motives, in turn, are linked to compulsive buying tendency online. Thus, the significant link between materialistic values and compulsive buying online was fully mediated by individuals' motives to seek an enhanced identity when buying online, an identity that is more ideal and happier.

CONCLUSION AND FUTURE TRENDS

Compulsive buying is clearly a detrimental consumer behaviour, psychologically and financially. It appears to be on the increase, at least as far as subclinical dysfunctional buying is concerned, which can be assessed by questionnaire-based measures. It is more prominent in younger people, and adolescents may be at particular risk of engaging in uncontrolled buying and spending. The central risk factors identified across a series of studies were individuals' endorsement of materialistic values, as well as buying motives that focus on seeking identity and enhancing mood. In addition, women's compulsive buying is also a strategy to deal directly with perceived identity deficits, over and above the identity seeking through consumption that is associated with materialistic values and the psychologically oriented buying linked to it. Furthermore, compulsive buying is not limited to the real-life shopping atmosphere of conventional shops and stores, but has started to occur also on the internet as a buying environment. Given the exponential growth of online buying, and the increasing sophistication of retail sites in mimicking visual and experiential aspects of conventional shopping, virtual compulsive buying could be a future trend that affects young consumers of both genders.

The research presented in this chapter provides convergent evidence from studies using different methodologies and samples that identity seeking constitutes an important dimension of compulsive buying. Identity seeking through consumption combines with a consumer culture infrastructure that reinforces it through advertising messages that stress "ideal identities", and through credit opportunities that are likely to over-indebt consumers. Changes in these factors could well help to curb compulsive buying, but are not likely in the near future, although changes to lender practices in the UK are under discussion (Elliott, 2005). It is, of course, not proposed here that identity seeking is the only psychological process involved in compulsive buying, only that it is a significant dimension that is likely to help improve understanding, prevention, and treatment of an increasingly prevalent behaviour detrimental to individuals' well-being. At the level of the individual, information and advice may help people to develop a more critical stance toward the unrealistic nature of the materialistic ideal, which proclaims that consumer goods offer sensible tools for solving emotional and identity-related problems. It would seem important to target individuals as early in life as possible, given that children as young as 8 years old already believe that having "cool things" will help them be accepted by their peers (see Chapter 8). Further implications are discussed in Chapter 9.

6 Does size matter? The impact of ultra-thin media models on women's body image and on advertising effectiveness

Emma Halliwell & Helga Dittmar

Synopsis

The "body perfect" ideal for women is ultra-thin, with media models typically underweight. Advertisers defend the continued use of this unhealthy and unachievable ideal with the argument that "thinness sells". Our exposure experiments show that:

- Ultra-thin media models make many women feel bad about their own body, whereas models with a healthy, average body weight do not.
- Internalisation of the thin ideal is a central vulnerability factor.
- Contrary to the "thinness sells" claim, advertising effectiveness is not compromised by models with a healthy body size.
- Average-size models promote diverse products as effectively as thin models: body-care items, appearance-related goods, and even weight-loss products.

Ms. Not Good Enough

© Jessica Barlow

Advertising is a core component of consumer culture, as we saw in Chapter 1. The primary aim of advertising is to facilitate product sales, of course, but the messages portrayed through advertising have much broader consequences for individuals' values, beliefs, and identity. There has been increasing concern and widespread public debate about whether the use of ultra-thin models in the media has a detrimental effect on women. In June 2000, the UK government held a body-image summit to discuss the relationship between media ideals and eating disorders, which is testament to the increasing profile of the link between the media and body image issues. The British Medical Association's (BMA) report discussed at the summit concludes:

> We consider that the media play a significant role in the aetiology of eating disorders . . . there is a clear need for more comprehensive research to be conducted on this issue.
>
> (2000, p. 25)

Despite extensive criticism of the use of ultra-thin models in advertising, the advertising industry argues that "thinness" sells, whereas "fatness" does not. The London-based Premier agency, which represents the top models Naomi Campbell and Claudia Schiffer, was reported as saying that agencies, advertisers, and magazines are only responding to consumer demand:

> Statistics have repeatedly shown that if you stick a beautiful skinny girl on the cover of a magazine you sell more copies . . . Agencies would say that we supply the women the advertisers, our clients, want. The clients would say that they are selling a product and responding to consumer demand. At the end of the day, it is a business and the fact is that these models sell the products.
>
> (Gillian, 2000, May 31, p. 7)

This claim that "thinness sells" helps to justify the use of ultra-thin models, regardless of possible detrimental effects on girls and women. This raises two distinct issues that need to be addressed. First, as noted in the BMA's report, it is important to unpick the relationship between exposure to ultra-thin models and women's well-being. Clearly, not all women are affected equally by media images. It would be helpful to understand factors that make women more or less vulnerable to negative exposure effects. Second, it is important to evaluate advertisers' claims that ultra-thin images are needed to produce effective advertising.

DOES THINNESS SELL?

The "thinness sells" argument is often employed to defend the use of ultra-thin models in advertising, but there is little research evidence to support this claim.

There is some evidence that a model's physical attractiveness has a positive effect on consumers' product attitude, willingness to purchase, and actual purchase (Caballero & Solomon, 1984; Kahle & Homer, 1985). Although the impact of model attractiveness is partly dependent on the product advertised, research supports the notion that highly attractive models are more effective than normally attractive models at selling appearance-related products (Bower & Landreth, 2001).

However, the influence of a model's body size on advertising effectiveness has remained virtually unresearched. Exceptions are a study that specifically investigates exercise promotion and a study that examines instructional frame and perceptions of model's attractiveness. A slim, as opposed to an average-size or overweight, model was the most effective image in promoting exercise (Shaw & Kemeny, 1989), but this single study focuses on a very specific behaviour, and one of the perceived benefits of exercise is weight loss. Thus, it is questionable whether the impact of model weight in this case would generalise to products in other domains. A recent study found that larger-size models were rated as more attractive when they were introduced with a non-traditional frame stating that they were from a magazine that uses adverts featuring "women who are heavier than the traditional model" rather than with a traditional frame stating that they were "ads from popular women's magazines" (Loken & Peck, 2005, p. 431). This suggests that drawing attention to the use of realistic images can make the models more appealing, but it does not address directly whether thinness is important for advertising effectiveness. So, whereas evidence suggests that models used in advertising need to be attractive to sell a product, there has been no compelling evidence that they also need to be extremely slim. We have conducted the first systematic series of studies that examine whether or not advertising is perceived as more effective when the product is promoted by ultra-thin models compared to models whose body size represents that of the average UK woman. However, before presenting this research, it is necessary to examine the impact that ultra-thin media models have on women.

THE PSYCHOLOGICAL IMPACT OF THIN MEDIA IMAGES ON WOMEN

Body image is central to the self-concept and to self-esteem, influencing psychological functioning and diverse behaviours (Cash & Pruzinsky, 2002; Halliwell & Dittmar, 2006). Body dissatisfaction, the experience of negative thoughts and esteem about one's body, is important to study because it is a precursor to a number of significant consequences, including negative self-perception, depressed mood, and disordered eating (Polivy & Herman, 2002; Thompson, 2004; Thompson et al., 1999). One of the most established perspectives on the development of body dissatisfaction is sociocultural theory, which views the mass media as particularly potent transmitters and reinforcers of sociocultural body ideals (Levine & Harrison, 2004; Thompson et al., 1999). The central proposal is that individuals come to feel bad about their bodies because they are exposed to unrealistic beauty ideals, which they then feel pressurised to achieve. However, there are diverse factors that make some individuals more vulnerable to negative media effects than others (e.g. Dittmar & Howard, 2004a, 2004b; Stice, Schupak-Neuberg, Shaw, & Stein, 1994). It seems that it is not so much sociocultural pressures *per se* that are detrimental in the long term to individuals' body image, but the extent to which they come to internalise these pressures as values, or ideals, related to their own appearance (Dittmar, 2005c).

Ultra-thin media models

To date, research on the mass media and body image has primarily focused on girls and women, and there are convincing reasons why: body dissatisfaction and disordered eating are disproportionately higher in women (Eating Disorders Association, 2007; Feingold & Mazzella, 1998), appearance is more central to their self-concept and evaluations by others (Fredrickson & Roberts, 1997; Grogan, 1999; Halliwell & Dittmar, 2003), and the female beauty ideal is now so ultra-thin that it is both unattainable and unhealthy (Groesz et al., 2002; Halliwell & Dittmar, 2004). Ultra-thin female models are drastically over-represented in magazines and television, so that only the tiniest minority of women have the body size shown in virtually all advertising (Fouts & Burggraf, 1999, 2000; Spitzer, Henderson, & Zivian, 1999).

As discussed in Chapter 1, the majority of media models are more than 15% underweight, and this has to be placed in the context of 15% underweight constituting a diagnostic criterion for anorexia (American Psychiatric Association, 2000). Body mass index (BMI) is a measure of weight relative to height, and the healthy range is from a BMI of 19 to 25. In contrast, media and fashion models' BMI is typically below 16, in the biologically underweight range. Comparisons of changing body ideals in the media against actual changes in the body sizes of women demonstrates that, whereas idealised women's bodies have been getting much thinner, actual women's bodies have been getting heavier (Spitzer et al., 1999; Wiseman et al., 1992). Thus, like an opening pair of scissors, the discrepancy between the thin body ideal and the reality of women's actual body size has been growing dramatically.

Associations between media exposure and body image

Numerous studies have demonstrated that the amount of time women or girls spend reading magazines or watching television is positively related to the amount of body dissatisfaction they report. For example, Gonzalez-Lavin and Smolak (1995, as cited in Thompson et al., 1999) found that girls who watched more than 8 hours of television each week reported greater body dissatisfaction than those viewing less. Subsequent research suggests, however, that it may only be particular kinds of media exposure that are problematic. Higher body dissatisfaction, weight concerns, and problematic eating behaviour is linked specifically to exposure to media that endorses and glamourises thinness, such as fashion magazines, soap operas, movies, or music videos (e.g. Borenkowski, Robinson, & Killen, 2000; Harrison, 2001; Tiggemann & Pickering, 1996). Moreover, parallels are frequently drawn between the decreasing size of the female body ideal and both escalating levels of women's body dissatisfaction and increases in the incidence of eating disorders (e.g. Grogan, 1999). However, concurrent trends in changing media presentations and the prevalence of body dissatisfaction do not demonstrate directly that media images *cause* dissatisfaction. Furthermore, although correlational studies suggest that the media does influence women's body image concerns, their findings do not allow cause–effect inferences. We do not know whether media exposure leads to heightened body image concerns, or whether individuals who are already concerned about their appearance actively choose to consume more body-focused media. Therefore, it is important to examine the effects of media exposure on body image concerns directly. Experimental studies are better able to address issues of causality, because they allow researchers to manipulate media exposure and then measure the immediate psychological impact of this manipulation on body image concerns.

Exposure experiments and vulnerability factors

Typically, experimental exposure studies compare women's reactions to viewing images featuring the ultra-thin ideal by comparing it with exposure to other types of images. Given that all other aspects are identical, systematic differences in women's reports after exposure to these different media images can be confidently attributed to the presence or absence of thin models. This research repeatedly finds that viewing ultra-thin models can and does lead to increases in body image concerns (e.g. Heinberg & Thompson, 1995, Irving, 1990; Posavac, Posavac, & Posavac, 1998), although there are some contradictory findings for particular groups of young women (e.g. Henderson-King & Henderson-King, 1997; Mills, Polivy, Herman, & Tiggemann, 2002). However, a meta-analysis assessed the results of 25 experimental studies and demonstrated that, on average, young women feel worse about their bodies after exposure to thin images than other types of images (Groesz et al., 2002).

The consistent finding that exposure to ultra-thin models is often associated with negative outcomes is perhaps best understood within a social comparison framework. As outlined in Chapter 1, comparing oneself to targets who are superior on relevant dimensions leads to negative emotions and lower self-evaluations (Wood, 1989). Given the large body-size discrepancy between the great majority of women and ultra-thin media models, comparisons should have negative consequences for their body esteem, because feeling inferior is most likely "when reaching the target's status would involve climbing a mountain rather than a molehill" (Collins, 1996, p. 52).

However, we know that exposure to idealised media images does not invariably lead to negative affect or lowered body-esteem (e.g. Halliwell & Dittmar, 2005; Joshi, Herman, & Polivy, 2004), and Polivy and Herman (2004) emphasise that individuals are not passive recipients of sociocultural pressures, but rather are active and critical in the ways in which they engage with them. This is consistent with demonstrations of diverse factors that make some girls and women more vulnerable to negative media exposure effects (cf. Levine & Harrison, 2004). Clearly, understanding such vulnerability factors is important for the development of interventions designed to protect girls' and women's body image. Diverse factors have been shown to moderate exposure effects, including trait body dissatisfaction (Posavac et al., 1998), self-monitoring (Henderson-King & Henderson-King, 1997), disordered eating symptoms (Pinhas, Toner, Ali, Garfinkel, & Stuckless, 1999), and habitual social comparison tendency (Dittmar & Howard, 2004b). Rather than review each of these, we focus instead on a construct that we believe might underlie several of these diverse factors and, therefore, might be a particularly central vulnerability factor, and useful target for interventions.

Social Comparison Theory states that comparisons with a superior target will only have an effect on self-evaluation if the comparison is on a dimension that is relevant and important to the person concerned (Stapel & Tesser, 2001). Therefore, comparisons with ultra-thin models in the media should only have an impact on women for whom appearance and thinness are salient. We already outlined in Chapter 1 that thin-ideal internalisation, measured by the relevant subscale of the SATAQ (Heinberg et al., 1995), captures the extent to which women have come to endorse the thin ideal as their personal goal. Given that the endorsement of ideal-body values is linked with body dissatisfaction, eating problems, and a greater propensity to make social comparisons concerning appearance, we propose that it is a significant vulnerability factor for negative effects when women are exposed to consumer culture beauty ideals.

In summary, then, there is consistent evidence that "body perfect" ideals in the media do impact on women's body image concerns. Moreover, research has begun to examine factors that protect some women from detrimental effects of media exposure. In contrast to the plethora of exposure experiments examining the impact of media images on women's body image, research in this area has not engaged with the issue of advertising effectiveness. So, whereas it has already done a good job of identifying potential risks associated with the use of unhealthily thin models, it has not investigated alternatives that could realistically be presented in their place. The majority of exposure experiments compare exposure to ultra-thin models with exposure to control images that contain no models. A few studies have compared exposure to ultra-thin and average-size models, and have found that average-size models do not increase body image concerns (e.g. Irving, 1990; Posavac et al., 1998), but these studies tend to confound thinness and attractiveness. That is, they compare exposure to thin, attractive models with exposure to average-size, less attractive models. This means that we cannot disentangle whether differences in body image concerns after exposure are due to differences in the body weight of the models, or their attractiveness, or both. Clearly, this is also problematic in terms of engaging with debates over using ultra-thin models in advertising, given that we already know that attractiveness sells.

DOES SIZE MATTER? A SERIES OF EXPERIMENTAL EXPOSURE STUDIES

To address the dual questions of whether models' body size matters for how women feel about their own bodies after media exposure on the one hand, and whether models' body size has any impact on advertising effectiveness on the other, we have conducted numerous experimental exposure studies; four are presented here.

Thin-ideal internalisation and advertising effectiveness (Experiment 1)

In this first experiment, our aims are to address both the issue of individual vulnerability and the "thinness sells" argument (Halliwell & Dittmar, 2004). We are interested in examining whether average-size models can be used effectively in advertising, and this means that we have to avoid confounding the effects of weight and attractiveness. Through a pilot study, we made sure that the average-size models we used are equally attractive as the ultra-thin models, so that we can be confident that any differences in the effect on women's body image concerns on the one hand, and on perceived advertising effectiveness on the other, are due to the body size of the model, and not her attractiveness.

This investigation also extends the examination of individual vulnerability factors that moderate the effects of exposure to thin models. As previously discussed, we predict that women who have internalised the ultra-thin ideal, rather than simply being aware of it, are most vulnerable to negative exposure effects. Specifically, we expect these women to report more anxiety about their bodies after viewing ultra-thin models than no models. In contrast, we predict that viewing average-size models is not associated with increased body-focused negative affect, because women do not engage in extreme upward comparisons about their weight.

Marks & Spencer, a prominent UK high street chain, conducted a large-scale survey of women's body sizes in the UK, and concluded that a dress size 14 is the norm for British women (Arlidge, 2000). This is equivalent to a European size 42, and a US size 10–12, which is slightly smaller than the average size of American women, size 14 (Young, 2000). Given that our study was conducted in the UK, we chose size 14 for the average-size model condition. As this represents the average dress size for the population we studied, it presents a more realistic comparison target for women than the ultra-thin ideal. These alternative models, compared to the traditional thin models, are not so drastically discrepant from women's view of their own body, or their view of how their body could potentially look. Therefore, women who place considerable importance on a slim physical appearance as a measure of self-worth may not be detrimentally affected by advertisements showing such models.

Our study used three exposure conditions: a control, or baseline, condition in which participants viewed adverts that did not feature any models or appearance-related information; an ultra-thin models condition; and an average-size models condition. In each condition, women participants viewed two adverts for deodorant. In the control condition, the adverts depicted landscapes, deodorant bottles, and slogans. To create the adverts for the ultra-thin models condition, images of two models featured in recent, popular women magazines' fashion spreads were selected. The average measurements listed on a model agency website (http://www.models1.co.uk) indicate that, typically, such models are a UK dress size 8 (European size 34, US size 4–6). To create the advertisements for the average-size condition, we used digital imaging software (Adobe PhotoShop) to adjust the body size of the models from the ultra-thin condition. Stretching the body of a typical, ultra-thin model until it represents that of the average UK woman, rather than using a different model, means that we can control all factors other than models' body size. The bodies were stretched by 25% of their original size, to a 30-inch waist, representing UK dress size 14 (Debenhams, 2001). An example of the same model at dress size 8 and, stretched, at dress size 14 is shown in Figure 6.1. Advertisements were created by using the same backgrounds and slogans as in the control condition, but scaling the products down in size, so that a model could be added.

To check that the manipulation of body size has not affected the perceived attractiveness of the models, we asked young women ($n = 32$) to rate either the size 8 or size 14 models on attractiveness. One of the two models was rated as significantly more attractive than the other, but this was the case regardless of her body size. So, the change in each model's body size did not influence her attractiveness. In fact, it is a bonus that there was a significant difference in attractiveness between the two models because this makes it possible to test the hypothesis that attractiveness is related to advertising effectiveness, and to assess possible interactions between model attractiveness and body size, which would not be possible if both models were equally attractive.

The study was presented on the internet, with a carefully constructed cover story about advertising and consumer preferences. Women were recruited through e-mail and directed to the study's web site ($n = 202$); the majority were

Figure 6.1 Model at dress size 8 (ultra-thin) and 14 (average-size).

Caucasian (96%) and UK residents (88%). The first web page introduced the research as an academic study assessing women's consumer preferences with regard to advertising. Participants were told that they would see two advertisements for deodorants and their task was to evaluate both, as well as to select the advert that most appealed to them. They were also told that the study examined "the kinds of people who prefer particular sorts of ads", and that they would therefore be asked about their personal attitudes and beliefs. To begin the experiment, participants clicked a button at the bottom of the screen, which alternately assigned them to one of the three exposure conditions.

All participants began by filling in a set of questions ostensibly about values in society and their individual attitudes. Embedded within these questions was the thin-ideal internalisation measure (SATAQ; Heinberg et al., 1995). This was followed by the presentation of two adverts, which—depending on exposure condition—featured either ultra-thin models, average-size models, or no models. After viewing each advert, women indicated their attitude to the advert, their attitude to the brand, and their intention to purchase the product (if cost was no concern). These are established and validated measures of perceived advertising effectiveness that are linked to actual buying behaviour (Wells, 1997). To support the cover story, participants then indicated which advertisement they preferred and gave a brief open-ended explanation for their choice. Then, crucially, participants indicated how nervous or tense they were feeling "right now" about various aspects of their lives, with the explanation that current mood can affect how people perceive adverts. Embedded within these questions was a shortened version of the Physical Appearance State and Trait Anxiety Scale (PASTAS; Reed, Thompson, Brannick, & Sacco, 1991), which assesses momentary negative affect associated with various weight-related body parts (such as waist, buttocks, or hips). Finally, to check whether participants were aware of the true purpose of the study, they were asked to state in their own words what they thought the specific purpose of this study was. All but five participants were completely unaware of the true purpose of the research (these five were excluded from the analysis). Women ended the survey by completing a demographics section, asking for age, income, relationship status, and weight and height (so that their BMI could be calculated).

Women were classified as either high or low on thin-ideal internalisation, based on a median split at a score of 4. Thus, this sample-based split coincides with a cut-off that is meaningful theoretically in terms of the six-point scale used, where 3 represents "slightly disagree" and 4 "slightly agree". Therefore, the half of the women in the high internalisation group, on average, agree with thin-ideal statements, whereas the half in the low internalisation group, on average, disagree with the internalisation statements. As predicted, women who internalised ideal-body values respond differently to viewing the images than women who had not. The mean levels of anxiety reported by women low and high on internalisation after exposure to each advertisement type are shown in Figure 6.2.

For women who have not internalised the thin ideal, there is no detrimental effect of viewing ultra-thin models on body-focused anxiety. In contrast, and as predicted, among women who have internalised the thin ideal as a personal goal, viewing the ultra-thin models leads to significantly higher levels of anxiety than viewing the average-size models or the control images. There is no difference in reported body-focused anxiety after viewing average-size attractive models compared to the control condition. In summary, these findings show that among women who do not internalise the thin ideal, viewing ultra-thin models does not have a negative impact. In contrast, among women who internalise ideal-body values, viewing thin models induces weight-related appearance concerns, whereas viewing average-size models

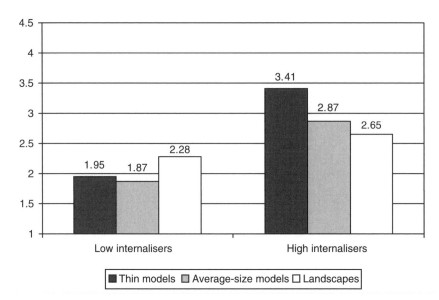

Figure 6.2 Body-focused anxiety by exposure condition for high and low internalisers. (*Note.* Adapted from Halliwell & Dittmar (2004), Does size matter? The impact of model's body size on advertising effectiveness and women's body-focused anxiety, *Journal of Social and Clinical Psychology*, *23*, p. 116, with kind permission of Guilford Publications.)

does not. Thus, model size does matter for body-related anxiety, at least among women who have internalised the thin consumer culture beauty ideal. But does it matter for advertising effectiveness?

Given that the no models control condition was qualitatively different from the two model conditions (where the same woman is depicted, but with different body sizes), the main interest was a comparison of the perceived effectiveness of adverts showing ultra-thin compared to average-sized models. As shown in Figure 6.3, perceived advertising effectiveness is virtually identical for each model, regardless of whether her body size is average or ultra-thin. Thus, advertising is seen as equally effective when models have an average, rather than a thin, body size. Not surprisingly, adverts featuring the more attractive model are rated as more effective than those featuring the less attractive model. In summary, the main result is that attractiveness influences perceived advertising effectiveness, but model size does not.

This research makes a crucial contribution to the debate about using ultra-thin models in advertising. It demonstrates that it is, specifically, the thinness of the models used in advertising, rather than their attractiveness, that is problematic as far as women's weight-related anxiety is concerned. Furthermore, it shows that thin-ideal internalisation is an important vulnerability factor for negative media effects. However, perhaps the most important finding is that, although model attractiveness increases the perceived

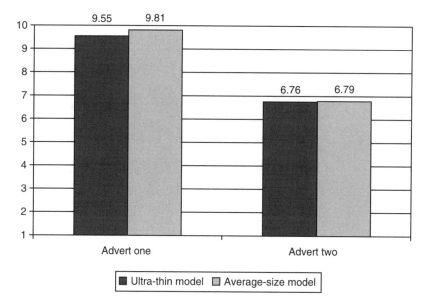

Figure 6.3 Perceived effectiveness of adverts featuring ultra-thin or average-size models. (*Note.* Adapted from Halliwell & Dittmar (2004), Does size matter? The impact of model's body size on advertising effectiveness and women's body-focused anxiety, *Journal of Social and Clinical Psychology*, *23*, p. 118, with kind permission of Guilford Publications.)

effectiveness of the adverts, the thinness of the models does not. Thus, this is the first evidence-based indication that advertising could use average-sized models without compromising effectiveness.

Of course, this is only a single study and these findings need to be corroborated. In addition to replicating the original research, the experiment reported next also assesses an additional factor that has been neglected in earlier research, the impact of an individual's social context on their vulnerability to negative media effects (Dittmar & Howard, 2004a). In our first experiment, which examined the self-relevance of thinness through thin-ideal internalisation, only high internalisers experienced a negative effect in comparisons with ultra-thin models. However, the salience of thinness-based social comparisons with media models is also likely to depend on women's social context. In addition to whether or not women endorse thinness as a personal ideal, the extent to which their immediate social environment focuses on, and promotes, a thin appearance ideal may also be important.

Professional hazards? Fashion employees compared to teachers (Experiment 2)

The aim of this study is to contrast professions that differ in their degree of emphasis on, and promotion of, thinness as an appearance value. It is part and parcel of the fashion advertising industry to produce what is defined as the ideal look for women, whereas this is obviously not the business of secondary education. Given this difference in salience, women employees in fashion advertising may be even more sensitive to the thin ideal than women teachers working in environments where educational values are strong. On the other hand, women may be drawn to specific professions because the salience of appearance-related values conforms to their own pre-existing beliefs (Stice, 1994). Whichever cause–effect direction, it is likely that profession as a social context increases or decreases women's vulnerability to the impact of thin media images.

Women in the fashion advertising industry are a particularly useful group to study because their professional environment highlights the thin ideal for women constantly and because they are engaged in the production of advertisements that use thin fashion models. In addition, their first-hand knowledge of images being altered and enhanced through computer-aided techniques, such as airbrushing or digital thinning, should make them particularly expert—and possibly critical—judges of advertising effectiveness. We chose secondary school teachers as a professional contrast group because teachers are primarily engaged with educational issues and standards in their working lives, because their professional environment does not emphasise the thin ideal for women as a socio-cultural value, and because their lack of involvement with the production of media images makes them lay—rather than expert—judges of adverts. In addition, their habitual level of exposure to thin images is likely to be less extreme than that of fashion advertisers, but comparable to the great majority of women in the UK, who are all recipients of advertising.

Thus, these two groups of women are likely to show weaker or stronger reactions when exposed to thin advertising models, but opposing sets of expectations can be formulated about the direction of the difference. On the one hand, the salience of, and constant exposure to, the thin ideal in fashion advertising may increase women's vulnerability to the impact of thin images. On the other hand, women in fashion advertising may become habituated to thin models precisely because of this constant exposure, and may therefore be "inoculated" against such images, because they are engaged in their production and aware of the sophisticated computer techniques used to create unrealistically thin and glamorous models.

In our study, profession represents a social context that differs in the salience and promotion of the thin ideal for women. In addition, we re-examined internalisation of the thin ideal as a moderator of women's vulnerability to the negative impact of exposure to thin models in advertising. Based on the findings of the previous experiment, we do not expect the body size of the models to impact on advertising effectiveness (as long as the models are seen as equally attractive). Again, we expect that women's body-focused affect is not affected by exposure to different media images, if their level of ideal-body internalisation is low. In contrast, we predict that different images have an impact on women with a high level of ideal-body internalisation. Specifically, body-focused negative affect should be higher after thin images than after average-size or control images. Furthermore, although we do not expect a difference in body-focused negative affect after exposure to average-size models and control images, we consider it possible that body-focused negative affect could be lower after average-size models than after control images, because women may experience a relief effect; "my body actually looks okay". Finally, we expect systematic differences between the women employed in advertising compared to those employed in education.

We recruited 156 participants, either from a large London-based fashion advertising company or from secondary schools in southern England. The women in fashion advertising were not models themselves, but were involved in the creation and promotion of fashion images through being employed in a diversity of administrative, design, and secretarial positions. The final sample consisted of 75 women from each profession, after six participants were excluded because a check at the end of the study revealed that they guessed the study's true focus on body image. On average, secondary teachers were older (37 years) than the advertising employees (28 years). The adverts used in this study were created using the same procedure as before, but the featured product was eau de toilette. Once again, a pilot study demonstrated that the manipulation of body size had not affected the perceived attractiveness of the models. The research was presented as a study on "advertising effectiveness and consumer personality". Groups of participants completed questionnaires during staff meetings in their usual professional environment, i.e. offices or classrooms. Thin-ideal internalisation was measured first, before respondents were exposed to one of three types of advertising image: ultra-thin models, average-size models, or landscapes (no models). They then indicated how effective they judged each advert they had seen and, finally, they completed the same measure of body-focused negative affect that we used in the first experiment.

We were surprised to find that there was no significant difference between advertising employees and teachers, either in the extent to which they had internalised the thin ideal (mean ratings 3.52 and 3.45) or in their overall body-focused negative affect (mean ratings 2.66 and 2.62). As expected, and replicating the findings from Experiment 1, the types of images have a different impact depending on whether women internalise the thinness ideal or not. However, the nature of this interaction is further affected by women's profession. These findings can best be understood if we examine women working in advertising and teachers separately. Figure 6.4 shows women's levels of body-focused negative affect in each exposure condition.

Regardless of profession, women who have not internalised ideal-body values are not negatively affected by exposure. However, among internalisers, women employed in fashion advertising and teaching respond differently to the images. The effect of exposure condition is much stronger amongst teachers, accounting for 55% in body anxiety difference, than amongst

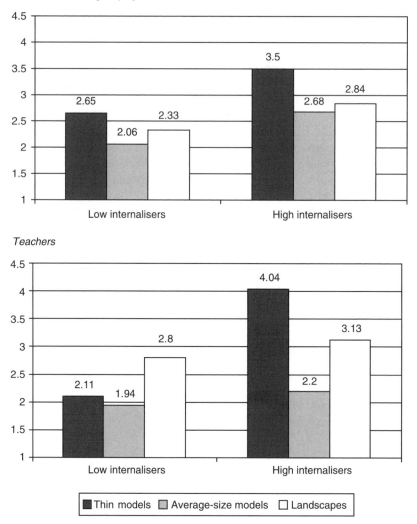

Figure 6.4 Levels of body-focused negative affect reported by women high and low in internalisation after exposure to three types of advertising image. (*Note.* Adapted from Dittmar & Howard (2004a), Professional hazards? The impact of model's body size on advertising effectiveness and women's body-focused anxiety in professions that do and do not emphasize the cultural ideal of thinness, *British Journal of Social Psychology*, *43*, p. 490, with kind permission of the British Psychological Society © 2004.)

women working in fashion advertising, where only 16% are accounted for by exposure condition. For high internalising women working in education, the effect of exposure to ultra-thin models is strong: body-focused negative affect is much higher after adverts with thin models than after other adverts. For high internalising women working in advertising, exposure to ultra-thin models is also associated with higher body-focused negative affect than exposure to average models or no model adverts, but the effect is not so pronounced. Constant exposure to the thin ideal and professional work with thin fashion models may have "hardened" these women to some extent against thin images making them feel bad about their body and weight, yet the negative impact of thin images on body-focused negative affect can still be demonstrated. There is no difference in levels of body-focused negative affect among women working in fashion after viewing average-size models compared to control images. In contrast, teachers report significantly lower levels of anxiety after exposure to average-size models compared to control images. Thus, high internalising teachers seem to experience significant *relief* when seeing models in adverts close in size to the national average for women, compared to the baseline body-focused negative affect reported in the control condition.

This study replicates Experiment 1 by demonstrating that exposure to ultra-thin models has a negative impact on body-focused negative affect amongst women who internalise the consumer culture thinness ideal. This is true for women employees in two very different professions, adding confidence to the generalisability of this finding. Yet, exposure to average-size attractive models, rather than being neutral, can also have a relief effect on body image concerns amongst some women. This suggests not only that the use of attractive average-size models in advertising could avoid exacerbating vulnerable women's body image concerns, but also that it can lead to a reduction in the body image concerns of some women, at least in the short term.

With respect to perceived advertising effectiveness, advertising employees tend to give less favourable ratings of all the adverts than do teachers. Of course, one would expect individuals who work in the field of advertising to be more critical of the images used in advertising. However, our main concern is whether the body size of models has an impact on effectiveness ratings amongst an expert group of women. As in Experiment 1, the results indicate that the models' body size does not affect advert evaluation and willingness to buy the advertised product. Moreover, this is true for both groups of women. Again, adverts showing attractive average-size models are perceived to be just as persuasive as adverts showing models that fit the current thin ideal. Although women in fashion advertising evaluate all adverts slightly less positively than teachers, this effect is entirely independent of model size.

This experiment increases confidence that it is, indeed, the thinness of the models used in advertising, and not their attractiveness, that is problematic as far as the reactions of women are concerned. Moreover, it also replicates our finding that average-size models seem to be as effective as ultra-thin models in advertising, so long as they are equally attractive. The finding that advertising effectiveness is not compromised by average-size models also holds for a group of women likely to be both expert and critical with respect to advertisements.

These first two experiments focus on advertising effectiveness for deodorant and eau de toilette, both products that do not have a direct link to women's appearance. Thus, the findings so far suggest that models with a healthy, normal body size could be used effectively in advertising for appearance-neutral products, but our argument that there are no commercial reasons for using thin models would become more persuasive if this effect could also be demonstrated for other consumer goods, particularly products relevant for appearance. In a research project funded by the UK government's Economic and Social Research Council (Dittmar & Halliwell, 2005), we specifically addressed this issue and compared the impact of models' body size on the perceived effectiveness of adverts for appearance-focused products, make-up, and thinness-enhancing products (diet foods).

Products relevant to appearance and weight loss (Experiment 3)

It could be argued that thin models may well be perceived as more effective when they advertise goods that are related to appearance, or, even more so, products that promote weight loss. Therefore, if our previous findings generalise to these types of product, this would much strengthen our argument that thin models are not necessary for effective advertising. In addition to examining advertisements for different products, we also developed a new methodology for creating ultra-thin and average size models for the adverts. The digital imaging technique we had previously used is clearly successful in altering body size while controlling for perceived attractiveness (Halliwell & Dittmar, 2004). However, this methodology has the disadvantage that it delivers average-size models that are artificial. Stretching distributes weight evenly over the body, whereas actual weight gain tends not to be uniform. Therefore, using the bodies of actual size 14 models is more realistic. However, to control attractiveness, it is necessary to use the same face for both thin and average-size models. We developed an innovation that uses actual bodies of models, as well as faces, and creates advertisements using separate faces and bodies that were selected independently according to specified criteria of attractiveness and body size. On the basis of pilot testing with 30 women, we selected models' bodies judged to represent best either UK dress size 8 or dress size 14. Using Adobe Photoshop, we mounted faces on bodies to create advertisements that showed either a thin or an average-size model, both with the same face. The same background, product, and slogan were used in both, as well as for the control condition, where no model was presented. The advertisements were then pretested with a further 40 women to check the manipulation of body size and attractiveness, as well as to assess whether they were perceived as realistic. An example of ultra-thin, average size, and control adverts for diet foods is shown in Figure 6.5.

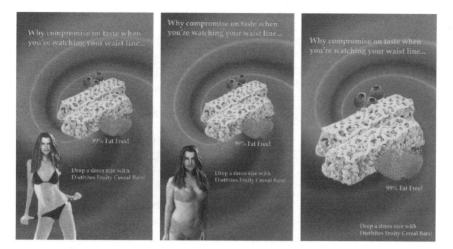

Figure 6.5 Diet food advert with ultra-thin model, average-size model, and no model.

We recruited 391 women, aged 18–30 years, to take part in a study examining "consumer culture". The women viewed adverts either for appearance-focused products, make-up, or thinness-enhancing products (diet foods), which featured ultra-thin models, average-sized models, or no models. After viewing each advert, women rated its effectiveness as in Experiments 1 and 2, but they also judged how credible, trustworthy, knowledgeable, and expert they think the model is. We compared adverts featuring thin and average-size models, carrying out two sets of analyses (in which we control for BMI and individual differences in general attitudes toward advertising): one with perceived advertising effectiveness and the other with model evaluations as outcomes. The mean ratings for the diet foods and make-up advertised by either thin or average-size models are shown in Figure 6.6.

Interestingly, the same models are seen as significantly less credible, trustworthy, expert, and knowledgeable when advertising diet foods than make-up, regardless of their body size. This suggests that women are critical and wary of weight loss advertising. What is perhaps even more significant is that, overall, our findings show that women have a significantly more positive view of average-sized models, even if the mean differences are small. Compared to ultra-thin models, they rate models with an average, healthy body size as more credible, more trustworthy, and more knowledgeable (although not more expert).

With respect to advertisements promoting products, we find that perceptions of advertising effectiveness are not systematically influenced by models' body size as a factor by itself, nor is there an interaction between models' body size and product advertised. Thus, in a large sample that has ample statistical power for detecting experimental effects, advertising effectiveness is not compromised by showing models with average body sizes, compared to

Model evaluation

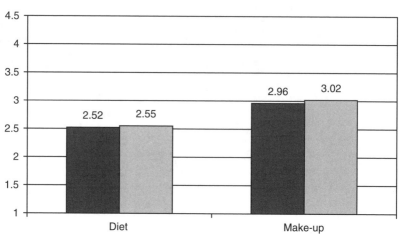

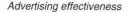

Advertising effectiveness

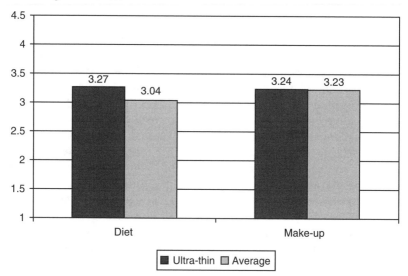

Figure 6.6 Ratings of adverts for diet products and make-up featuring ultra-thin or average-size models.

ultra-thin models. Moreover, there is no evidence that ultra-thin models are more effective in advertising products that are directly related to weight loss, compared to make-up. This finding suggests that average-sized models can be used effectively when advertising different types of products, even products related to weight loss.

With respect to how women feel about their bodies, evidence that exposure to ultra-thin models can lead to body image disturbance has important implications because longitudinal research indicates that body image disturbance, in turn, predicts eating-disordered symptoms among young women (Cattarin & Thompson, 1994; Killen et al., 1996; Stice & Agras, 1998). Therefore, we believe that finding alternatives to ultra-thin models can go some way to protecting vulnerable women and girls from developing body-image problems, and thus potentially starting on one of the pathways toward developing an eating disorder. To this end, our findings that advertising for appearance-neutral, appearance-related, and thinness-enhancing products is not compromised by using realistic, healthily sized models is extremely encouraging.

However, this research has focused on non-clinical groups of women who do not have extreme body image issues or disordered eating patterns. It would also be interesting to know something about the impact of media images on women who have already experienced an eating disorder. Women with eating disorders report that they are strongly influenced by idealised bodies in the media (Murray, Touyz, & Beumont, 1996). Additionally, Hamilton and Waller (1993) found that women with eating disorders overestimate their body size to a greater extent after they view female models than do non-eating-disordered women. Yet, to our knowledge, the final study reported here is the first experimental investigation of the impact of media images on attitudinal body image among women with a history of eating disorders.

Women with a history of eating disorders (Experiment 4)

This study examines the impact of exposure to ultra-thin and average-size media models on the body image concerns of women who have a history of eating disorders, and also the perceived effectiveness of these models in advertising (Halliwell, Dittmar, & Howe, 2005). We hypothesise that, as for women without a history of eating disorders, exposure to ultra-thin models in the media leads to increased body-focused negative affect. In terms of differences in levels of body-focused negative affect after exposure to average-size models compared to control images, we expect that women would certainly not feel worse after average-size models, and possibly feel better, thus showing a relief effect like the teachers in Experiment 2. However, it was unclear to us whether the findings relating to advertising effectiveness and models' body size would replicate, because women with experience of eating disorders may be more critical of larger body sizes.

We used a very similar design to that in the previous experiments, with two experimental conditions each represented by two adverts for perfumes featuring women models. However, in this study the control adverts were for different products, pocket computers. Participants were recruited through the Eating Disorders Association in the UK. Questionnaire packs were sent to 150 women randomly selected from a list of women who had self-identified that they "had an eating disorder" or "were recovering from an eating disorder", and had indicated that they would be happy to participate in research. Each questionnaire included two advertisements, and 50 women each received advertisements featuring ultra-thin models, average-size models, and control images. The response rate was 51%, spread roughly equally across the three exposure conditions and the final sample consisted of 76 women, with a mean age of 32 years. After seeing each advertisement, advertising effectiveness was assessed. Under the guise of asking for "more information about the sort of person you are", women then rated how they felt right now about a wide variety of different aspects, such as their finances, or personal qualities. This section again included the body-focused negative affect items. Figure 6.7 shows the mean levels of body-focused negative affect reported by women in each exposure condition.

Contrary to our expectation, women's levels of body-focused negative affect are not higher after viewing ultra-thin models compared to other media images. Exposure to ultra-thin images does not increase body-focused negative affect among women with an eating disorder history, thus not replicating findings with women who do not have an eating disorder history. However, this may be due to a "ceiling effect", because women with eating disorders generally experience greater concern about their body than women who do not have an eating disorder history (Cash & Deagle, 1997). In the present study, body-focused negative affect amongst women who had not been exposed to appearance-related stimuli is 3.8 on a five-point scale, whereas among women

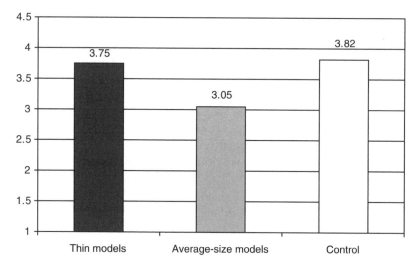

Figure 6.7 Body-focused negative affect among women with an eating disorder history after viewing ultra-thin models, average-size models, or control images. (*Note.* Adapted from Halliwell, Dittmar & Howe (2005), The impact of advertisements featuring ultra-thin or average-size models on women with a history of eating disorders, *Journal of Applied and Community Psychology*, *43*, p. 410 with kind permission of John Wiley & Sons, Ltd © 2005.)

of similar ages without an eating disorder history, body-focused negative affect after viewing a control image was 2.7 on the same scale (Dittmar & Howard, 2004b). As levels of body-focused negative affect are so high for these women in the absence of appearance-related stimuli, exposure to ultra-thin models may do little to inflate this anxiety further. In contrast, there is a significant effect in how they respond to models with an average, healthy body weight: body-focused negative affect is significantly lower after viewing average-size models than after no models. This suggests that exposure to average-sized models leads to a relief effect, compared to baseline levels of body-focused negative affect, where exposure appears to reduce body image concerns.

Replicating previous findings, there is no significant difference in perceived advertising effectiveness, regardless of whether the advertisements display ultra-thin models or average-size models. Thus, in line with research among women without a history of eating disorders, the size of the model used in advertising does not have a significant impact on the advertisement's perceived effectiveness.

CONCLUSION

In taking stock of the findings presented in this chapter, we address first the strengths and weaknesses of the reported exposure experiments, and then discuss some of their implications with respect to prevention and intervention, both at the level of individual girls and women, as well as at the social level of advertising policies.

Strengths and limitations of research

In summary, our findings are consistent with a growing body of research indicating that exposure to ultra-thin models in advertising has an immediate negative effect on many women. In contrast to much of the research in this area, which focuses on student women, our research demonstrates that adult women in quite diverse professions and of different ages are also susceptible to negative exposure effect. So, this is clearly not just an issue for young women. In addition, we demonstrated in Experiments 1 and 2 that internalisation of the consumer culture "body perfect" ideal as a personally important value is a crucial vulnerability factor in this process.

The consistency of these findings among diverse samples of over 800 women is a strength of our research, but there are also potential limitations due to the experimental methodology used that need addressing. First, exposure to ultra-thin models in everyday life sometimes involves little attention, where women flick through magazines, walk past billboards, or only half-watch the TV running in the background. In contrast, in typical experimental studies women are exposed to images long enough so that they look at them intently, and they are also asked to engage in additional tasks (such as evaluating the adverts) that ensure concentrated and thorough processing of each image. Although this inducement of high attention may be beneficial with regard to experimental control, it may not reflect adequately women's everyday exposure to ultra-thin images. In one of our studies (Brown & Dittmar, 2005), we examined this potential limitation through exposing women to ultra-thin models in one of two different ways. In one exposure condition, they saw the advertisements with ultra-thin models each for 10 seconds and evaluated them (high attention). In the other exposure condition, they saw advertisements with ultra-thin models as quick flashes only, lasting a mere 150 ms (low attention): 150 milliseconds was chosen as the length of exposure because, although clearly above the threshold needed for perception, this time is sufficiently short to prevent elaborate processing (Blair & Banaji, 1996). Thus, respondents are able to perceive these images, just about, but they can only process them at a low level of attention. We again find that exposure to thin models increases body-focused anxiety for women high on thin-ideal internalisation, but most importantly, we demonstrate that this effect occurs regardless of whether women pay full attention to the thin images or see them only fleetingly. Thus, we can show that negative exposure effects occur even when women pay little attention to ultra-thin images.

As with the majority of studies in this field, only the immediate impact of exposure to media images is measured, limiting conclusions to short-term effects. However, if negative effects can be demonstrated after a single exposure, and for low attention levels, the effect of a lifetime of exposure to ultra-thin images, on a daily basis, is likely to be even more damaging. It would be valuable to research the long-lasting effects of media exposure, and some studies are starting to address this (e.g. Tiggemann, 2006).

Another strength of the studies reported here is that they are the first systematic set of experiments to document, across different groups of women, and across a range of different products, that perceived advertising effectiveness is not compromised by the use of alternative images: models with a healthy body size. Our advertisements were produced specifically for the research, rather than constituting actual, commercial advertisements, but although this needs to be acknowledged as a limitation, the research images are comparable to those that appear in magazines, and the dimensions of advertising effectiveness examined are well established and validated (Wells, 1997). Still, there is clearly more work to be done investigating adverts for different products and in different media. For example, to date we have focused solely on print advertising and the impact of body size, and the moving images of TV advertising would be a useful focus for future research.

Implications for prevention and intervention

Our findings with respect to what makes women vulnerable to negative media effects, and presumably other sociocultural sources of pressure towards thinness, suggest that interventions aimed to prevent or reduce thin-ideal internalisation might be beneficial. Strategies that prevent or lower thin-ideal internalisation in girls and women may thus help to protect them from the potential negative impact of advertising (see Levine & Harrison, 2004, for a recent review). For instance, several media literacy interventions demonstrate that it is possible to increase women's scepticism about the desirability of media that depicts a thin beauty ideal, and that making them more critical may have some effect on internalisation (e.g. Irving & Berel, 2001; Posavac, Posavac, & Weigel, 2001). A meta-analysis of the effectiveness of such programmes shows that their success is significant, with a moderate effect on reducing thin-ideal internalisation, and a small effect on reducing dieting and eating pathology (Stice & Shaw, 2004). Programmes that increased resistance to thinness pressures and boosted self-esteem worked better than information alone, particularly with at-risk respondents. Yet, given that thin-ideal internalisation appears to start at a much younger age than previously supposed (see Chapter 8), early prevention may be the most promising option. This issue is addressed more fully in the concluding chapter.

It is also important to challenge the production of these unrealistic images. Taken together, the results of our research suggest that attractive, average-size models could be effectively used in advertising to promote a range of diverse products, even those directly related to appearance and weight loss. Not only would this advertising be effective, it would not heighten body-focused negative affect in vulnerable women, and in some cases it may actually relieve body image concerns. Specifically, average-size images appear to lead to improvements in body image among high internalisers in professions that are not appearance-focused and among women who have a history of eating disorders. Although there is no indication that advertising policies may change any time soon, there are some signs that a backlash against the "cult of the skinny" may be starting. Research like ours is receiving increasing media attention (see CBC Newsworld, 2006), and this may have helped to highlight the dangers of ultra-thin models sufficiently, so that prestigious fashion houses in Madrid and Milan decided in September 2006 to ban fashion models who are underweight, insisting on a BMI of 18.5 or above (e.g. Frith, 2006; Kay, 2006).

However, we would not want to suggest that a shift in the models used in advertising would altogether "cure" women's body dissatisfaction. A huge amount of work discusses cultural ideals of femininity and beauty. Our research focuses on thinness, only one dimension of beauty, even if particularly important. It would be simplistic to suggest that glamorising thinness alone can account for the cultural and historical imbalance in the prevalence of eating disorders or body image concerns, or to isolate thinness as the sole target for interventions. Eating disorders reflect a multiplicity of sociocultural concerns, including concerns about "femininity and feminism, about the body, about individual control and consumption within consumer society" (Malson, 1998, p. 6). Similarly, the current preoccupation with thinness is best understood as a reflection of political, economic, and religious pressures (e.g. Chernin, 1981; Faludi, 1991; Seid, 1994; Stern, 1997; Wolf, 1991), as well as of consumer culture. Indeed, it follows that successful prevention programmes must challenge many fundamental underlying cultural values (Steiner-Adair, 1994).

Considering this, the suggestion that policy changes within the fashion and advertising industry could be beneficial to women can only ever be one factor among others that may help prevent body dissatisfaction. Yet advertising plays a particularly potent role in influencing cultural standards of attractiveness and depicting women's actual bodies as deviant from what is acceptable on numerous dimensions (Kilbourne, 1994). We propose that our research suggests the use of average-size models in advertising as an evidence-based, relatively immediate, and straightforward intervention strategy that could be of some benefit (see Chapter 9 for a more detailed discussion). To this end, we believe that the findings presented here are encouraging, and potentially offer an alternative to the damaging focus on thinness.

7 Think "ideal" and feel bad? Using self-discrepancies to understand negative media effects

Helga Dittmar & Emma Halliwell

Synopsis

We still know little about the psychological mechanisms through which people come to feel bad about their own bodies after seeing idealised media models. Using a self-discrepancy framework, we test models in our exposure experiments, which show that:

- Our own self-discrepancy measure, the Self-discrepancy Index, is particularly useful in the body-image domain.
- Ultra-thin media models cause body anxiety in vulnerable women through making salient discrepancies between their own body and weight and the "body perfect" ideal.
- Negative exposure effects also occur in men, in whom idealised muscular media models cause greater body anxiety through the activation of self-discrepancies specific to the male ideal body.

Mr. No Muscles

© Jessica Barlow

So far, we have established two things. First, advertising typically uses models whose bodies represent a standard of ideal beauty that is unrealistic and unattainable, which means that its pursuit is likely to lead to ill-being (Chapter 1). Second, we present persuasive evidence that, for many women, exposure to ultra-thin female models leads to heightened body dissatisfaction, particularly when they have internalised the thin ideal as a personal value (see Chapter 6). Yet two important research gaps need to be addressed. First and foremost, we need an understanding of the psychological processes through which individuals come to feel bad about their bodies in response to idealised media models. Whereas there is some understanding of vulnerability factors that make individual women more or less responsive to thin models in advertising, we still know little about the mechanism whereby seeing ideal models in the mass media leads individuals to negative evaluations and emotions about their own body. Second, little attention has been paid so far to idealised male models as a cause of men's body dissatisfaction, but there are good reasons to suppose that men have started to experience negative effects in response to models that have become increasingly muscular:

> Mirror, mirror on the wall . . . are muscular men the best of all? Is this overconcern with body size a new obsession? Perhaps. In the past few years, we have been increasingly exposed to half-naked, muscular male bodies (e.g., Calvin Klein underwear ads). Evidently, even brief exposure to these images can affect a man's view of his body.
>
> (Clark, 2004)

Obviously, there is a pronounced difference between the "body perfect" ideals for women and men (see Chapter 1). In contrast to the ultra-thin female ideal, the male ideal body is lean, but muscular, and has a V-shape with broad shoulders and a trim waist. Concerns with appearance and bodily attractiveness have become more central for men (Pope et al., 2000), in parallel with an exponential growth in the number of muscular male bodies being displayed in the mass media, particularly in advertising (Rohlinger, 2002). Thus, men are increasingly exposed to a body ideal that is unattainable for the great majority, which may lead them to experience negative effects on their body image, too.

SELF-DISCREPANCIES, BODY IMAGE, AND MEDIA EXPOSURE

There is a strong link between how people feel about their bodies and their general sense of self-worth (Harter, 1999), so there is good reason for proposing that body image is a central aspect of identity. As argued in Chapter 1, we can conceptualise people's thoughts and beliefs about their body as a domain of their self-concept, representing their actual self. If we want to understand the psychological mechanism through which media exposure can make them feel bad about themselves, then we need a theoretical perspective that offers two things. First, it has to incorporate notions of the ideal body individuals wish or strive for, representing their ideal self, which is likely to be influenced by sociocultural beauty ideals. Second, it has to offer a theoretical link between thoughts and emotions, addressing the question of why thinking about an ideal body would make people experience negative emotions about their own body, such as dejection and anxiety. We believe that this "think ideal and feel bad" sequence can be best understood by drawing on Self-discrepancy Theory (e.g. Higgins, 1987), and have conducted a series of studies in which we develop and test models that use discrepancies between the actual and the ideal bodily self to explain when and how negative media effects occur, both for women and for men.

Self-discrepancy Theory

As proposed in Chapter 1, Self-discrepancy Theory presents a particularly useful framework because it proposes that discrepancies, or gaps, within an individual's self-concept are causes of negative affect, such as anxiety, depression, body dissatisfaction, and unhealthy behaviours, including disordered eating. It assumes that an individuals' emotional vulnerabilities result from discrepancies in their beliefs about themselves. Initially, Higgins and colleagues (Higgins, 1987) focused on three domains of the self: actual self, ideal self, and ought self. The actual self is a representation of the attributes that an individual believes he or she possesses. The other domains of the self act as self-directive standards, or self-guides. The ideal self is a representation of the person that individual would ideally like to be, whereas the ought self concerns attributes the individual believes she or he ought to possess. Mismatches between self-guides were proposed to have specific emotional consequences, where actual–ideal discrepancies lead to dejection and actual–ought discrepancies lead to agitation. However, empirical research often shows that actual–ideal self-discrepancies are related to both depression and anxiety, thus suggesting that they are linked to negative affect generally (e.g. Ozgul, Heubeck, Ward, & Wilkinson, 2003; Tangney, Niedenthal, Covert, & Barlow, 1998). Actual–ideal self-discrepancies are also linked to body dissatisfaction, whereas actual–ought discrepancies were not uniquely predictive (Strauman et al., 1991). Higgins (1999) argues that differential emotional effects occur only when the magnitude and relevance of self-discrepancies is sufficiently large. Although there is support for predictions involving ought self-discrepancies amongst clinical samples (e.g. Weilage & Hope, 1999), among non-clinical populations, the size of ought discrepancies may not be sufficiently large or accessible to be related to any detectable change in agitation (Higgins, 1999). In summary, actual–ideal self-discrepancies have been shown consistently to be associated with negative affect, whereas actual–ought self-discrepancies appear unlikely to provide a useful focus for research on body dissatisfaction among non-clinical populations (Halliwell & Dittmar, 2006).

Self-discrepancies, body image, and gender

The accessibility of discrepancies depends on the recency of activation, the frequency of activation, and the applicability to the situation. Only discrepancies that are accessible, according to this definition, are likely to influence the experience of affect (Higgins, 1999). With respect to the ultra-thin ideal, we therefore expect that women hold frequently activated and generally applicable appearance-related self-discrepancies. However, throughout the past 30 years, there has been increasing emphasis on ideal male body images in the media and among men themselves, as discussed later in this chapter. Therefore, it is likely that men's appearance-related self-discrepancies have also started to become salient and accessible due to increasingly frequent activation.

Empirical research relating self-discrepancy theory to body dissatisfaction or eating-disordered symptoms is sparse. Early research, assessing general self-discrepancies, supported links between actual–ideal discrepancies, body dissatisfaction, and bulimic-type eating (e.g. Strauman et al., 1991), but assessing self-discrepancies in general may elicit only a limited number of self-descriptors that are specifically related to appearance. More recently, there has been a trend of assessing content-specific self-discrepancies, in order to elicit self-descriptions in a particular domain (e.g. Forston & Stanton, 1992; Katz & Farrow, 2000; Strauman & Glenberg, 1994). There is some evidence that domain-specific discrepancies are stronger predictors than general discrepancies, particularly when the outcome measure is relevant to the specific domain. For example, Forston and Stanton (1992) found that actual–ideal self-discrepancies in the appearance domain were predictive of bulimic symptoms among student women, yet general actual–ideal self-discrepancies were not. Szymanski and Cash (1995) also supported theoretical associations involving ideal appearance-related self-discrepancies, but instead of respondent-generated self-discrepancies they used a fixed-item measure of appearance-related discrepancies that focuses on various body sites.

How can self-discrepancies be measured?

There is a debate concerning the measurement of self-discrepancies, the reasons for which will become clear. Higgins and colleagues devised the Selves Questionnaire, in which respondents list 10 traits or attributes that describe their actual self and 10 traits to describe various self-guides (Higgins, Bond, Klein, & Strauman, 1986). They then rate the extent to which they possess, or would like to possess, each attribute. However, instead of asking respondents to report only those aspects of the self that are most important or accessible to them, some studies have employed researcher-generated measures of self-discrepancies (e.g. Szymanski & Cash, 1995; Tangney et al., 1998). These fixed-item measures typically present respondents with a list of characteristics and ask them to rate how similar or different they are to their self-guide on each characteristic. The only previous study that explicitly compared fixed-item with respondent-generated measures found that both assessment tools displayed essentially same relationships with other variables (Tangney et al., 1998). However, these findings may not replicate in self-discrepancies that focus specifically on appearance, where it is much less clear what would constitute a comprehensive set of descriptors. The fixed-item measure used by Szymanski and Cash (1995) requires participants to rate their appearance along 11 physical attributes. It was originally developed to assess women's self-discrepancies, but has subsequently been validated and used with men. However, it is unclear whether these 11 items all tap appearance discrepancies that are salient, particularly to young men. This concern is consistent with arguments put forward by Higgins (1999), who considers the concept of accessibility central. Higgins argues that cued responses recorded by fixed-item methods assess discrepancies that are available, but not necessarily accessible. They assess self-discrepancies that individuals *can* think about when asked, but not necessarily ones that they *do* think about habitually. Psychologically, therefore, it may be important to measure only those aspects of individuals' self-concept that are salient in their day-to-day functioning where, for instance, thinness-related thoughts may be available to both men and women, but chronically accessible only to women.

Higgins' Selves Questionnaire provides a measure of congruency between various self-states. Participants rate the extent to which they believe they possess, or ideally should possess, each attribute they have listed (Strauman & Higgins, 1987). Subsequently, matches are coded through synonyms that differ by no more than one point on the rating scale, whereas mismatches are represented by synonyms that differ by two or more points, or by direct antonyms. The discrepancy score is calculated by subtracting the total number of matches from the total number of mismatches. However, in our previous research, we have developed a different respondent-generated measure that focuses solely on discrepancies in the self-concept (Dittmar, 2005a; Dittmar, Beattie, & Friese, 1996; Halliwell, 2002). Thus, instead of deriving a self-discrepancy measure from matching respondents' descriptions of different self-states, our measure is designed to tap respondents' self-discrepancies directly. Respondents are asked to complete sentences using the format "I . . ., but I would like . . ." and then rate each self-discrepancy they generate in terms of its magnitude and psychological importance. The resulting Self-discrepancy Index (SDI) has shown construct validity in Dittmar's work on consumer behaviour, where it was linked with uncontrolled emotional buying (see Chapter 5), and in Halliwell's research (2002), where it was related to negative affect, both general and specific to one's body. We therefore decided to use the SDI in our research. Two questions arise, however: how does the SDI compare with a fixed-item measure of self-discrepancies and how does it compare to Higgins' methodology?

The Self-discrepancy Index, body satisfaction, and eating

The first study we carried out has two main aims directly relevant to this chapter (Halliwell & Dittmar, 2006).[10] First, it provides a systematic comparison between fixed-item and our own participant-generated measure of appearance-related self-discrepancies. Second, it examines appearance-related self-discrepancies in both young women and young men, using them to predict three outcomes: general negative affect, body-focused negative affect, and body dissatisfaction. The sample consisted of 158 students, 81 women and 77 men, with an average age of 22 years and an average BMI of 22, which reflects a healthy body weight. All participants completed a questionnaire that included six measures. The participant-generated measure of appearance-related self-discrepancies was an adaptation of the general Self-discrepancy Index (SDI) to focus on appearance specifically (Halliwell, 2002). Participants completed up to five sentences of the format "I . . . , but I would like . . ." describing aspects of their appearance that they would ideally like to change (to elicit subjectively meaningful self-discrepancies directly), using any word or set of words they liked. They then rated each self-discrepancy statement, in turn, in terms of perceived size and importance, which were multiplied to calculate the SDI, as an indicator of self-discrepancy salience. The SDI was completed first so that only accessible discrepancies were reported. Respondents then completed the fixed-item measure of appearance-related self-discrepancies (Szymanski & Cash, 1995), where they rated discrepancies concerning 11 attributes: height, skin complexion, facial features, hair texture/thickness, muscle tone/definition, body proportions, weight, chest size, physical strength, physical coordination, and overall appearance. To measure affect, participants rated how often, during the last month, they had experienced diverse negative mood states (e.g. dejected, sad, nervous), both in general, and specifically with respect to their body. Body satisfaction was measured through general feelings of physical (un)attractiveness and (dis)satisfaction with appearance (Appearance Evaluation subscale; Cash, 1990).

The correlation between the two types of self-discrepancy measure was significant, but rather low ($r = .28$), suggesting that the two measures are distinct. We also found that young women reported significantly greater actual–ideal self-discrepancies than young men, which supports the argument that appearance discrepancies are likely to be more chronically accessible for women. When the content of participant-generated discrepancies was compared to the ratings on the fixed-item measure, it was apparent that the fixed-item measure prompted men and women to report discrepancies, albeit small discrepancies, which were not evident in the unprompted responses. For example, physical strength was never mentioned by women, yet their mean rating score was 1.76, and men did not spontaneously list physical co-ordination, yet scored 1.35 on the rating scale. This supports the argument that fixed-item measures may prompt available discrepancies, whereas respondent-generated measures assess accessible discrepancies only. We therefore expect them to be superior predictors of body image.

Table 7.1 shows the strengths of gender and appearance-related self-discrepancies as predictors of general negative affect, body-focused negative affect, and body dissatisfaction, separately for the fixed-item measure and the SDI. The first finding to note is that there were no significant gender differences in the outcome measures, thus young women and men reported similar degrees of body dissatisfaction and negative feelings about their bodies. This supports the notion that young men's feelings about their bodies can be just as negative as young women's, even if their appearance-related self-discrepancies are not as salient and chronic. The second, and main, finding was that the SDI proved to be a powerful predictor of all three outcome variables, whereas the fixed-item measure predicted only appearance evaluation, and less strongly than the SDI. Across both women and men, increasing scores on the SDI were linked with more negative affect generally, more negative affect about one's body, and lower appearance evaluation. Thus, it was concluded that—with respect to such firmly established self-guides as actual–ideal appearance-discrepancies—the SDI seemed better able to tap accessible self-discrepancies, thus predicting evaluative and affective body image outcomes more powerfully.

These findings support the use of respondent-generated self-discrepancies, but they leave the question open of how the SDI we developed compares with the more standard measure developed by Higgins and colleagues. As part of a larger research project (Dittmar & Halliwell, 2005), we carried out a direct comparison of the SDI and the Selves Questionnaire. Women respondents

Table 7.1 Appearance-related self-discrepancy measures as predictors of young women's and men's general negative affect, body-focused affect, and appearance evaluation

	General affect	*Body-focused affect*	*Appearance evaluation*
Gender (G)	.13	.05	.08
Fixed-item (FI)	.04	.19	−.36*
Self-discrepancy Index (SDI)	.64***	.36*	−.59**
FI × G	−.02	.09	.00
SDI × G	−.31*	−.01	.12

$*p < .05$; $**p < .01$; $***p < .001$. Relationship status was controlled for.
Adapted from Halliwell & Dittmar (2006), Associations between appearance-related self-discrepancies and young women's and men's affect, body image, and emotional eating: A comparison of fixed-item and respondent-generated self-discrepancy measures, *Personality and Social Psychology Bulletin, 32*, p. 454, with kind permission of Sage Publications © 2006.

completed each measure twice, once unprompted (i.e. general) and once with respect to appearance as a specific domain. Given that weight and body size are particularly central to women, we also derived weight-related self-discrepancy measures, through coding responses and calculating self-discrepancy scores only with respect to those statements that specifically referred to weight loss and a smaller size of body or body parts. The analyses reported by Dittmar and Halliwell (2005)[11] showed that *within* each type of measure, appearance- and weight-related self-discrepancies were highly inter-correlated, both when self-discrepancies were general (SDI, .73; Higgins, .66), and when appearance had been prompted (SDI, .60; Higgins, .45). This con-firms that women's appearance concerns are highly focused on body size. In contrast, correlations *between* the two types of measures were low to moder-ate, ranging from .09 (*ns*) for general self-discrepancies overall to .27 for weight-related self-discrepancies (when appearance was not prompted). This suggests that the SDI measures self-discrepancies in a distinctly different way to Higgins' Selves Questionnaire.

The central aim of this comparison was to assess the relative predictive power of the two types of self-discrepancy measure for body image. Validated outcome variables were selected, which comprised thin-ideal internalization (Thompson et al., 1999), body esteem (Mendelson, Mendelson, & White, 2001), body-focused anxiety (see Chapter 6), and restrained eating, dieting (Van Strien, Frijiter, Bergers, & Defares, 1986). The predictive power of the SDI compared to the Selves Questionnaire with respect to these four meas-ures is shown in Figure 7.1, where the percentages refer to the amount of variability in the outcome variables that is predicted by each of the two self-discrepancy measures, in its two forms: unprompted and with appearance prompted.

The pattern of findings shows that prediction is improved for each type of measure when appearance is prompted. This makes sense, given that the outcome measures are linked to the appearance self-concept domain, and supports the use of domain-specific self-discrepancy measures. The second main finding is that the SDI outperformed the Selves Questionnaire, and that this finding is particularly powerful when appearance was prompted as the domain for respondents to think about. The amount of variability in outcome variables explained is considerable, especially for the evaluative and affective dimensions of body image, but also significant for thin-ideal internalisation and the extent to which women engage in dieting behaviour. A further finding is that specific weight-related self-discrepancies are even stronger predictors than overall appearance-related self-discrepancies for all variables, except thin-ideal internalisation. Thus, weight-related self-discrepancies may be of particular importance. In summary, the SDI devel-oped in our previous research offers a superior measure of self-discrepancies in the context of body image. Based on these findings, we have used the SDI in preference to Higgins' Selves Questionnaire in all our research on media effects, including the studies reported in this chapter.

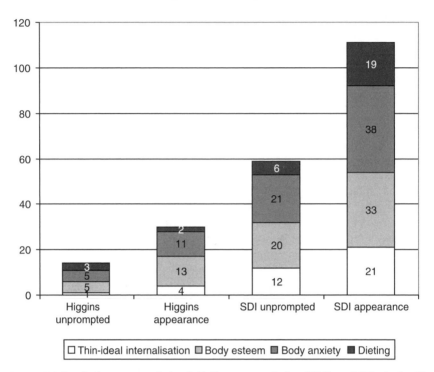

Figure 7.1 Predictive power of the Self-discrepancy Index (SDI) and Higgins' self-discrepancy measures for body image (percentages refer to variability accounted for).

WHEN WOMEN THINK "THIN" AND FEEL BAD

Notwithstanding the importance of demonstrating that thin ideals in the media have a negative effect on many women's body image, what is of most interest from both a social psychological perspective and a concern with reversing or preventing such negative effects is an understanding of the *process* through which this impact occurs. In terms of vulnerability factors, we have already shown in Chapter 6 that negative media exposure effects occur only for women who have internalised the thin ideal as their personal appearance value system. This means that body size and weight are highly salient and accessible domains of their identity, and of their ideal self. We have already argued that self-discrepancies provide a useful framework for understanding the process through which media exposure leads to heightened negative emotions about one's own body. Yet previous studies (e.g. Strauman et al., 1991), including our research reported in the last section, examined actual–ideal self-discrepancies as pre-existing stable individual differences. This is also true with respect to media exposure, where the only previous study linked such pre-existing self-discrepancies to media exposure in adolescents (Harrison, 2001). However, rather than examining self-discrepancies as pre-existing, chronically accessible constructs, they can also be conceptualised as *temporarily* accessible constructs activated by environmental input—such as thin models in advertising.

Ideal-body self-discrepancy activation as a psychological process

In explanations of the origins and activation of self-discrepancies, there is an important distinction between temporarily accessible self-discrepancies that are associated with transiently experienced emotions, and chronic self-discrepancies linked to a chronic vulnerability to particular emotions (Higgins, 1987). In contrast to previous research, we propose to examine temporary self-discrepancies activated by environmental input: ideal models in advertising. This conceptualisation is consistent with evidence that temporarily accessible constructs can have a stronger influence on information processing than chronically accessible constructs (Bargh, Lombardi, & Higgins, 1988). Thus, exposure to thin models can give rise, there and then, to weight-related self-discrepancies, because women's bodies are almost invariably larger than the media ideals. To the extent that such negative self-thoughts are activated in women, it is likely that they lead to the experience of negative affect about body and weight: "think thin and feel bad". Recent evidence that activated of appearance-related cognitive structures can mediate some effects of exposure to thin models (Brown & Dittmar, 2005; Hargreaves & Tiggemann, 2002) is consistent with this proposal, but there is no previous research that examines the impact of specific temporarily accessible self-discrepancies—primed by media exposure—on body dissatisfaction. These considerations led us to expect that temporary accessibility of weight-related self-discrepancies mediates the impact of media exposure. We also propose that these self-discrepancies are activated through exposure to thin media models only in those women who have internalised the ideal of a thin body. We thus expect thin-ideal internalisation to moderate exposure effects on women's body-focused negative affect, through the activation of weight-related self-discrepancies.

A new model of media exposure effects in women

This proposal can be depicted as a diagram (Figure 7.2), offering a new model of media exposure effects in women. Our model is novel in proposing a causal role of temporarily accessible self-discrepancies for the experience of body-focused negative affect after exposure to thin media models. It offers a further new contribution to the research literature by conceptualising thin-ideal internalisation as a moderator of the proposed psychological process whereby the exposure–negative affect link occurs through weight-related self-discrepancy activation (mediation). This extends previous demonstrations that thin-ideal internalisation moderates media effects.

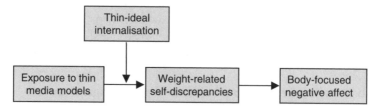

Figure 7.2 New media exposure model for women (with thin-ideal internalisation as moderator and weight-related self-discrepancy activation as mediator).

The structure of the model emerges when we consider the time sequence in which we expect variables to exert an impact on women's anxiety. Thin-ideal internalisation is a psychological individual difference variable, which exists prior to exposure, whereas we conceptualise the activation of weight-related self-discrepancies as an immediate reaction to exposure. Whether or not this reaction occurs should be influenced by whether or not women internalise a thin body as their personal ideal, i.e. thin-ideal internalisation should act as a moderator. Given that we propose weight-related self-discrepancies as a mediator, we expect these self-thoughts to lead to the experience of weight- and body-focused anxiety, i.e. affective responses to exposure.

Two experiments to test the model

To test the proposed model, we conducted two experiments that exposed women either to ultra-thin models or to a control condition (in which no models are shown). We expect that women would feel worse about their bodies after seeing ultra-thin models, compared to no models, if they have internalised the thin ideal, thus replicating previous findings (e.g. Dittmar & Howard, 2004a, 2004b; Halliwell & Dittmar, 2004). Yet the central aim is to test directly whether the heightened body-focused negative affect after thin-ideal exposure is mediated by weight-related self-discrepancy (WRSD) activation as the most proximal process leading women to experience negative body-focused affect. Given that we think that this effect is moderated by thin-ideal internalisation, we use two-sample structural equation modelling (SEM; as in Chapters 3, 4, and 5) to test the model for women who have internalised the thin-ideal as a personal value versus those who have not (Dittmar, Halliwell, & Stirling, in press).

The sample in our first experiment consisted of 87 women; 41 were exposed to advertisements for deodorant featuring ultra-thin models and 46 saw control advertisements containing no models (using landscapes as the backdrop for the same products). Their average age was 27 years, and the average BMI was normal: 22. Just over half were students (58%), and the remainder were in employment, about half working in professional occupations. The measures and procedure were very similar to those described in Chapter 6. We used a web-based questionnaire with the same advertising effectiveness cover story, and assessed whether respondents had remained unaware of the study's true purpose. Respondents also completed the same thin-ideal internalisation scale as described before (embedded among fillers about general attitudes toward advertising) and, right at the end, they completed the same body-focused anxiety measure. The innovation was that women completed the SDI directly after exposure, disguised as a measure of "your ideals", which allegedly can influence the perception of advertisements. Using only statements that referred explicitly to weight or body size, we derived a specific WRSD index from these data.

Using their average score on the thin-ideal internalisation scale, we classified women as having internalised the thin ideal as their personal value if they score 4 or above, which means that they agree with internalisation items. Women who score below 4 are classified as non-internalisers. Preliminary SEM analyses confirmed that thin images significantly increase body-focused negative affect compared to the control condition for women who have internalised the thin ideal ($\beta = .30$), whereas there is no negative effect for non-internalisers ($\beta = .04$). The same pattern of findings emerges with respect to WRSD scores, which are significantly higher after thin model than control advertisements, but again only for women who have internalised the thin ideal ($\beta = .45$ versus $\beta = -.00$). Our proposal of WRSD activation is further supported by the finding that, for these women, 34% of self-discrepancy statements refer explicitly to weight and body size in the experimental condition, compared to 12% in the control condition. In contrast, for non-internalisers there is no difference after thin models (17%) compared to control images (17%). Thus, thin models compared to a baseline of stimuli unrelated to appearance increase the WRSD for thin-internalisers as well as negative body-focused affect.

Next, we test the full proposed model directly, including both a direct path from exposure to negative affect, and an indirect path through WRSD. We find that there is no longer a significant direct path from exposure condition to thin-internalisers feeling badly about their bodies ($\beta = .10$ compared to $\beta = .30$ initially), and we can confirm statistically that the fit of the proposed model with our data does not deteriorate when the direct path from exposure to affect is deleted for both groups of women. The final findings are shown in the top half of Figure 7.3.

Exposure to thin models in advertising activates significantly stronger weight-related self-discrepancies in women who have internalised the thin ideal, compared to the control condition, and these WRSDs in turn are linked to heightened negative affect about their own bodies. No such negative exposure effects occur for women who have not internalised the thin ideal as their personal value. Thus, thin-ideal internalisation—an indication of the psychological importance attached to thinness as a personal goal—emerges as a significant vulnerability factor, making women susceptible to a negative impact of thin media images through activating negative self-thoughts about

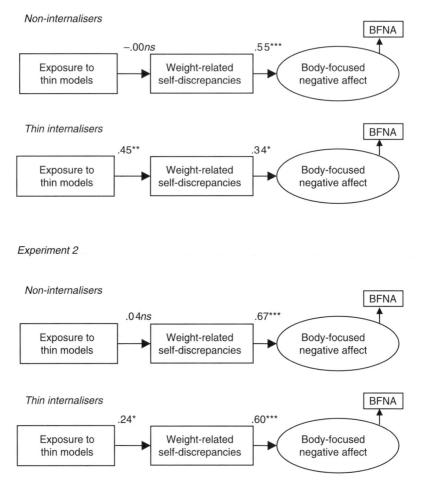

Figure 7.3 Structural equation models for women (Experiments 1 and 2). * *p* < .05; ** *p* < .01; *** *p* < .001; ns, not significant.

weight and body size, which, in turn, lead to the experience of body-focused anxiety. This finding provides support for the causal mechanism proposed in our model through which exposure to thin media ideals makes women feel worse about their bodies. The higher anxiety reported by women after seeing ultra-thin models is fully mediated by the activation of self-thoughts that focus on the gap between their actual and ideal self in terms of wanting to be thinner than they are.

We carried out a second experiment, which had two main aims. First, confidence in the robustness of our findings would increase if they replicate in a new, larger sample of young women. Second, in our first experiment we simply exposed women to advertisements that featured thin models, but research—albeit in a different domain—suggests that direct emphasis on the thin body size of the advertising models could further raise the salience of the ultra-thin beauty ideal (e.g. Aaker, 1999). Thus, although thinness is not a personally salient characteristic for non-internalisers, direct emphasis on models' thin body size may make the cultural importance of thinness sufficiently salient so that exposure to thin models may have an effect even on their body image. On the other hand, thin-ideal internalisation may function as a highly stable vulnerability factor, so that its absence protects women against exposure effect, no matter whether the thinness of advertising models is especially emphasised or not. Thus, an examination of advertisements with the same thin models, but emphasising their thin body size in one exposure condition and not the other, is an extension that can help assess the generalisability of our model across different levels of exposure to the thin ideal. There are no previous studies which address this issue.

The second experiment involved 155 women respondents with an average age of 26 years and an average BMI of 23, which falls into the healthy range. This time, we used three exposure conditions: 50 women were exposed to thin models promoting deodorants (no emphasis), 52 saw the same thin models, but promoting figure-hugging clothes (emphasis on models' body size), and 53 women were in the neutral control condition without any models. The advertisements were the same as in Experiment 1, and the additional set was created by removing the deodorant bottles and attaching the brand labels to the body-revealing clothes worn by the thin models. The measures and procedure were virtually identical to those in Experiment 1.

In two-sample SEM analyses, we examined whether there are systematic differences in women's responses to thin models, depending on whether they simply see the models (no emphasis) or whether the thin body size of the models is highlighted through the promotion of figure-hugging clothes (emphasis on models' body size). We found that there is no significant difference either with respect to WRSDs or body-focused negative affect, and this was the case for non-internalisers as well as internalisers (all $\beta < .14$). Thus, the effect of thin models on women's body image is the same, regardless of whether they are simply featured in advertisements or if their thin body size is emphasised through a focus on their body-revealing and figure-hugging clothes. Thus, the absence of exposure effects in non-internalisers is not affected by an added emphasis on models' body size, suggesting that thin-ideal internalisation is a stable value orientation, not malleable by environmental input. This provides support for the generalisability of the proposed model across different thin model exposure conditions.

We next examine whether our model replicates in this larger, new sample of women, using the same set of two-sample SEMs as in Experiment 1, focusing on the comparison between thin model exposure (collapsing across deodorant and clothes) and the control condition. Preliminary SEM analyses again confirm that thin models significantly increase body-focused negative affect compared to the control condition for women who have internalised the thin ideal ($\beta = .22$), whereas there is no significant negative effect for non-internalisers ($\beta = .12$). The same pattern of findings emerges with respect to WRSD scores, which are significantly higher after thin model than control advertisements, but again only for women who have internalised the thin ideal ($\beta = .24$ versus $\beta = .04$). Thus, the finding replicates that thin models, compared to a baseline of stimuli unrelated to appearance, increase WRSDs for thin-internalisers as well as negative body-focused affect. Next, we test the full proposed model directly, including both a direct path from exposure to negative affect, and an indirect path through WRSDs. We find again that there is no longer a significant direct path from exposure condition to negative affect for thin-internalisers ($\beta = .09$ compared to $\beta = .22$ initially), and we can confirm statistically that the fit of the proposed model with our data does not deteriorate when the direct path from exposure to affect is deleted for both groups of women. These final findings are shown in the bottom half of Figure 7.3.

The findings from Experiment 1 replicate in all respects. For women who have internalised the thin ideal, exposure to thin models activates significantly stronger WRSDs than exposure to neutral images, which in turn are linked to heightened negative affect about their own bodies. No such negative exposure effects occur for women who have not internalised the thin ideal as their personal value. Thus, thin-ideal internalisation emerges again as a significant vulnerability factor for negative media exposure effects, where thin media ideals lead women to a "think thin, feel bad" sequence. The central finding, replicating Experiment 1 and thus providing support for the proposed model in a larger and more diverse sample of women, is that the higher anxiety reported by women after seeing ultra-thin models is fully mediated by the activates of self-thoughts that focus on the gap between their actual bodily self and a thinner ideal self. Thus, the activation of self-discrepancies with respect to the ideal body plays a powerful role, helping us to understand the psychological mechanism through which women come to feel bad about their bodies after exposure to ideal media models. The next question that arises is how men respond to ideal male models in the media, given the recent proliferation of such images in advertising (e.g. Rohlinger, 2002).

WHEN MEN THINK "MUSCULAR" AND FEEL BAD

Sociocultural emphasis on the ideal male body is growing, and the media portrays an increasingly muscular ideal that is becoming unattainable for the majority of men (Pope et al., 1999). It is important to study the causes of male body dissatisfaction because it can lead to significant negative consequences, such as negative self-evaluation, depressed affect, and unhealthy muscularity-enhancing behaviours, such as steroid abuse, exercise addiction, or unbalanced diet regimes (Cafri, Thompson, Ricciardelli, McCabe,

Smolak, & Yesalis, 2005). As we saw, there is powerful and consistent evidence that unrealistic female media models have a detrimental effect on many women's body image, but little attention has been paid so far to idealised male models as a cause of men's body dissatisfaction.

Men's body dissatisfaction and the male body ideal

Male body dissatisfaction is becoming widespread. A series of US surveys examining changes in men's and women's concerns over 25 years show that appearance dissatisfaction doubled in women, but increased almost threefold in men, from 15% in 1972 to 43% in 1996 (Thompson et al., 1999). In 1996, 63% of men were unhappy with their mid torso, and 45% expressed dissatisfaction with their muscle tone. These surveys may not be entirely representative of the general population, but increases in male body dissatisfaction are also evident in two studies that used more tightly controlled sampling (Furnham & Calman, 1998; Raudenbusch & Zellner, 1997), although not in a third (Cash, Morrow, Hrabosky, & Perry, 2004). A recent review (Cafri et al., 2005) identified body dissatisfaction as a salient factor for boys and men, documented in different parts of the world, including both Europe and North America. Concerns with appearance and bodily attractiveness have become more central for men, termed the "Adonis complex" (Pope et al., 2000), and men are ostensibly just as likely as women to exercise for appearance-related reasons (Strelan & Hargreaves, 2005).

As discussed in Chapter 1, sociocultural pressures are growing that encourage a muscular body ideal for men: ideal male bodies are increasingly displayed in the mass media, particularly in advertising, which present an unattainable ideal for a majority of men. Content analyses of *Playgirl* centrefolds show men who have become increasingly muscular (Leit, Pope, & Gray, 2000), men's health and fitness magazines promote the message "burn fat, build muscle" (Labre, 2005), and this ideal is communicated to boys through toy action figures, whose muscularity has increased to such an extent that it exceeds that of body builders (Pope et al., 1999). Young men aspire to the lean, well-toned ideal with a V-shaped, muscular torso: when asked to rate their ideal body shape, they preferred a body larger than their current size, and, in particular, a substantially larger upper body (Stanford & McCabe, 2002). Links between media exposure and men's body dissatisfaction have been demonstrated in a few correlational studies (e.g. Hatoum & Belle, 2004; Morrison, Morrison, & Hopkins, 2003), but controlled experimental exposure is best suited to gauging the immediate psychological impact of idealised media images.

Acute exposure to idealised media models in men

Experimental studies that expose women to the ultra-thin female ideal are numerous, whereas we could locate only ten such experiments with a body dissatisfaction outcome measure that included male respondents and, of these, only four focused specifically on male models and men. The findings of the six studies that sample both women and men are mixed, with some showing negative effects on men's body image (e.g. Grogan, Williams, & Conner, 1996), and others not (e.g. Kalodner, 1997). This lack of consistency is most likely due to a number of factors, including demand characteristics and using male images that were attractive, but not necessarily epitomising the muscular ideal (cf. Dittmar et al., 2006). For women, it is not the general attractiveness of idealised models but the specific "body perfect" characteristic of thinness that has a detrimental effect on their body image. Thus, it is important in studies with men to use male models that embody the male ideal of a lean and muscular body.

Four exposure experiments focused specifically on men and used carefully selected male media models. In a comparison of TV advertisements that showed either ideal or non-ideal men, male students reported feeling more depressed after seeing muscular advertising models (Agliata & Tantleff-Dunn, 2004). College men's self-rated body satisfaction decreased after viewing images of muscular men, but did not change after exposure to non-muscular men (Lorenzen, Grieve, & Thomas, 2004). Although it is likely that the observed differences in men's responses are, indeed, the consequence of ideal male images increasing body dissatisfaction, it cannot be ruled out conclusively that they are due to a relief effect after the non-ideal men instead, i.e. decreased body dissatisfaction. Thus, it is preferable to use a control condition that consists of neutral images without any men or other body-related stimuli. Indeed, two studies offer such a comparison. One found that men who viewed advertisements with muscular male models reported heightened body dissatisfaction, compared to men who saw advertisements that contained only the products (Baird & Grieve, 2006), and the other found that male students exposed to advertisements with muscular men reported a greater discrepancy on a perceptual measure between their own muscularity and their ideal level of muscularity, compared to a control group who saw neutral advertisements (Leit, Gray, & Pope, 2002).

In summary, the evidence so far is suggestive, but does not yet demonstrate consistently that idealised male models cause body dissatisfaction in men. This is the first aim of a series of experiments we conducted. As in our research with women, we used a carefully constructed cover story to counteract demand characteristics, and checked whether our respondents had guessed the true purpose of the research. We compared exposure to idealised, muscular male models with a no-models control that can serve as a baseline of men's body dissatisfaction. In addition to examining acute exposure as a cause of male body dissatisfaction, the question arises of how such a negative effect can best be theorised. Given that ideal-body internalisation has not been shown to be a vulnerability factor among men, both in the general research literature on body image and in a previous exposure experiment (Agliata & Tantleff-Dunn, 2004), we could not simply adapt our media exposure model for women. Rather, given that processes underlying negative media effects in men have not been previously examined, the development of an appropriate model for men is the second aim of our research.

A domain-specific self-discrepancy activation model of media exposure effects

We have already shown that self-discrepancies are useful for understanding negative media exposure effects in vulnerable women, and we also demonstrated at the beginning of this chapter that actual-ideal self-discrepancies are more predictive of body image outcomes when they are specific to the domains of appearance, particularly those aspects of appearance that are central to sociocultural ideals. This is consistent with current models of the self-concept, which view it as multi-faceted, consisting of diverse self-representations, as outlined in Chapter 1. Thus, individuals are likely to have a number of self-discrepancies that relate to different domains, e.g. appearance or body ideal, which become more or less accessible in different situations, such as men being exposed to the male body ideal compared to not being confronted with such self-relevant information. Situational context, although not exposure specifically, has been shown to moderate the self-discrepancy–affect link (Boldero & Francis, 2000). Using the same logic as for women being exposed to ultra-thin models, we propose that exposure to ideal male models should give rise, there and then, to specific body-related self-discrepancies in men, because their bodies are often less muscular and fit than the media ideals.

If exposure to body ideals gives rise to temporary self-discrepancies in men that are specific to the domain of body build and muscularity, rather than generalised, then the emotional responses to these self-discrepancies may also be strongest in that specific domain, i.e. negative affect about body build and muscularity should be stronger than negative affect about other domains of the self. If this effect can be shown not only for a non-appearance domain of the self, but also for aspects of appearance not specific to the ideal male body, this would constitute particularly good support for the proposed model. In short, we propose to examine muscularity and body build as a specific self-domain for men, which is likely to be important for both temporary actual–ideal self-discrepancies and affect after exposure to muscular media models. There is no previous research that examines the impact of specific temporarily accessible self-discrepancies, primed by media exposure, on men's body dissatisfaction.

These considerations led us to develop a domain-specific self-discrepancy activation model, which may help explain men's increased body dissatisfaction after exposure to models that epitomise the male muscular ideal. We suggest that such exposure gives rise to negative affect in men (feeling bad) that is more strongly associated with their muscularity and body build than with negative affect in other appearance or self domains. We further expect that the psychological process directly associated with this negative emotional effect is the temporary activation of actual–ideal self-discrepancies that are specific to the male ideal body domain. This proposed mediation is captured by the sequence of men thinking "muscular" and then feeling bad about their own body's build and muscularity after exposure (see Figure 7.4).

We examine this model in a series of exposure experiments, addressing four hypotheses. First, we expect that exposure to ideal male models leads to increased body dissatisfaction in men, compared to neutral images. The consistent demonstration of such an effect across several studies would support the proposal that ideal media exposure causes male body dissatisfaction, at least in the short-term. Second, this negative exposure effect should manifest itself more strongly in men's dissatisfaction with their body build and muscularity, rather than with other appearance-related attributes, or attributes unrelated to appearance. Third, exposure to ideal male bodies should lead to the activation of men's actual–ideal self-discrepancies in a domain-specific way: self-discrepancies concerning the ideal male body should increase, but not self-discrepancies related to other aspects of appearance, or aspects of the self unrelated to appearance. Such a finding would support the likelihood that domain-specific self-discrepancy activation is a significant psychological process associated with increased male body dissatisfaction after exposure. Thus, the fourth hypothesis is that the proposed link between exposure and ideal-body-focused negative affect is mediated by actual–ideal self-discrepancies that are specific to the ideal male body.

Four experiments to test the model

All our studies use two exposure conditions: advertisements showing idealised male media models or no models. The models were chosen to present a physique considered ideal by men, i.e. physically fit and toned with a V-shaped, muscular upper body. Through pilot work in each study, we ensured that the male models were seen as typical of the male body ideal, and that young men wished that their bodies looked like these images. Exposure to these models should stimulate self-thoughts and negative affect in men exposed to them, which we measured only once: after exposure to the advertisements. The carefully constructed cover story about advertising effectiveness, with self-thoughts and current mood portrayed as possible influences on how people perceived ads, enabled us to imbed outcome measures among fillers. We also ensured that our samples consisted of heterosexual men, given that body image and appearance ideals differ according to sexual orientation

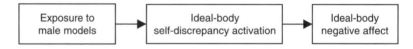

Figure 7.4 Domain-specific self-discrepancy activation model of negative media exposure effects on men's body satisfaction.

(e.g. Siever, 1994). Most of the respondents' BMI fell into the normal range, but we nevertheless controlled for BMI in all statistical analyses.

In our first study, we sampled young men ($n = 78$) from diverse backgrounds, including both students and employees, with a mean age of 20 years. The procedure was very similar to that described in Chapter 6: men completed a questionnaire in which they evaluated advertisements for a (fictitious) night club that either depicted toned, V-shaped, muscular models or no models. Imbedded among fillers, they then completed four scales from the Multiple Body–Self Relations Questionnaire (Cash, 1990), which had been validated with men. As predicted, exposure condition had a significant and sizeable impact on body dissatisfaction across the four scales taken together, such that body dissatisfaction was higher after seeing male media models, compared to the no models baseline. However, by itself, only the fitness evaluation scale was significantly affected by exposure. This documents that men evaluated their body as less fit after exposure to idealised male media images, compared to the control. Decreased fitness evaluation after exposure may indicate self-discrepancies between an actual bodily self and an ideal, more muscular and fitter self, and it is to a direct assessment of self-discrepancy arousal that we turn next.

Study 2 examines whether negative media exposure effects replicate in a different sample of young men, who were exposed to photographs of ideal male models or to control photographs, depicting mobile phones. Second, it investigates whether exposure to ideal male images gives rise specifically to body-related self-discrepancies, rather than to discrepancies in a domain unrelated to appearance. Third, it enables us to explore qualitatively which particular body-related self-discrepancies men report after exposure. The sample comprised male students at two UK universities ($n = 80$), aged 22 years on average, half of whom saw ideal male models and half neutral images without any human figures. Using the SDI, we then asked respondents to report actual–ideal self-discrepancies in two different domains. The first domain was concerned with shopping behaviour, chosen to be unrelated to the body, asking them to report on aspects they would ideally like to change, such as expensive or impulsive purchases of consumer goods. The second domain was concerned with appearance, asking respondents to focus on how they would ideally like to look. Two main findings emerged, which support the domain-specific activation model. First, compared to mobile phone advertisements, exposure to ideal male models did not significantly raise self-discrepancies in the shopping behaviour domain. In contrast, and as hypothesised, self-discrepancies in the appearance domain were affected by exposure, such that SDI scores were significantly increased, compared to the control condition. Second, we examined the content of men's self-discrepancy statements separately for the two exposure conditions. We developed a coding scheme[12] that categorised self-discrepancy statements as either related to the male ideal body or referring to other appearance-related self-discrepancies. Statements concerning the male ideal included: fitness and athleticism, height and weight, muscularity, broader shoulders and more bulk, belly, and biceps. An example of muscularity is "I am quite toned, but I would like to be more muscular". Other appearance-related self-discrepancies included references to general appearance, skin, hair (both head and body), facial features (including glasses and ears), and miscellaneous. An example of facial features is "I have aggressive-looking eyes, but I would like kinder eyes". We found that the balance between statements that refer to the male ideal compared to other aspects of appearance is significantly different: two-thirds of self-discrepancy statements made by men in the control condition refer to other appearance-related self-discrepancies (66%) compared to one-third about the male ideal (34%), whereas after exposure to ideal media images the distribution shifts to half of self-discrepancies referring to the male ideal. In particular, references to fitness and muscularity increase almost fourfold. Thus, this study shows that men's self-discrepancies in the appearance domain are larger and more psychologically salient after exposure to male media models, and that the content of those self-discrepancies is also more likely to focus specifically on aspects central to the male ideal. The next task in examining the proposed domain-specific self-discrepancy activation model is to study both self-discrepancies and men's negative affect after exposure.

The final two experiments use different advertisements and samples of young men, but the design is so similar that analysis and findings of both studies can be reported together. In Study 3a, young men aged 22 years on average and prominently students ($n = 60$) were exposed to three advertisements for deodorant, showing either idealised male models or only the products (control condition). Instead of using a paper-and-pencil questionnaire, Study 3b was presented on the internet, where 71 young men with a mean age of 23 years were exposed to two deodorant advertisements that showed either male models or no models (see example adverts in Figure 7.5).

After exposure, we used the SDI in its general format without any prompt, so that we could examine unobtrusively the extent to which men are spontaneously thinking about self-discrepancies related to the ideal male body. To derive different SDIs from these data, self-statements were coded into three types: ideal-body self-discrepancies (IB-SDI; e.g. wanting to be more muscular), other appearance-related self-discrepancies (OA-SDI; e.g. wishing they had curly hair), and appearance-unrelated self-discrepancies (AU-SDI; e.g. wanting to be less shy). In terms of affect, we used a similar measure to that described throughout Chapter 6, but this time using three types of items: ideal-body negative affect (IB-NA; e.g. muscle tone, shoulders, and upper body), other appearance-related negative affect (OA-NA; e.g. buttocks, legs), and appearance-unrelated negative affect (AU-NA; e.g. income, personal relationships).

Our domain-specific self-discrepancy activation model is predicated on muscular male models leading to self-discrepancies and negative affect that concern the ideal male body, rather than other aspects of the self. The

Figure 7.5 Deodorant advertisement with and without idealised male model.

findings are reported in detail in Dittmar et al. (2007); we only highlight the most important results here. When modelling the impact of exposure condition on self-discrepancy activation, we find, across both experiments, that the only significant changes in men's self-discrepancies reported in response to idealised media models were increased discrepancies in the ideal-body domain, but not in the other domains, unrelated to appearance or related to other appearance aspects. This is exactly what we would expect in support of the hypothesis concerning domain-specific self-discrepancy arousal: Exposure to idealised models leads men to think of their ideal self in terms of having a more muscular and powerfully built upper body, whereas other self-discrepancies do not increase. The findings for affect were more complex, but they did show, within each study, that associations between exposure and negative affect were strongest for the ideal-body domain, about twice as strong as associations with the other domains. Thus, the link between exposure and IB-NA proved significantly greater than the links with negative affect in other domains of the self: After seeing male models, men feel particularly bad about their lack of muscularity and upper body build.

Having demonstrated, separately, that ideal male models make men think "muscular" as well as feel bad about their body size, we now turn back to the model shown in Figure 7.4. This model puts them together by proposing that the increase in ideal-body negative affect after exposure is mediated by, or takes place through, temporary self-discrepancy activation that is specific to the ideal-body domain. Figure 7.6 shows the findings when this model is tested in Studies 3a and 3b. Mediation tests were significant in both, and the model was supported because both parts of the indirect path, that from exposure to IB-SDI and that from IB-SDI to IB-NA, proved significant, and

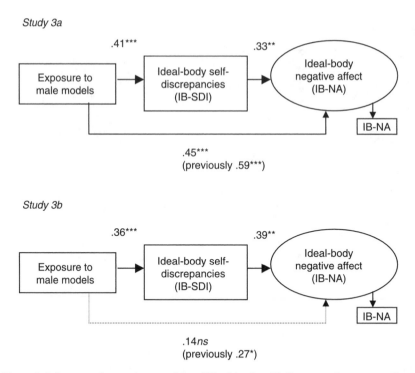

Figure 7.6 Structural equation models of ideal-body self-discrepancies as a mediator of the exposure–negative affect link (unmediated exposure–affect link in parentheses). * $p < .05$; ** $p < .01$; *** $p < .001$; *ns*, not significant.

the strength of the direct path between exposure and IBNA was reduced (previous path coefficients are shown in parentheses).

Ideal images of fit, muscular, V-shaped men typically used in advertising do cause increased body dissatisfaction in young men. Negative effects on body image replicate in four acute exposure experiments; the use of different samples (both students and non-students), image stimuli, and modes of exposure increases confidence in the robustness of this finding. In terms of possible consequences of body dissatisfaction, there is recent concern over the growth of unhealthy body-shaping behaviours among men designed to increase muscularity (Cafri et al., 2005). The present findings suggest that exposure to male media models may play a role in promoting the specific kind of body dissatisfaction that may lead to such behaviours. As predicted, negative exposure effects were found to be specific to particular dimensions of men's self-concept and affect, rather than general. Exposure to idealised models leads men to think of their ideal self in terms of having a more muscular and powerfully built upper body, whereas other self-discrepancies do not increase. Thus, the self-discrepancies that men experience as greater and more psychologically salient after exposure are domain-specific: they concern the ideal male body as part of their self-concept. This temporary activation and accessibility of specific self-discrepancies—men thinking "muscular"—carries over to negative affect, but again in a specific way—men feeling particularly bad about their lack of muscularity and upper body strength. Thus, the present findings support a new model of media exposure effects on body image in men that identifies the temporary activation of ideal-body self-discrepancies as the psychological process associated with increased negative affect about one's body in response to idealised media models.

CONCLUSION AND FUTURE RESEARCH

We have presented a range of research findings that, cumulatively, provide good evidence for our theoretical models in which temporary, exposure-activated self-belief patterns are used to understand negative media effects. The psychological processes through which the mass media act as a strong influence on individuals' body dissatisfaction and body-shaping behaviours were only poorly understood previously (e.g. Levine & Harrison, 2004; Polivy & Herman, 2004; Thompson et al., 1999), and we believe that the domain-specific self-discrepancy activation models we have developed so far can offer an explanation for understanding acute exposure effects. The ideal-ised models typically used in advertising lead both women and men to feel bad about their bodies, because they think about their self in terms of the discrepancies between the "body perfect" ideal depicted in advertising and their own bodies, thus focusing on their shortcomings. This "think ideal, feel bad" sequence is in evidence for women who have internalised the thin ideal as their personal value system, whereas the research on men does not examine vulnerability factors. This is clearly an area for future research. Given that not all men are likely to be affected by media exposure to the same extent, the model could be extended to account for vulnerability to domain-specific tem-porary self-discrepancy activation. A likely moderator is whether or not men are actively engaged in changing their body size and muscularity (Halliwell, Dittmar, & Orsborn, in press).

Our findings also have implications for the theory and measurement of self-discrepancies. First, they suggest that the SDI may be a particularly useful assessment tool for predicting affect and behaviour in particular domains, such as body image and body-shaping behaviours. Second, the present findings imply that research on domain-specific self-discrepancies may be useful for self-domains likely to be linked to unhealthy behaviours. For instance, ideal-body self-discrepancies may be particularly useful pre-dictors of men's behaviours designed to increase muscularity, and of women's behaviour intended to promote weight loss.

A major direction for future research emerges, which builds on the findings that self-discrepancies that focus on "body perfect" ideals lead to increased body dissatisfaction after exposure to idealised media models. A research priority is to examine the development of ideal-body self-discrepancies in young children, particularly in the context of unhealthy sociocultural role models they may identify with early on, such as dolls for girls or action man toys for boys. We have started research on young girls' exposure to different dolls, including Barbie, which is reported in Chapter 8.

8 What is beautiful and who is "cool"? Consumer culture and socialisation

Robin Banerjee & Helga Dittmar

Synopsis

Children appear especially vulnerable to the "body perfect" and material "good life" ideals of consumer culture, and at an increasingly younger age. If we want to build a foundation for protecting them, we need to understand consumer culture socialisation better. This chapter aims to contribute through showing that:

- Children come to internalise body and material ideals during their identity development.
- Girls as young as 5–7 years old want a thinner body after exposure to images of thin dolls such as Barbie.
- Materialism is a significant aspect of 8- to 11-year-old children's lives, because they believe that, to be popular among their peer group—to be "cool"—they have to have the right material goods.

How to be cool and beautiful   © Jessica Barlow

One of the most striking aspects of consumer culture today is that messages about what is beautiful and who is "cool" are deliberately targeted at children from a young age, making materialistic and appearance norms and values a key focus of their socialisation experience. This chapter examines how children respond to material goods marketed at them, such as dolls, and what they believe material goods can do for them in the context of their peer relations.

With respect to sociocultural beauty ideals, children as young as 3 years already hold weight stereotypes that "fat is bad" (Cramer & Steinwert, 1998). Dolls and toys marketed at young children embody sociocultural ideals. In the previous chapter, we saw that idealised male bodies, increasingly displayed in advertising, present an unattainable muscular ideal for a majority of men. To young boys, this ideal is communicated through toy action figures, such as GI Joe, whose muscularity has increased to such an extent that it exceeds that of body builders (Pope et al., 1999). For girls, the ultra-thin beauty ideal is even more pervasive. Barbie doll is *the* cultural icon of female beauty, with 99% of 3- to 10-year-olds in the US owning at least one Barbie (Rogers, 1999). Yet, Barbie is so exceptionally thin that, in a flesh-and-blood woman, her weight and body proportions are not only unattainable, but also unhealthy. This is worrying because dolls, such as Barbie, can provide "aspirational role models" for young children (Pedersen & Markee, 1991; Turkel, 1998):

> I looked at a Barbie doll when I was 6 and said, "This is what I want to look like." I think a lot of little 6-year-old girls or younger even now are looking at that doll and thinking, "I want to be her".
>
> (model Cindy Jackson, CBS News, 2004)

With respect to the psychological importance of consumer goods and money, there are increasing concerns that today's children are more materialistic than ever. Recent reports on children in both the US and the UK have suggested that "being rich" is their top aspiration (Brown, 2005; Schor, 2004), and the conclusion from a national US survey is that the "acquisition and accumulation of possessions have become preoccupying behaviours for them" (Goldberg et al., 2003, p. 278). Pre-adolescent children are a market segment that is targeted heavily by advertisers for a range of consumer goods—clothes, accessories, shoes, mobile phones, music and electronic items—and statistics estimate that 8- to 14-year-olds spent $300 billion across the globe in 2003 and influenced another $350 billion spend by their parents (Lindstrom, 2004). Furthermore, there is evidence that even quite young children are knowledgeable about the symbolic and status meanings associated with consumer goods (Achenreiner & John, 2003; Driscoll, Mayer, & Belk, 1985). For example, preferences for advertised brand names may be present in children as young as 2 years old (Hite & Hite, 1995).

The specific socialisation mechanisms that promote and strengthen materialistic beliefs, values, and behaviours in children remain underexplored in psychological research. However, there is good reason to argue that children's materialistic values are intimately connected with their peer experiences: A US poll is reported to show 41% of parents took the view that "kids feel they need all of these products *in order to fit in*" (Schor, 2004, p. 185, emphasis added). Thus, materialism has become a significant aspect of children's everyday lives, because they believe that, to be popular among their peer group—to be "cool"—they have to have the right games, clothes, shoes, and a host of other material goods. There seems to be a peer culture in which material goods are central, particularly in children's relationships with their peers. Children may be most vulnerable to the internalisation of materialistic values if they perceive peer pressure for having "cool" things, and if they believe that they can use material goods to become more popular and accepted. As we saw in Chapter 4, pursuing materialistic goals as a means of improving social status or gaining power seems particularly strongly associated with lower well-being in adults. This evidence provides salient reasons for examining the origins of, and motives for, materialism earlier in development.

SOCIALISING BODY AND MATERIAL IDEALS

For young children, fantasy and play are vital parts of socialisation where they internalise ideals and values (Sutton-Smith, 1997). With respect to beauty ideals, dolls provide a tangible image of the body that can be internalised as part of the child's developing sense of identity and body image (Kuther & McDonald, 2004). In terms of the material good life, children may watch celebrities' homes on TV and be told that the people who own such expensive stuff are successful, with a wonderful and interesting life. As argued in Chapter 1, a developmental account of how body and material ideals are socialised though dolls, toys, and consumer goods more generally, should begin by considering them as role models from a symbolic interactionist perspective (Mead, 1934). Material objects can function as embodiments of cultural presentations that gradually become internalised into children's developing sense of identity (Dittmar, 1992a). At the same time, children are known to become increasingly concerned about self-presentation, peer-group norms, and evaluations by their peer group (Banerjee, 2002a, 2002b; Parker & Gottman, 1989). Peer-group interaction may therefore represent a particularly important direct context for the socialisation of body and material ideals through consumer goods marketed to a youth audience.

Material objects and identity development

The central Meadian concept of *taking the perspective of the other* can help explain how material objects can function as socialisation agents, where the symbolic meanings associated with the object (thin is beautiful, popular people buy brand X) are eventually internalised as aspects of one's ideal self

(Dittmar, 1992a). As outlined in Chapter 1, the symbolic meanings of objects can serve as an imaginary point of view from which to see one's own bodily or material self, where young children come to understand the meaning of perfection or popularity through engaging with objects that embody cultural ideals. Thus, the primary meaning of the term "role model" from a Meadian perspective is a cultural representation that becomes internalised to form part of the child's emerging identity. This identity development takes place through different phases of play, where initially a child can adopt only a single perspective. With respect to dolls or other material objects, children initially understand their most simple meaning though observing, directly or on TV, others' interactions with these goods, or their comments about them. During play with dolls, or other objects, they enact this simple meaning directly through identification: a girl playing with Barbie may identify with her "beauty" through pretending to be Barbie, in the same way in which a boy may identify with the muscles and power of a toy action figure. Through social interaction and communication, such as in the family and peer groups, children come to develop a more complex representation of their material objects as part of their identity, where their toys function as role models, signifying material and appearance values of consumer culture that are internalised as part of children's ideal identities. Later, when children come to understand that there are multiple perspectives one can take towards these objects, they may still continue with their identification, but they may also start to be critical of their toys or dolls, as we will see later in this chapter with respect to Barbie. First, we consider developmental work on children's concerns with how they present themselves to others.

Self-presentational concerns in children

Psychological research over the last decade has demonstrated that even young children are aware of motivations to control one's behaviour and appearance in order to make desired impressions on others. Such self-presentational motivations are likely to underpin children's aspirations to meet the ideals and standards embodied in material products such as dolls and other toys. Empirical work on self-presentation in primary school children highlights rising concerns about how they are evaluated by their peers, and consumer messages about what is beautiful and who is "cool" may therefore become particularly important at this time.

Research investigating children's explanations of fictional characters' self-presentational behaviour in hypothetical scenarios (e.g. a character who is showing off to his peers) has consistently demonstrated that, whereas younger children tend to explain others' behaviour by referring to descriptions of an actual or assumed state of affairs (e.g. "he said he's good at football, because he *is* good at football"), older children recognise that people can intentionally control their behaviours in order to shape their public identity (e.g. "she wants them to think she's great"; "he doesn't want them to think he's a baby"). Such awareness of self-presentational motives has been found in children—typically from around 8 years of age—when questioned about a variety of different self-presentational tactics, including self-promotion and ingratiation (Aloise-Young, 1993; Bennett & Yeeles, 1990a; Watling & Banerjee, in press a), showing off (Bennett & Yeeles, 1990b), modesty (Banerjee, 2000; Watling & Banerjee, in press b), and disclaimers (Bennett, 1990). Moreover, primary school children also come to recognise that self-presentational behaviour may be adjusted to meet the demands of particular social contexts: Children in primary school increasingly recognise how different self-descriptions would be needed to convey a positive impression to audiences with different preferences, such as peers compared to adults (Banerjee, 2002c). To summarise, the evidence indicates a substantial rise in awareness of self-presentational motives during the primary school years, with children from around 8 years of age demonstrating increasingly sophisticated insights into how their public identity can be shaped by means of self-presentational strategies.

What developmental factors underlie the increasing interest in self-presentation during childhood? Interestingly, it appears that the cognitive prerequisites for understanding self-presentation, such as the capacity for reasoning about other people's beliefs, are in place by around 5 or 6 years of age (Banerjee & Yuill, 1999a). However, as indicated above, children usually do not refer spontaneously to concerns about social evaluation until around the latter half of primary school (Banerjee, 2002a, 2002b; Banerjee & Yuill, 1999b). Thus, it seems that it is the *motivation* to control their public identity that becomes generally important at around 8 years of age. This coincides with a related transition in peer group processes, whereby children become increasingly focused on acceptance by their peer group, through adherence to peer group norms and favourable social comparisons, as a major social goal (Erwin, 1993; Parker & Gottman, 1989). Therefore, it seems highly likely that if materialistic values and norms are perceived as relevant to peer group acceptance, they could become a major focus of primary school children's self-presentational efforts.

It is important to note that consumer products are often marketed to particular age groups, so that messages about what is beautiful and who is "cool" are attached to age-targeted goods. For example, very young girls may be interested in Barbie dolls, but may later identify with Bratz dolls instead. Similarly, even though self-presentation processes become generally salient from around 8 years of age, the particular behaviours, characteristics, and possessions that are perceived as important for peer group acceptance, and consequently for self-presentation, may vary with age. In fact, one specific self-presentational goal does appear to be salient for children even at the start of primary school, namely the desire to match gender norms and standards in front of same-sex peers. Banerjee and Lintern (2000) found that young boys in the first years of primary school were significantly more likely to describe themselves as gender-typed (in terms of toys and activities) when in front of same-sex peers than when alone. This finding is compatible with evidence that peer groups can often punish (through ridicule or exclusion) counter-stereotypical behaviour at a young age (Fagot, 1977; Langlois & Downs, 1980). Thus, even though pre-adolescence may be a time when self-presentational efforts to be evaluated positively by one's peer group are generally salient, some ideals may become an important focus of self-presentation in children as young as 5 years of age.

THE THIN BEAUTY IDEAL, DOLLS, AND YOUNG GIRLS' BODY IMAGE

One of the most established perspectives on the development of body dissatisfaction—a negative evaluation of one's bodily identity—is socio-cultural theory (Levine & Smolak, 1996; Thompson et al., 1999), which views the mass media, and thus consumer culture, as powerful transmitters and reinforcers of socio-cultural body ideals (Dittmar, 2005c; Levine & Harrison, 2004; Pope et al., 1999). The thin "body perfect" ideal for girls is, of course, present in many aspects of their socio-cultural environment (such as advertising, TV, and peer groups), but dolls like Barbie—due to their iconic status—are likely to act as salient role models, at least for very young girls.

Barbie as the embodiment of the female socio-cultural body ideal

"Every half-second, somewhere in the world another Barbie is sold" (Schor, 2004, p. 22), with increasingly younger girls being targeted. Launched in the early 1960s, Barbie is the best-selling fashion doll in every major global market, with worldwide annual sales of about 1.5 billion dollars (Mattel, 2003).

Barbie's body proportions, as a cultural icon of female beauty, have received much criticism (e.g. Brownell, 1991), and research confirms that her body proportions are unrealistic, unattainable, and unhealthy when applied to a flesh-and-blood woman. When fashion dolls, including Barbie, were compared to the typical fashion model and the Greek ideal of beauty, standardised bust measurements of fashion dolls showed that adult women would assume heights of 6'2"–7'5", or 1.88–2.26 metres (Pederson & Markee, 1991). Using anthropometry (a branch of anthropology that deals with comparative measurements of human body parts based on mathematical formulations), Norton, Olds, Olive, and Dank (1996) were able to scale Barbie's proportions to determine how they would be reflected in adult women's body size dimensions. After measuring the circumference of diverse body sites, deviations were calculated between Barbie and different groups of US women, and expressed as z-scores that represent probabilities of occurrence. Unsurprisingly, fashion models were thinner ($z = -.76$) than a cross-section of 18- to 35-year-old women, and anorexic patients were thinner still ($z = -1.31$).

The average *z*-score of Barbie was −4.17, representing a probability of less than 1 in 100,000 women having her body proportions. Z-scores were even more extreme for particular body parts, scientifically emphasising the sheer unreality of Barbie's body proportions. Were Barbie a flesh-and-blood woman, her waist would be 39% smaller than that of anorexic patients, and her body weight would be so low that she would not be able to menstruate (Rintala & Mustajoki, 1992).

Body dissatisfaction in girls

Most research with children has been conducted during adolescence and late pre-adolescence (e.g. Riccardelli & McCabe, 2001), and there are few studies with very young children. What findings exist show early awareness of social pressures towards thinness. Children 4–6 years old were shown to favour a thin body (Musher-Eizenman et al., 2003). Girls report higher levels of body dissatisfaction than boys and a stronger desire to be thinner (Oliver & Thelen, 1996), which increases with age: 40% of girls aged 8–9 years wanted to be thinner, compared to 79% of girls aged 11–12 years (Maloney, McGuire, & Daniels, 1988). A recent study on 5- to 8-year-old girls concluded that girls' desire for thinness emerges around age 6. Using a figure silhouette rating task, Lowes and Tiggemann (2003) found that, on average, girls as young as 5 years already desired a body thinner than their current figure, but that this discrepancy became more pronounced in 6- to 8-year-old girls. Thus, girls' body dissatisfaction starts to emerge at a very young age, possibly from 5 years. The question that interested us was whether exposure to the thin ideal could be shown to be a *cause* of 5- to 8-year-old girls' feelings of unhappiness with their bodies and their desire to be thinner. Thus, we carried out the first experimental exposure study with such young girls (Dittmar, Halliwell, & Ive, 2006).

The impact of exposure to images of dolls on young girls' body image

In this exposure experiment with 162 girls aged 5–8 years, we compare the effects of exposure to Barbie-doll images with exposure to neutral images (which contained no body-relevant cues), but also with exposure to images of Emme, a new doll based on the full-figured eponymous American super-model launched in 2002. For young girls, Barbie dolls can serve as ultra-thin body ideals, and Emme dolls as an alternative that presents a realistic body size that is backed by the American Dietetic Association as an aid in promoting a more positive body image for young girls (Mendelsohn, 2003). Figure 8.1 gives an example of Emme doll.

Given the recent conclusion that girls' desire for thinness emerges around age 6 (Lowes & Tiggemann, 2003), we decided to sample girls aged 5–8 years. They were in Years 1, 2, and 3 of the UK's National Curriculum school

Figure 8.1 Emme doll. (*Note.* "EMME®" is a registered trademark of EMME
Associates Inc. http://www.emmesupermodel.com. Reproduced from
the internet with kind permission of Tonner Inc. with Emme Model
Model Press Agency © 2006.)

structure (Year 1 is equivalent to US kindergarten, Year 2 to first grade, and
Year 3 to second grade). This is the first study to use an experimental
exposure paradigm with such young children, thus offering a methodologic-
ally rigorous examination of ultra-thin dolls as a *cause* of girls' feelings of
unhappiness with their bodies and their desire to be thinner. It addresses
three main research questions: Do images of Barbie have an immediate negative impact on girls' body image? Does exposure to images of a doll with
more realistic body proportions result in the same detrimental effects? Is
the impact of exposure to Barbie images age-related, so that effects differ
depending on school year group?

Applying the account of dolls as role models to this research specifically
suggests that girls' identity development involves different phases of play,
where young children initially imitate, and identify with, "beautiful" Barbie
in a direct, non-reflexive manner, but then—gradually—come to internalise

thinness as a salient feature of what it means to be beautiful. Once inter-nalisation is completed, and the thinness ideal has become part of girls' self-concept, they may become able to take a more reflexive stance toward Barbie, by being able to consider her from multiple perspectives, including their own younger self. This may mean that Barbie "has done her work" as a thinness role model, and may therefore no longer act as a direct influence on girls' body image. Suggestive support for such a change in reactions to Barbie comes from 10- to 14-year-old US girls' retrospective accounts of their experiences with Barbie dolls (Kuther & McDonald, 2004). All girls report periods of intensive identification when they were very young, and Barbie's importance as an aspirational role model was highlighted: "She is like the perfect person when you are little that everyone wants to be like" (p. 48). However, this phase of identification is later supplanted by anger, where all girls report some aggression, such as "I cut off all of Barbie's hair and burned the clothes" (p. 46). Thus, Barbie ceases to function as an aspir-ational role model much before the age of 10 years, and some girls voice concerns over her negative impact: "I think she is too thin and does not show the best example for young kids . . . when they [my friends] were younger they wanted to be like her because she was thin, now . . they would die" (p. 48). Thus, identification with Barbie appears to occur early, but is then followed by a distancing process.

This proposal, that exposure to Barbie dolls may no longer exert a direct effect on older girls' body image, is strengthened by considering develop-mental theories, which converge in identifying a transition in the relationship between the sociocultural environment and children's self-concept that impacts on self-evaluation. According to Bandura's Social-Cognitive Theory (e.g. 1986, 1989), "in the course of development, the regulation of behavior shifts from predominantly external sanctions and mandates to gradual sub-stitution of self-sanctions and self-direction *grounded in personal standards*" (Bussey & Bandura, 1999, p. 690, emphasis added). This emphasis on personal standards posits a greater involvement of the child's self-concept in evaluative self-reactions as a key developmental shift. For young girls, the thin body ideal appears an important personal standard that becomes internalised as part of their developing self-concept, and—drawing a parallel between overt behaviour and children's thoughts and feelings regarding their bodies—it would be expected that the sociocultural environment, as exemplified by thin Barbie dolls, exerts a direct influence on younger girls, so that they would express a desire to be thinner as a consequence of exposure to Barbie-doll stimuli. In contrast, older girls may no longer react to Barbie-doll stimuli in this direct way because they have already internalised the thinness ideal as a personal standard, and their desire to be thin has become more of a function of this internal, cognitive self-concept structure, rather than a reaction to environmental thinness stimuli. This expectation is further supported by changes in the nature of children's social comparisons (Ruble, 1983), which, from about age 7, assume a greater importance for children's self-evaluation, although young children are interested in, and do make, social comparisons. Therefore, we expect that younger girls' response to thin-bodied dolls like Barbie is the desire to be thinner themselves, which should *not* occur in response to full-bodied dolls, such as Emme, nor in the control condition. In contrast, older girls' (already internalised) desire to be thin may be unaffected by short-term exposure to Barbie dolls, which may have ceased to function as an aspirational role model. This raises the interesting question of how they respond to dolls with a full-bodied figure, given that Emme clashes with their internalised thinness ideal. These hypotheses can be summarized in the form of a single model (see Figure 8.2), which can be tested through multi-sample structural equation modelling, with the three year groups constituting different samples.

Our research assesses effects on girls' body image in an experiment that uses three exposure conditions: Barbie-doll images, Emme-doll images, and neutral control images. Girls are exposed to one set of these stimuli in the form of a picture book that each girl looks through while being read a story about "Mira", which consists of six happy scenes around the themes of shopping for clothes and getting ready for a birthday party. We created three types of picture book, to expose girls to different image stimuli in the three conditions. Each picture book contained six images, laminated and bound, which show Barbie dolls, or Emme dolls, or neutral pictures without any depictions of bodies. After the story, we assessed girls' body image, making sure that we used measures suitable for such young girls. The Revised Body Esteem Scale (Mendelson, White, & Mendelson, 1996) is an evaluative measure of body image that assesses children's thoughts and feelings about their body, including general appearance, beliefs about how

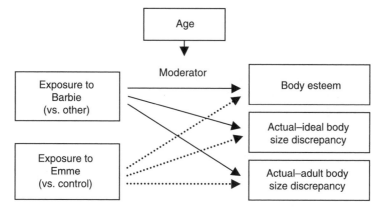

Figure 8.2 Model of the impact of exposure to different dolls on girls' body image. (*Note.* Reproduced from Dittmar, Halliwell, & Ive (2006), Does Barbie make girls want to be thin? The effect of experimental exposure to images of dolls on the body image of 5–8-year-old girls, *Developmental Psychology*, *42*, p. 286 with kind permission of the American Psychological Association © 2006.)

others evaluate their looks, and also specifically their weight. Girls expressed their (dis)agreement with diverse statements by picking one of three smiley faces, representing "no" (downturned mouth), "in between" (straight line mouth), or "yes" (upturned mouth). Among fillers, such as "I love watching the Teletubbies", were the body esteem items, such as "I'm pretty happy about the way I look" or "I really like what I weigh". In addition, we decided to complement this evaluative measure with pictorial measures of body size dissatisfaction, where girls indicate both their actual body size and their ideal body size. Collins (1991) developed a figure rating scale for children from the original version for adults (Stunkard, Sorensen, & Schulsinger, 1983), which shows a series of seven line drawings of female figures, ranging from extremely thin to obese. From a line of young girls' figures, each girl picks, and colours in, the figure whose body looks most like her own body now, imagining she is looking in a mirror (actual body shape). Then, on a second line of the same figures, she coloured in the figure that shows the way she wants to look like the most (ideal body shape). Finally, each girl colours in the adult figure that shows the way she would like to look like when she is grown up (adult ideal body shape). Body shape dissatisfaction scores were computed by subtracting actual from ideal body sizes.

As we would expect, the two pictorial measures show strong positive associations ($r = .65–.69$), which demonstrates that the extent to which girls desire a different—usually thinner—body shape is similar, but not identical, when they are asked about right now and when they are asked about their ideal body shape as an adult. Neither of these body-shape discrepancies is significantly related to overall body esteem, the evaluative measure of body image, demonstrating that body shape dissatisfaction is independent of evaluative body dissatisfaction. Next, we assess the impact of exposure condition on girls' body image. Two comparisons between the three image exposure conditions are of central interest: first, the effects of exposure to Barbie dolls compared to the other images, and, second, exposure to Emme dolls compared to neutral stimuli that contain no information about bodies at all. Averaging across the three body image measures, girls' body dissatisfaction is significantly higher after Barbie doll images than after other images, but there is no difference between exposure to Emme doll and the control. These findings provide support for the hypothesis that exposure to Barbie dolls causes an increase in girls' body dissatisfaction, and that this negative effect is specific to thin dolls, and not observed after exposure to dolls with a body size that resembles the average woman.

Furthermore, the detrimental Barbie-doll effect shows age-related differences, as expected. In order to examine year-group differences in more detail, and to assess exposure effects on specific aspects of body image, we carried out multi-sample structural equation modelling (EQS 6.1; Bentler, 1995), with two exposure contrasts—Barbie vs. other, and Emme vs. control—as predictors of body esteem, actual–ideal body-size discrepancy, and actual–adult-ideal body-size discrepancy. The resulting model has excellent fit, and the findings are shown in Figure 8.3, separate by girls' year group.

For the youngest girls, aged 5½–6½ years, the two main findings are that Barbie-doll exposure significantly depresses overall body esteem, and increases discrepancies between girls' actual and ideal body size, such that they desire more extreme thinness after seeing Barbie-doll images than after seeing other images. Discrepancies between actual and adult ideal body size are unaffected. Emme-doll images have no significant impact on any body image measure, including actual–adult ideal body-size discrepancy.

The pattern of findings is similar for girls who are 6½–7½ years old, but it is amplified. The negative effects of Barbie-doll images are stronger, both in terms of decreasing body esteem, and increasing actual–ideal body-size dissatisfaction in the direction of girls wanting to be thinner. In addition, there is now also a significant effect of Barbie exposure on girls' discrepancies between their actual body size and their ideal body size as an adult woman, such that girls desire more extreme thinness when grown up. As for the younger girls, Emme-doll images have no impact, including actual–adult body-size dissatisfaction. Thus, the detrimental impact of Barbie-doll images on girls' body image is more pronounced at this age, and also includes their aspirations for an adult woman's body size.

For the oldest girls, aged 7½–8½ years, findings are radically different. Barbie-doll images no longer have any direct negative effect on girls' body image—all paths to body dissatisfaction outcomes are non-significant. The only significant finding for these girls is a negative effect of Emme-doll images, which increase the discrepancy between actual body size and ideal adult body size, such that girls desire more extreme thinness when grown up after seeing the full-bodied Emme dolls.

In summary, the main findings of this experiment are twofold. First, they show that very young girls experience heightened body dissatisfaction after exposure to Barbie-doll images, but not after exposure to Emme dolls (or neutral control images). This demonstrates that it is not body-related information conveyed by dolls *per se* that has a direct impact on young girls' body image, but specifically by dolls that represent a distortedly thin body ideal like Barbie. These ultra-thin images not only lower young girls' body esteem but also decrease their satisfaction with their actual body size, making them desire a thinner body. This detrimental effect is already evident for girls aged 5½–6½ years, but is more pronounced among 6½–7½-year-olds. Both lowered body esteem and wanting a thinner body are indicators of body dissatisfaction, which can lead to serious consequences (see Chapters 6 and 9). Previous research on girls' body dissatisfaction has focused on adolescents or pre-adolescent children from age 8 onwards, but this study highlights the need to begin earlier in the quest for body image disturbance, the onset of which appears to be at a younger age than previously thought.

Second, Barbie-doll images do not result in negative effects on the body

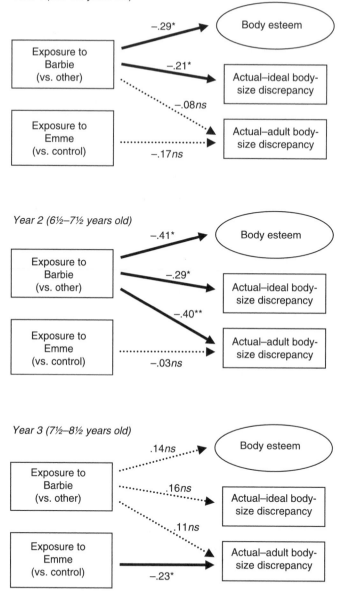

Figure 8.3 Structural equation models of exposure to different dolls on girls' body esteem and desired body shape, separated by year group. * *p* < .05; ** *p* < .01 (both one-tailed); *ns*, not significant. (*Note.* Reproduced from Dittmar, Halliwell, & Ive (2006), Does Barbie make girls want to be thin? The effect of experimental exposure to images of dolls on the body image of 5–8-year-old girls, *Developmental Psychology, 42*, p. 289 with kind permission of the American Psychological Association © 2006.)

image of the oldest group of girls, aged 7½–8½ years. It seems likely that developmental changes in self-processes, where responses to sociocultural stimuli become more reflexive due to the greater involvement of children's self-concept, can help explain this finding. It seems likely that there is a sensitive phase when girls use Barbie dolls as aspirational role models, which may end around 7–8 years of age because girls have internalised the thin beauty ideal by then, and their desire to be thinner is more a reflection of that internalised standard than a direct response to environmental stimuli. If this account is accurate, then concern about Barbie as a powerful socialisation agent of an unhealthy, ultra-thin, and unachievable body ideal cannot be dismissed easily on the grounds that her influence may be short-lived—"it's something they grow out of" (model Cindy Jackson, CBS News, 2004). Although possibly true at a surface level, the damage has already been done if it is the case that thin dolls like Barbie are a highly significant, if not the only, vehicle through which very young girls internalise an unhealthily thin ideal. The unanticipated finding that older girls report a greater desire to be thin when adults after exposure to Emme dolls (compared to neutral control images) deserves comment, because this suggests that more realistically sized dolls may not prevent body dissatisfaction in girls aged over 7 years, but can have the undesirable, opposite effect of increasing it. For these older girls, if they have already internalised the thinness ideal, the depiction of a full body could represent a possible, but feared, future self (Markus & Nurius, 1986; Ogilvie, 1987; Ogilvie & Clark, 1992). This interpretation, that thinness-internalised girls see full-bodied Emme as implying a threat that they, too, may end up *not* thin when they are older, is supported by the finding that the negative impact of exposure to Emme dolls manifested itself only in an increased desire to have a thinner *adult* body, not a thinner body right now. This study has a range of implications which are addressed in the conclusion to this chapter.

MATERIALISM AND PEER RELATIONS IN CHILDREN

The research described above shows how certain consumer goods can communicate messages about bodily ideals that form part of young children's socialisation experience. These messages clearly have significant potential to influence children's belief and value systems, and hence their identity. However, it is also true that there are individual differences in the extent to which people internalise and act on the body-image and materialistic values emphasised in consumer culture. Our research on materialism in children confirms not only that such individual differences can be measured from a young age, but also that those differences are systematically related to children's peer experiences.

Materialism in children

Just a small number of studies in recent years have focused on materialism during childhood. However, this research does make it clear that we can find meaningful differences between children in the endorsement of materialistic values. In one important investigation, Goldberg et al. (2003) developed— and provided extensive validation for—a Youth Materialism Scale (YMS) with a sample of 9- to 14-year-olds. Their original item pool was picked from two widely used adult materialism scales (Belk, 1985; Richins & Dawson, 1992), which were then reworded for children. Their 10-item YMS scale reflects a single factor, but covers a range of issues identified as important in adult research: acquisition of material goods as a life goal, an indicator of success, and a main route to happiness (see Chapter 4). It has good psychometric properties and was validated in preliminary work by comparing those scoring in the top and bottom quartiles of the YMS. Materialistic youths were found to be less satisfied with what they currently owned, expected their parents to spend more on their birthday and Christmas presents, allocated a greater amount of windfall money to themselves rather than to altruistic pursuits, and attached greater value to a future job that would earn lots of money. Furthermore, in Goldberg et al.'s main study of 9- to 14-year-olds, children high on materialism: had more interest in new products; shopped more frequently; saved less; watched more, and were more influenced by, advertising, particularly when presented by celebrity endorsers; liked school less; and reported somewhat poorer grades. Thus, the materialistic youths appeared more preoccupied with consumer behaviours and were less committed to schooling.

Other research has also confirmed inverse links between materialism and psychological well-being among 11- to 18-year-olds, with evidence that materialism predicted greater anxiety, lower happiness, and poorer self-esteem (Kasser, 2005). This evidence is complemented by research connecting high levels of materialism with unhealthy psychological and behavioural profiles in adolescence, such as more behavioural problems, worse psycho-social adjustment, and more frequent health-risk behaviours (Kasser & Ryan, 1993; Williams, Cox, Hedberg, & Deci, 2000). Finally, as presented in Chapter 5, a sample of 16- to 18-year-olds in the UK was found to have much stronger materialistic values than adults, and materialistic values were by far the strongest predictor of tendencies toward compulsive buying, which entails overspending and being preoccupied with shopping (Dittmar, 2005a). Over 40% of these adolescents were identified as showing buying attitudes and behaviours that have pathological components. Therefore, the task of identifying the developmental factors responsible for individual differences in materialism must be regarded as highly important.

Two main pathways into materialistic value internalisation have been proposed: the experience of insecurity, and the exposure to social models that encourage materialistic values (Kasser et al., 2004). In general, studies of the origins of values have tended to focus on socialisation patterns within the family (Kilby, 1993), and the little research on materialistic values is no exception. Goldberg et al. (2003) demonstrate that more materialistic youths tend to have more materialistic parents, which suggests a family value transmission route. Furthermore, some investigations conclude that young adults with strong materialistic values are more likely to have experienced "broken" family homes (Rindfleisch et al., 1997), where materialism as a route to happiness is emphasised (Roberts et al., 2003), or, more generally, "maternal and social environments that were less supportive of their growth, self-expression, and intrinsic needs" (Kasser, Ryan, Zax, & Sameroff, 1995, p. 912). However, these researchers also acknowledge that peer groups constitute an important socialisation environment that deserves systematic study. Indeed, the research described below shows that peers may be important with respect to both pathways into materialism: their rejection can contribute to feelings of insecurity, and they can act as prominent social models who influence the endorsement of materialistic values.

Peer relations and materialism in children

Prior to our own research, only one exploratory study considered children's materialistic values with respect to peer groups. Children reported the extent to which they wished to enhance their image among their peers, were willing to conform to their peers' expectations, and tended to learn from them or seek information, all with particular reference to the acquisition and use of goods and brands (Achenreiner, 1997). A positive and significant correlation emerged between materialistic values and susceptibility to peer-group influence, but this study does not assess children's actual peer relations—that is, their true status or popularity among their peers—or their perceptions of peer group pressures.

As discussed earlier, the developmental increase in concerns about social comparison, self-presentation, and peer-group acceptance means that children's peer relations, and especially their perceptions of pressure to conform to peer group norms, may well play a critical role in the socialisation of materialistic values. However, peer pressure has so far typically been studied in the context of negative outcomes for adolescents (e.g. substance abuse or misconduct; see Urberg, 1999), and its emergence as part of the increasingly important peer group processes in primary school has received little attention to date.

In our own recent work (Banerjee & Dittmar, in press), we suggest that perceptions of peer-group pressure, and consequent adoption of materialistic values, are likely to be associated with higher levels of peer rejection. We know already that there are substantial individual differences among children in the extent to which they are accepted by their peers. These differences are usually assessed using sociometric procedures that require all children in a class to nominate peers with whom they most and least like to play (e.g. Coie

& Dodge, 1983, 1988; Newcomb, Bukowski, & Pattee, 1993). Peer rejection is indicated by receiving high numbers of negative nominations, which has been linked with a negative profile of high aggression and/or social withdrawal, and low sociability and poor leadership skills (see Newcomb et al., 1993, and Gifford-Smith & Brownell, 2003, for reviews). Moreover, peer rejection appears to be relatively stable over time (Coie & Dodge, 1983).

We propose that rejected children are especially at risk for heightened perceptions of peer-group pressure, which in turn may lead to greater endorsement of materialistic values. First, we expect peer-group pressures to be perceived especially strongly by rejected children, since they are likely to have heightened concerns about peer-group acceptance. Indeed, evidence from research on social anxiety indicates that children rejected by their peers are more fearful of negative evaluation than children who are popular or have an average peer status (La Greca & Stone, 1993). The link between peer rejection and perceived peer pressure is further supported by observations that deviation from group norms results in negative evaluation by one's peers (see Abrams, Rutland, & Cameron, 2003; Schachter, 1951). Second, we predict that higher perceptions of peer-group pressure are associated with increased materialism. If material goods and attributes do become the focus of peer-group activities and interests—which, of course, is a central goal of toy and clothing manufacturers' marketing strategies (Lindstrom, 2004; Linn, 2004; Schor, 2004)—then perceptions of peer-group pressure should have significant consequences for the adoption of materialistic values. We investigate these hypotheses with children in the last three or four years of primary school, a time when peer-group acceptance is a dominant social goal (Parker & Gottman, 1989).

A new measure of perceived peer culture pressure

We began our research on this topic by developing a new questionnaire to measure 7- to 11-year-old children's perceptions of peer-group pressure, since no such instrument existed for this age group. This work is informed in part by Brown, Clasen, and Eicher's (1986) Peer Pressure Inventory, which assesses adolescents' perceptions of how much they are encouraged by their friends to do, or not do, certain activities, with respect to five domains: peer involvement, misconduct, conformity to peer norms, school involvement, and family involvement. Our new scale began with a pool of age-appropriate items relating to all of these topic areas, but this pool was then refined and expanded through consultation with academic colleagues as well as practising educational psychologists. In particular, we included a wide-ranging set of items concerned with behavioural, attitudinal, and material peer-group norms, such as clothing and activity choices or preferences relating to television, films, and music. Given existing evidence indicating that children in this age range vary in their appreciation of social evaluation concerns (Banerjee,

2002a), we anticipate that they also vary in their perceptions of pressure to conform to aspects of this "peer culture".

In our first study, 240 children aged 7 to 11 years answered a series of 31 questions about perceived peer pressure to have or display a certain characteristic by circling "Never", "Sometimes", "Often", or "Always". The question stem was always "Do other children make you feel that you should . . ." (e.g. "Do other children make you feel that you should dress in certain clothes?"). Thus, the scale is designed to measure children's subjective feelings of pressure from peers. Interestingly, our factor analysis shows that almost all the items load neatly onto either a factor we labelled *Peer Culture*, involving general behavioural norms, material characteristics, low family involvement, low academic involvement, and misconduct, or a *Positive Behaviours* factor, involving high family involvement, high academic involvement, and good conduct. Thus, rather than having factors that reflect different content domains, we have a separation of attributes and characteristics that would be prized by adults from those that are specifically related to peer culture, which presumably are those that are valued by the children themselves.

With attention to both conceptual content and factor loading strength, we proceeded to refine our scale. We selected 11 *Peer Culture* items, which covered key domains of materialistic norms (music, clothes, food, looking older), socialising patterns (having boyfriend/girlfriend, playing with certain others, going to certain parties, talking or behaving in certain ways), and negative behaviour patterns (ignoring parents, damaging things, being tough and getting into fights). We also chose six items regarding positive, adult-valued behaviours. These two scales were found to have good internal consistency, and are not significantly correlated with each other. Interestingly, further analysis shows that the *Peer Culture* scores remain similar across the 7- to 11-year age range, whereas pressure to engage in the adult-valued behaviours (e.g. hard work, good conduct) tends to decrease with age.

This preliminary study suggests that material characteristics form an important and integral dimension of a *Peer Culture*; in fact, pressure to dress in certain clothes was the highest loading item for this factor. This finding adds credence to our hypothesis that peer culture may play a key role in the emergence of materialistic values in particular children. In contrast, perceptions of pressure from peers regarding items that adults typically regard positively (academic diligence, good conduct, etc.) load neatly onto an entirely separate factor, supporting Berndt's (1979) assertion that there is "an isolation of parents from peers that is consistent with the idea of two worlds, one world for family and one world for peers" (p. 615).

In a subsequent validation study, 131 children aged 8–11 years completed our peer-pressure scale, and we also asked them questions about hypothetical stories where a same-sex protagonist either resisted or conformed to peer-group suggestions about material goods, such as pressure to get a particular new and popular brand of trainers. This study not only replicates the factor structure of our peer-pressure scale but also shows that children who perceive greater *Peer Culture* pressure expect more negative social outcomes for the story protagonists who resist material peer culture suggestions. In other words, a child who feels relatively greater pressure to fit in with a *Peer Culture* believes more strongly that other children would not want to be friends with the central story character after s/he resists peer-group pressure to get the new popular trainers by saying "No, I like the ones I have". Thus, our preliminary work gives us good reason to expect that children who perceive high levels of *Peer Culture* pressure could turn to material goods and values as a key defensive response when threatened by peer rejection.

Survey with children on rejection, peer pressure, and materialism

Our next study directly investigates the hypothesis that perceived *Peer Culture* pressure predicts individual differences in materialism. Moreover, we anticipate that children who are high on peer rejection would be especially vulnerable to perceptions of peer-group pressure. Such a link would be consistent with adolescent work showing that peer pressure and conformity to peers are strongly associated with the drive to become more popular (Santor, Messervey, & Kusumakar, 2000). Our study involved administering our peer-pressure questionnaire and Goldberg et al.'s (2003) materialism scale to 171 children aged 8–11 years, as well as collecting sociometric nominations from each child about his or her most- and least-liked classmates.

We once again replicate the factor structure of the peer-pressure scale, showing that pressure to conform to material norms does indeed form part of a wide *Peer Culture* dimension. In our main analysis, we use structural equation modelling to assess the fit of the theoretical model specified earlier, whereby the association between peer rejection and materialism is mediated by *Peer Culture* peer pressure. Figure 8.4 shows the resulting model, which has very good fit (controlling for gender and school socio-economic status). Our analysis confirms that peer rejection predicts greater perceptions of *Peer Culture* pressure, which in turn predicts greater materialism, but also shows a direct path from peer rejection to materialism.

To summarise, children with higher levels of peer rejection perceive greater peer pressure regarding *Peer Culture* characteristics, and such perceptions of peer pressure are, in turn, associated with stronger endorsement of materialistic values. In this analysis, we controlled for gender and for school effects related to socio-economic status—whereby materialism scores are higher in the low-SES schools, consistent with findings for British adolescents (Dittmar & Pepper, 1994). Thus, the investigation suggests that children experiencing higher levels of peer rejection, partly because of their increased perceptions of pressures regarding peer culture norms in order to "fit in", are likely to be more vulnerable to the permeation of materialistic values into childhood peer culture.

The fact that an additional direct path from rejection to materialism was significant suggests that related factors other than perceptions of *Peer*

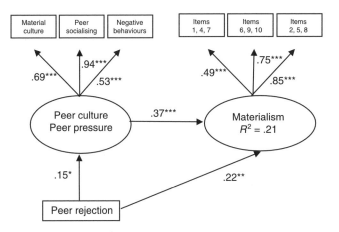

Figure 8.4 Structural equation model of relationships between peer rejection, peer culture, peer pressure, and materialism in 7- to 11-year-old children. $*p = .05; **p < .01; ***p \leq .001$.

Culture pressure could also contribute to materialism. For example, negative family patterns, such as low warmth, rejection, and harsh discipline have been implicated in peer difficulties and antisocial behaviour (e.g. see Dodge & Pettit, 2003; Finnegan, Hodges, & Perry, 1998), and these could also independently contribute to materialism (e.g. Kasser et al., 1995; Rindfleisch et al., 1997; Roberts et al., 2003). Nonetheless, the results confirm that perceived pressure to conform to the peer culture does indeed, as hypothesised, carry significant weight in mediating the relationship between peer rejection and materialism.

Social motives: "Children like you more if you have 'cool' things"

A critical remaining question concerns the mechanism by which perceived *Peer Culture* pressure may relate to materialism. We suggest that if peer rejection is indeed linked to greater perceptions of peer-group pressure, as we found in the study described above, this should offer strong social motives for materialism: having the right games, clothes, and other material goods would be seen as important, or even necessary, for social acceptance. The role played by such social motives in childhood materialism has not been addressed in research to date, but work with adults suggests that social motives could play a critical role in generating the negative correlates of materialism (see Chapter 4). Srivastava et al. (2001), for example, demonstrate that the connection between perceived importance of money and low subjective well-being is explained by negative motives related to social comparison, power, and status. In a similar way, Christopher and Schlenker (2004) show that fear of negative evaluation can explain the relationship between materialism and negative affect. In the developmental context, it seems likely that children who are rejected by their peers and perceive greater peer pressure to conform to group norms will be especially likely to endorse such negative social motives for material consumption. This proposition is supported by the validation study discussed earlier whereby children high on *Peer Culture* pressure predicted more negative social outcomes for story protagonists who resisted peer-group suggestions regarding popular material products.

In our most recent study, we asked children explicitly about their endorsement of social motives for materialism. We gave 183 children aged 8–11 years our *Peer Culture* pressure scale and the materialism scale, and collected sociometric nominations. In addition, children responded to four statements regarding social motives for materialism, such as "If you haven't got the right things/clothes, other children laugh at you" or "Children like you more if you have 'cool' things". Once again, we find that peer rejection predicts higher levels of perceived *Peer Culture* pressure, and that *Peer Culture* pressure in turn predicts higher materialism. However, we also find that agreement with the items about social motives for materialism is strongly associated with both *Peer Culture* pressure and materialism. In our main structural equation analysis, we are able to demonstrate that endorsement of social motives does indeed mediate the effect of *Peer Culture* pressure on materialism. Figure 8.5 shows a conceptually coherent sequence from peer rejection, to perceived *Peer Culture* pressure, to social motives for materialism, and finally to materialism itself.

Thus, extending the results of our earlier studies, we find that children who perceive higher levels of pressure to conform to peer culture tend to subscribe to the view that having or not having certain material goods will have significant impacts on the quality of peer interactions and relationships, and this view seems to make it more likely that they endorse materialistic values. Importantly, these psychological processes are likely to be more significant

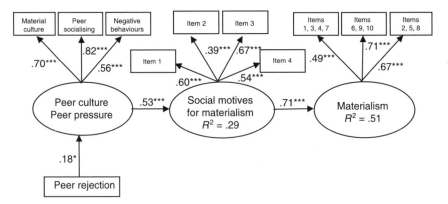

Figure 8.5 Structural equation model of relationships between peer rejection, peer culture, peer pressure, social motives, and materialism in children. *$p < .05$; **$p < .01$; ***$p \le .001$.

for materialism than the fact of peer rejection itself; in this study, peer rejection is related to materialism only insofar as it predicts greater perceived peer pressure and consequent social motives for materialism.

CONCLUSIONS AND FUTURE RESEARCH

These two research programmes, on body ideals and materialistic values, are related through the overarching theme of children's responses to, and internalisation of, consumer culture ideals. However, the specifics of the studies reported in this chapter are sufficiently different in terms of research questions addressed and implications, so that it makes sense to discuss them separately, starting with the doll-exposure study, and then considering children's materialism in the context of peer relations.

Children's body image

The findings of our exposure experiment suggest that Barbie dolls' ultra-thin body proportions provide an aspirational role model for very young girls that *causes* body dissatisfaction. Girls today are swamped by ultra-thin ideals, not only in the form of dolls but also in comics, cartoons, television, and advertising, along with all the associated merchandising, but Barbie appears to occupy a strong and special role in girls' developing body image (Kuther & MacDonald, 2004), so that exposure to images of Barbie doll can lead to detrimental effects, at least when girls are young enough to identify with Barbie doll. The finding that older girls no longer show this negative effect does not imply that they have outgrown the influence of the thin socio-cultural ideal. Rather, it seems likely that they move on from Barbie dolls to other, age-appropriate, socio-cultural sources of ideal body information, such as magazines or computer games. For example, in the immensely successful Tomb Raider series played by older children, Lara Croft's body proportions are similar to Barbie's.

In terms of potential limitations, it may be argued that the experiment's findings are generalisable only to those sociocultural contexts that are characterised by an extreme thinness ideal and that market dolls that embody this ideal to very young girls. However, given the increasing globalisation of consumption, as well as the thinness ideal in the mass media, the present findings may well generalise beyond Northern America and Europe. An interesting example is Fiji, a culture with a traditionally full-bodied female beauty ideal until the arrival of Western mass media; the *New York Times* described the introduction of American TV in Fiji as leading to elevated body image concerns with thinness: "TV trims Fiji girls' body image" (http://www.library.uchc.edu/bhn/cite/nyt/1731tele.html). More generally, the extent to which the findings of this book are likely to apply cross-culturally is discussed in Chapter 9.

Furthermore, like most other experimental exposure studies in this area, the present research investigated the effects of short-term exposure on body image. However, if negative effects can be demonstrated after a single exposure to images of thin dolls, repeated exposure may well be more damaging. However, the age-related differences in exposure effects found are consistent with a developmental model, in which there is a sensitive period for girls' identification with Barbie doll and internalisation of the thin ideal. These issues can be addressed fruitfully in future research that is longitudinal and which examines girls' thin-ideal internalisation directly. More generally, longitudinal research on the impact of dolls and toys as consumer culture sources of body ideals in both girls and boys would help to advance our understanding of how body image develops as part of children's identity and to inform early interventions that can help protect children's body image.

Children's materialism

With respect to the internalisation of materialistic values, the findings from our research programme so far provide clear empirical support for the widespread assumption that childhood peer processes are intimately linked with materialism (e.g. Schor, 2004). Nonetheless, many tasks for future research remain. Not least is the question of what impact high levels of materialism in childhood may have for behaviour, emotion, and long-term psychological outcomes. First, the translation of materialistic values into consumer behaviour needs attention: Do children with greater endorsement of material values in fact spend—or influence their parents to spend—more, or at least differently? Goldberg et al.'s (2003) self-report data certainly indicate that more materialistic youths shop more frequently and save less, and the Youth Materialism Scale itself includes items with clear implications for consumer behaviour. Evidence from work with adults indicates that high materialism is linked with patterns of compulsive buying and over-spending, with significant financial and psychological consequences (see Chapter 5). Based on the present research, we might expect that children with negative peer relations, who perceive greater pressure to conform to a material peer culture, may be particularly vulnerable to developmental trajectories involving this kind of problematic consumer behaviour.

More generally, the role of materialistic values in connecting peer antecedents with cognitive and emotional outcomes needs research attention. It seems highly doubtful that greater materialism would help to advance the cause of rejected children who are seeking more social acceptance. Most evidence points to a profile of prosocial and socially competent behaviours as predictive of positive peer status (Gifford-Smith & Brownell, 2003; Newcomb et al., 1993). These kinds of characteristic clearly relate more closely to the intrinsic values of affiliation and self-development highlighted by Kasser and Ryan (1993), whereas an extended focus on extrinsic, materialistic goals could plausibly inhibit positive social relations and thereby lead to the maladaptive emotional outcomes already known to be connected with adolescent and adult materialism (e.g. Burroughs & Rindfleisch, 2002; Kasser & Ryan, 1993). Thus, we would expect negative outcomes for highly materialistic children. To date, no studies have examined the consequences of individual differences in materialism during childhood, and this emphasises the need for longitudinal research that identifies the social antecedents and the emotional and behavioural consequences of materialism in childhood.

The impact of material and bodily ideals central to consumer culture on children's, adolescents' and adults' identities and well-being is evaluated further in the next chapter, which also discusses implications for intervention at both the social and the individual level.

9   What is the price of consumer culture? Consequences, implications, and the cage within

Helga Dittmar

Synopsis

Instead of bringing greater freedom, individuality, and happiness to people, consumer culture can exert a powerful psychological toll, curtailing a positive sense of who we are, our welfare, and even our health. This chapter evaluates the "price" of consumer culture in three ways:

- The rigorous evidence throughout the book documents that the search for "body perfect" and material "good life" consumer culture ideals has a negative impact on vulnerable children, adolescents, and adults.
- Intervention is necessary to prevent or reverse the internalisation of unrealistic and unhealthy bodily and material ideals, at the level of individual and social change.
- Consumer culture is a "cage within" because its unrealistic ideals lead many people to experience identity deficits and negative emotions, which they then seek to remedy through the futile and damaging pursuit of a better identity through consumption.

Consumer culture perpetuates a number of myths, with the idealised images of the "body perfect" and the material "good life" as two central aspects. As we have seen throughout the book, the impact of these idealised images on children's, teenagers', and adults' identity and well-being is often negative. These research findings therefore fly in the face of the much-heralded benefits of consumer culture, whereby individuals are supposedly empowered and liberated through greater spending power, greater choice of consumer goods, and greater uniqueness and self-expression through consumption. Taking stock of my research programme, I argue in this concluding chapter that consumer culture also means entrapment, and possibly entrapment of the worst kind, because people are often unaware of its pervasive influence. They do not realise that it is virtually impossible to escape from internalising aspects of its warped parameters as aspects of their own identity. In short, consumer culture can become a "cage within": Its bars are invisible and its power pernicious, precisely because its myths appear to "well up and rise out of our [own] depths, our [own] inner instincts, desires, or aspirations" (Rose, 1996, p. 187). While we believe we are expressing our selves, we are, in fact, developing, monitoring, and moulding our identities with respect to the unrealistic images of consumer culture. A similar conclusion is expressed by Kilbourne:

> Much of advertising's power comes from this belief that it does not affect us. As Joseph Goebbels said "This is the secret of propaganda: those who are to be persuaded by it should be completely immersed in the ideas of the propaganda, without ever noticing that they are being immersed in it". Because we think advertising is trivial, we are less on guard, less critical, than be might otherwise be. While we are laughing, sometimes sneering, the commercial does its work . . . [C]onsumer culture encourages us not only to buy more, but to seek our identity and fulfillment through what we buy, to express our individuality through our "choices" of products . . . On this deeper level, rampant commercialism undermines our physical and psychological health, our environment and our civic life, and creates a toxic society.
>
> (2006, pp. 10–12)

Thus, consumer culture as a "cage within" entails a form of alienation (in a broad, rather than a Marxist, sense), from ourselves and our intrinsic psychological needs. Of course, not everybody is affected by consumer culture to the same extent, so individual differences in vulnerability need to be taken into account. However, given the increasing globalisation of consumer culture, this may be more a matter of asking how people can achieve some measure of resisting the "cage within". What factors can be identified that help individuals resist its influence? These issues are addressed in the final section of this chapter.

THE EVIDENCE: CONSEQUENCES OF CONSUMER CULTURE

Before addressing possible interventions, and questions of vulnerability and of generalisability to other cultures, the main research findings presented throughout the book are summarised briefly to offer an integrated, evidence-based picture of the effects that idealised images in consumer culture have on how individuals see themselves, what they aspire to, and how well they are. Running through the research in the book in order, it is clear that there is a close link between treasured personal possessions and identity that has to be seen in a non-evaluative light: it is neither good nor bad. Buying motives, too, are not easily classifiable as benign or detrimental, although there is some hint that emotional and identity-related concerns can precipitate excessive spending. This foreshadows findings that materialism is often bad for well-being, particularly a new type of materialistic value endorsement that is more specific than the older notion of materialism as a focus on needs provision and material comfort (as understood, for instance, by Inglehart, 2006). Yet, consumer culture imagery is not only concerned with the "good life" of affluence, but at the same time with the "body perfect". Striving for, and internalising, the values of an increasingly unattainable and unhealthy ideal appearance leads to body dissatisfaction, traditionally mainly in girls and women, but now also increasingly in men. Such pursuits are likely to become even more pathological in the future, given that the Department of Health reports that the actual body sizes of an increasing percentage of adults and children in the UK are becoming overweight and obese (Zaninotto, Wardle, Stamatakis, Mindell, & Head, 2006). At the core of body dissatisfaction is a discrepancy between a person's perceived body and their ideal body, which leads to negative thought and emotions, bound to rise further as a growing number of individuals have increasingly larger bodies. Thinking ideal and feeling bad means putting yourself at risk, because body dissatisfaction is associated with a variety of negative outcomes, including negative self-perception, depressed mood, and diverse unhealthy body-shaping behaviours (e.g. Cash & Pruzinsky, 2002; Grogan, 1999; Thompson et al., 1999).

Links between personal possessions, buying motives, and identity

The close association between material possessions and identity development through the symbolic meanings of objects is not negative in and of itself. The findings in Chapter 2 demonstrate that treasured personal possessions often play an important, and positive, role for identity maintenance and continuity, even if the specifics vary by gender and culture. Favourite material possessions can help individuals to sustain a sense of who they are, particularly during periods of change or crisis. As symbolic markers of personal history, they provide a life record of who, and where, people have been over time, aiding their sense of inner stability and self-continuity. However, material objects serve a diverse array of functions for people. We saw in Chapter 3 that, when people buy new consumer goods, psychological buying motives are at least as important as the functional and economic concerns with product quality and good value for money that are the supposed hallmarks of the "rational" consumer. For certain people, and in certain contexts, psychological buying motives take over. There was an early indication in Chapter 3 that two motives in particular make it likely that individuals spend more money than they intend or, possibly, can afford. These are captured in the slogans of "retail therapy" and "I shop, therefore I am", which refer to when people buy goods for emotional reasons, in order to repair or enhance their mood and sense of happiness, or for identity-related reasons, in order to construct a sense of who they are, and particularly who they would ideally like to be, both in their own eyes and those of other people.

As becomes clear in Chapters 3, 4, and 5, these two sets of motives, emotional and identity-related, are closely intertwined. Individuals do not just want to feel better, they want to feel better about themselves. However, material goods are unlikely to deliver these hoped-for benefits when people seek long-term solutions to identity deficits, insecurity, and unhappiness. Often, goods provide nothing more than a momentary high, where people fantasise about who they would like to be, and where browsing through goods and purchasing seems to offer an avenue for moving closer to that ideal person, which then quickly turns into a dead end. Thus, these beliefs—that the acquisition and ownership of material goods solves problems with identity and happiness—often turn out futile hopes.

When materialistic value endorsement is bad for well-being

Both Chapters 4 and 5 demonstrate that the pursuit of these beliefs has negative consequences for individuals' well-being. The beliefs that material goods and affluence lead to a better and happier self are core components of a materialistic value orientation, which increasingly characterises mass-consumer societies. It is important to draw a clear distinction between a broader conception of materialism and the more specific notion of materialistic value endorsement as highlighted in this book. Materialism is often seen as a strong emphasis on money and material possessions as a life goal, and although this is undoubtedly a central materialistic concern, the research findings reported in Chapter 4 support the proposal that this broad type of materialism is not invariably detrimental to subjective well-being, i.e. people's evaluation of how satisfied they are with their life and how much positive emotions outstrip negative emotions over time. People pursue money and possessions for diverse reasons, and this pursuit is linked with lower subjective well-being only when individuals experience stress and tension, because their materialistic, self-oriented orientation clashes with values that are oriented towards the welfare of others, or when they pursue money and possessions for the "wrong" reasons. "Wrong" in this context means the pursuit of material goods for motives that are unlikely to find fulfilment, and are therefore unrealistic.

Striving for wealth and goods in order to feel happier is linked negatively to well-being, particularly for individuals on lower incomes. The strongest negative association with well-being for everybody, not only in the UK, but also Iceland, was found for the motive of overcoming self-doubt. Thus, material goods seem ill-suited to affect the repair of identity deficits or provide a sense of increased happiness. The pursuit of these money-making motives is likely to detract people from investing their time, energy, and other resources in activities that are more likely to bring fulfilment, and therefore contribute towards psychological and physical health, such as intimate, fulfilling personal relationships or community involvement. Notwithstanding that unrealistic motives are not the same as extrinsic motivation, these findings are consistent with Self-determination Theory in a broad sense, because they imply that strivings unlikely to lead to the fulfilment of intrinsic psychological needs, such as relatedness to others or autonomy, produce ill-health. However, there are also differences between its implications, at least as originally formulated, and the present findings. It is not the pursuit of money and possessions *per se* that is detrimental for well-being, but rather their pursuit for unrealistic, toxic motives.

When Inglehart (2006) talks about post-materialist values, he refers to a move away from concerns with financial security and material needs towards concerns with self-expression, self-actualisation, and happiness. A concern with material provision may be an old form of materialism, characteristic of earlier generations, whereas the concerns of this book are with a new form of materialism that is characterised by beliefs in the importance of identity construction, identity improvement, and happiness, but emphasising that the very route towards achieving these goals is through the avenue of acquiring and consuming material goods. Such concerns have also been identified, and criticised as a form of power, in various social science disciplines, including sociology (e.g. Ritzer, 1995; Rose, 1996). This new form of materialism, characterised by unrealistic beliefs about the psychological benefits of money and material possessions is linked not only to lower subjective well-being, but is also a major factor that makes individuals vulnerable to excessive, dysfunctional consumer behaviours. Materialistic value endorsement emerges as a major predictor of compulsive buying tendencies, both in conventional shops and on the internet, exerting its influence through emotional and identity-related buying motives (see Chapter 5). Worrisome future trends were identified, with younger people more prone to compulsive buying. Moreover, the new materialism seems to play a fundamental role for children as young as 8 years old, who believe that being popular and "cool" is best achieved through having the right material goods. Chapter 8 suggests that consumer culture has an early and profound effect on children's processes of identity development and on their well-being, particularly in the context of peer relations, a potent socialisation environment. Yet, as we have seen throughout the book, the idealised images profiled by consumer culture do not only embody the "good life" in material terms, but also the "body perfect".

Putting yourself at risk: Think "body perfect" and feel bad

A feature in *Observer Woman* (Spencer, 2006), entitled "Thin! How women got devoured by the cult of the skinny" is worth quoting at some length, because it vividly, and caustically, captures the psychological power of the ultra-thin beauty ideal for women:

> She is far too thin. Everybody says so. In those shrunken hot pants and skinny red vest she looked positively ravenous, like an urchin from Oliver Twist – albeit one with this season's Prada handbag and hair extensions.

But just how skinny is Victoria Beckham? . . . We do know that she wears jeans with a miniscule 23-inch waist – the size, apparently, of a seven-year-old child . . . VB is not alone, of course, but merely the leading exponent of a New Look which has come to dominate our lives. Other exemplars include Lindsay Lohan, Mischa Barton, Nicole Richie, Kate Bosworth, Amy Winehouse – women relatively new on the celebrity radar who skitter across the pages of magazines, coat hangers furnished with tennisball boobs and expensive shoes, not a shred of fat to share among them. You might not give a tossed salad how much these bony birds weigh . . . [but] it matters because hyperthin has somehow become today's celebrity standard and, as a result – almost without us noticing – the goalposts have moved for all of us. With every image . . . with every shot, an inch or an ounce is shaved off the notional ideal female form which governs our relationship with our bodies and with the world. Images of Lindsay Lohan's chest bones, desperately reaching out to greet strangers, or Keira Knightley's xylophone of vertebrae, countable at 30 paces, have burned themselves into our consciousness so that uber-thin no longer looks odd. It no longer shocks . . . Looking now at pictures of Linda Evangelista in her supermodel prime, or Elizabeth Hurley in her safety-pin Versace frock, they look – unbelievably – a bit on the heavy side, even though at the time they seemed radiantly slim. To achieve this mental switcheroo, something seismic has happened, enough to make a body mass index of 10 (the BMA recommends something in the region of 22) look nearly normal to our rewired brains. When you rub your eyes, though, and snap yourself out of the reverie, you realise this isn't glamorous. It's cadaverously, dangerously thin.

(p. 26)

The research findings presented in Chapters 6 and 7 provide ample evidence that exposure to the ultra-thin female models typically used in advertising and the mass media is toxic for many women. They think of themselves in terms of having a body that is larger than their desired thin ideal, and this identity deficit or gap makes them feel negative emotions about their body and themselves. Although this negative effect does not occur for all women, it does occur for those who internalise the thin ideal as a personal value system. Moreover, the pursuit of the ultra-thin ideal is likely to lead to unhealthy and extreme body-shaping behaviours. This may be particularly worrisome for adolescent girls, whose self-esteem and body-esteem is especially low (Clay, Vignoles, & Dittmar, 2005), and who are exposed to websites that glamourise anorexic images and behaviours:

In the darker recesses of the internet, where teenagers increasingly reside, Victoria Beckham has become a macabre pin-up among subscribers to the web's many pro-ana websites. Here, anorexics exchange tips on how to starve themselves effectively . . ., together with "thinspirational" images of their favourite celebrities. "I envy her thin legs and chest" writes one Posh fan. "She has beautiful bones sticking out of her chest". Beautiful bones? Hardly, says Dr. Dee Dawson [from a London clinic for eating disorders]. "With a body like that, she'll be osteoporotic very early, she's unlikely to be menstruating, her muscles are being eaten from within – even her heart will have wasted away . . . You can count every single one of her ribs, and then you come to those domes of bosoms that there's no way she could produce herself. If she had the right breasts to go with that frame, she'd have nipples and nothing else!".

(p. 27)

Unfortunately, the influence of consumer culture kicks in way before adolescence. As reported in Chapter 8, girls as young as 5–7 years old want to be thinner than they are, and feel worse about their body and weight, when they are exposed to an age-relevant icon of the ultra-thin ideal: Barbie doll. Parallel effects on boys remain yet to be studied. We also saw throughout Chapters 6, 7, and 8 that alternative, attractive images of female beauty that feature models or dolls with a body size resembling an average, healthy body weight do not lead to body dissatisfaction in girls and women. Moreover, contrary to advertisers' claims that "thinness sells", we could demonstrate across different studies and consumer goods that average-size models do not compromise advertising effectiveness. This important point is discussed further in the next section on implications for responsible advertising.

The final point to make is that appearance, beauty, and the "body perfect" have long been central to the identity of many women and girls, who learn early that they are looked at and evaluated by their appearance. The unhealthy impact of the ultra-thin consumer culture ideal on girls and women has therefore been of concern for some time, but there are recent changes, albeit not desirable ones. The main change seems to be the rise of the muscular consumer culture ideal for boys and men, leading to similar negative exposure effects and psychological identity deficit dynamics as occur for women. Thus, gender differences may well be diminishing, but not in the direction of women turning away from the ultra-thin ideal. Rather, they appear to be in the direction of men, too, coming to be affected by an unrealistic beauty ideal that is likely to encourage unhealthy muscle-gain behaviours, at least in certain groups of men (Halliwell, Dittmar, & Orsborn, in press). Although it is not possible to document a direct causal link between mass-media exposure and eating or other clinical disorders, such as muscle dysmorphia (Cafri et al., 2005), we know that body dissatisfaction is a major risk factor for such disorders. And the often negative influence of exposure to idealised media models on both female and male body image is solidly documented in this book.

In summary, the unachievable and biologically inappropriate nature of the ultra-thin ideal for women especially, but also of muscularity for men, means that the pursuit of the "body perfect" is likely to put both psychological and physical health at risk. One might raise a counter-argument here, and say that striving for thinness or fat-less muscularity surely has to be good in the context of the recent statistics and projections of rising obesity in the UK, US, and other developed countries, making overeating the number one body problem, rather than anorexia or overexercising. The report to the UK Department of Health (Zaninotto et al., 2006) states that, among adults aged over 16 years, well over half weigh too much, 55% of women (33% overweight and 23% obese) and 65% of men (43% overweight and 22% obese). The corresponding percentages among children and adolescents aged 2–15 years are 31% of girls (15% overweight and 16% obese) and 32% of boys (15% overweight and 17% obese). As if these figures were not scary enough, the projections for 2010—if current trends continue unchecked—are a further rise in obesity of 11% for men, 5% for women, 2% for boys and 6% for girls. There are many reasons for this obesity wave (junk food, an eating culture of grazing and snacking, lack of exercise), which cannot be discussed here, but what is pertinent for this chapter is to at least comment on the unrealistic consumer culture body ideals in the context of an increasing number of increasingly fatter people. It was already mentioned that unhealthy eating regimes—whether aimed at weight loss or muscle gain—can flip into binge-eating episodes because individuals cannot keep up the strict constraints of their diets. Thus, paradoxically, striving for a thinner or fitter body may actually contribute towards weight gain or weight cycling (frequent weight fluctuations). On a psychological, rather than physical, level unrealistic media models are likely to make the discrepancies between the ideal body and individuals' actual (increasingly fatter) body even larger, leading to greater body dissatisfaction, and thus greater risk of unhealthy eating or body-shaping behaviours. Thus, the pursuit of the "body perfect" may have even greater costs in an increasingly obese society, where the sheer momentousness of the task may lead yet more people to extreme measures, such as surgery to remove fat, decrease stomach size, or change the shape of body parts (Thompson, 2004).

Yet the research findings in this book also document that some individuals are more vulnerable than others to negative effects from consumer culture ideals. We saw that those people who internalise "body perfect" and material "good life" ideals as personal values are worst affected, but there were also differences between people from different social categories, such as gender or SES background, as well as for people from countries other than Western mass-consumer societies, such as Croatia. These findings raise two important questions: Which identity positions make people more vulnerable? To what extent can we generalise to other cultures? These are addressed later in this chapter, in the section on "Questions of vulnerability and generalisability".

IMPLICATIONS FOR INTERVENTIONS

The main focus in this section is on implications for individual and social change, but it is worth pointing out briefly that there are also implications for various psychological theories. The media exposure effect models examined in Chapter 7 are an important example, because they suggest fruitful future research using a refinement of Self-discrepancy Theory, examining the potential usefulness of studying domain-specific self-discrepancies in the context of self-domains linked to unhealthy behaviours, such as body identity and extreme body-shaping behaviours. Moreover, although speculative at this stage, there could be a domain-matching phenomenon, whereby associations between self-discrepancies and affect are strongest when the specific domain of discrepancies within individuals' self-concept is matched with a corresponding domain of negative affect, as well as behaviour. Another example concerns the framework of Self-determination Theory. This book is in broad agreement with their proposal that pursuits unlikely to fulfil intrinsic psychological needs undermine psychological health and happiness, but offers an innovation, or extension, through its specific focus on identity and identity-related psychological processes involved in producing negative consumer culture effects (Dittmar, in press).

However, the main concern here is with the implications for interventions aimed at improving or, even better preventing, the damage caused through the pursuit of consumer culture ideals. One can think of such applied implications on two levels. At the level of the individual, there are interventions aimed at remedying aspects of identity or well-being that have been negatively affected (through therapy or treatment) or, even better, at preventing such negative effects occurring in the first place (through advice or education). At the social level, the concern is with changing policies and practices that are detrimental for individuals' identity and well-being. This might imply substantive social change.

Interventions aimed at individuals

The findings on compulsive buying (Chapter 5) have implications for consumer advice and treatment. Current treatments focus mainly on debt counselling or on psychopharmacological agents, such as selective serotonin re-uptake inhibitors (SSRIs) like Prozac, which are commonly used as antidepressants. However, it is unclear whether medication is effective; for instance, two randomised control trial studies showed fluvoxamine—an SSRI—to be no more effective than a placebo (Black, Gabel, Hansen, & Schlosser, 2000; Ninan et al., 2000). Treatment approaches that concentrate on aiding clients to develop realistic budget plans and strategies for long-term debt reduction provide vital help, but are unlikely to address clients' concerns with identity sufficiently. From the perspective developed in this book, treatment needs to focus on underlying beliefs and buying motives, in addition to alleviating symptoms, if long-term relief is to be provided. Indeed, recent treatment programmes include a focus on identity seeking and maladaptive beliefs about the psychological benefits of consumer goods (e.g. Benson, 2006), and there is now empirical evidence that cognitive behavioural treatment is effective (Mitchell, Burgard, Faber, Crosby, & de Zwaan, 2006).

With respect to the prevention of compulsive buying tendencies specifically, as well as links between materialistic value endorsement and lowered well-being more generally, the present findings suggest the benefits of guiding individuals toward critical reflection on materialistic values, both in terms of their personal value system and media literacy aimed at critical reflection on advertising messages that emphasise unrealistic psychological benefits from buying new consumer goods. It has to be acknowledged, however, that such attempts to curb a materialistic value orientation are probably a difficult route, because they run counter to the prevailing economic and consumer climate, which is geared toward increasing consumption. In addition, there may even be a tension internal to liberal-democratic styles and rationales of government that contributes towards the continuation of materialistic values.[13] For this reason, critical reflection on materialistic values might stand the best chance of providing a basis for prevention and consumer education when it is encouraged early, such as pre-adolescents being advised in their school curricula about unrealistic expectations of material goods, and about why and how to avoid uncontrolled spending and buying. The early prominence and importance of materialism among children (documented in Chapter 8) emphasises the need for such an intervention as part of personal and social education, ideally before secondary school. We can only wish that the pervasive power of advertising could be cured as easily as suggested by the spoof pill in Figure 9.1.

The other major direction for intervention concerns "body perfect" ideals, where the unrealistic nature of these ideals, as well as related patterns of self-beliefs, could be targeted in order to reduce or prevent the centrality of body size as a source of self-worth, whether thin or muscular. The reason why such interventions are so important is because body dissatisfaction puts individuals at risk of psychiatric illness, including eating disorders. The Chairman of Council of the British Medical Association, Ian Bogle, puts it aptly:

> Eating disorders have one of the highest mortality rates of all psychiatric illnesses, and are an increasing problem of modern Western societies . . . If we can identify risk factors that may trigger eating disorders in vulnerable individuals, then we may be able to reduce the number of young people who develop eating disorders . . . There is a need for more realistic body shapes to be shown on television and in fashion magazines, and to reduce young women's exposure to extremely thin models. We should also provide children and young people with the skills and information to resist media messages of bodily perfection.
>
> (British Medical Association, 2000, pp. 1–2)

Figure 9.1 Front cover of the *New Internationalist*, September 2006. (*Note.* Reproduced with kind permission of the *New Internationalist* © 2006.)

Implications for social and advertising policies are discussed further below, but with respect to intervention strategies targeted at individuals there are several options. First, interventions that question, and possibly lower, internalisation of the thin ideal should help protect girls and women from the potential negative impact of advertising. Indeed, a study that combined experimental exposure to thin media images with two brief interventions found that young women's body image worsened after exposure if they had internalised media ideals (consistent with findings presented in Chapters 6 and 7), but that critical appraisal of thin media images prior to exposure prevented this adverse effect (Yamamiya, Cash, Melnyk, Posavac, & Posavac, 2005). Another study used videos presented by psychologists as interventions, which focused either on the artificiality of media images (use of professional make-up, digital alteration to remove blemishes or increase thinness), or their biological inappropriateness (women's genetically predisposed weight is higher and cannot be influenced by dieting), or a combination of both (Posavac et al., 2001). Studying vulnerable young women, already high on body dissatisfaction, they found that all three interventions prevented negative exposure effects. This worked through decreasing social comparison with thin media models (see Chapter 1), shown by women giving fewer "idealising" responses, expressing the desire to look like or be like media models, and more "discounting" responses, questioning the realism of media images or recognising the conflict these models present with biological realities for women and the health issues that they raise. A meta-analysis (Stice & Shaw, 2004; see Chapter 7) confirms that such programmes are effective in reducing not only thin-ideal internalisation and body dissatisfaction, but also dieting and disordered eating.

Current educational programmes tend to target women and older girls, often during adolescence (e.g. Levine & Piran, 2004), but the findings in Chapter 8, demonstrating a heightened desire to be thinner in girls as young as 5–7 years after "body perfect" exposure, suggest the need for early prevention of thin-ideal internalisation. Interventions using age-appropriate materials should be targeted at young girls, making them aware that the thin beauty ideal is both unattainable and unhealthy, encouraging a more realistic body ideal, and emphasising non-appearance-related sources of self-esteem. Furthermore, interventions designed to increase awareness and critical reflection with respect to unachievable or unhealthy body ideals need to be adapted to the muscular ideal in order to reduce or prevent muscularity-focused body dissatisfaction in young men or, even better, boys.

The need for such interventions may become ever more urgent, given that unrealistic and extreme body ideals of female ultra-thinness and male muscularity are also portrayed in new mass-media channels, increasingly consumed by children and adolescents, such as computer games and music videos. For example, we can demonstrate that music videos, watched most heavily by 12- to 19-year-olds, increase body dissatisfaction in adolescent girls (Bell, Lawton, & Dittmar, 2007). Moreover, these unhealthy body ideals for adolescents, reinforced by multiple mass-media venues, are becoming increasingly discrepant from adolescents' actual body sizes, given that levels of overweight and obesity are hitting an unprecedented high, as discussed already. This implies the need for a more radical approach to intervention, complementing individual change with social change.

Social policy and social change

To counteract unhealthy body ideals, different mass-media models would seem an obvious solution, implying the need for more responsible advertising policies. This idea is not new, given that the BMA's report (2000) concludes that "if young women are to feel that they are valued for their intrinsic qualities and achievements rather than simply their looks, then we clearly need to address the ways in which contemporary Western culture encourages women to develop a preoccupation with body size and body image, and to perceive weight as their greatest health care concern" (p. 43). Although the report focuses mainly on women, it does recognise that "young men also face the pressure to be physically perfect, and are presented with unrealistic images of how they should look, which may precipitate eating disorders or other unhealthy behaviours such as the abuse of steroids" (p. 44). The report's recommendations for changes in the mass media are formulated with respect to women (p. 47), but are easily applicable to men [as indicated in the square brackets added]:

1. Broadcasters (or programme makers) and magazine publishers should adopt a more responsible editorial attitude towards the depiction of extremely thin women [extremely muscular men] as role models, and should portray a more realistic range of body images
2. Producers of TV and printed advertisements should consider more carefully their use of thin women [muscular men] to advertise products, in particular the ITC should review its policy on the use of thin [muscular] models to advertise products other than slimming [muscle-enhancing] aids

These recommendations, that mass-media producers and advertisers change their use of unrealistic and unhealthy media models, and the Independent Television Commission its advertising policy, were discussed with the UK Government at a body image summit held at 10 Downing Street as long ago as 2000. Although the ban, in several European cities, in September 2006, of fashion models who are underweight is a welcome challenge to the "cult of the skinny" (see Chapter 6), no responsible advertising policies about models have been put in place and little has happened by way of changes in advertising strategies. The research reported in Chapter 6 could be crucial here because it adds further fuel to the need and appropriateness of different media and advertising policies by providing the first systematic evidence that average-sized models, as long as they are attractive, do not compromise advertising effectiveness. This raises the question of why unhealthy models continue to be so prominent, but the structure of consumer culture is such that the unreality of these models is best suited to creating the largest identity deficits in the greatest numbers of consumers, which, in turn, is likely to help sales of the myriad products promoted by the promise that they help to increase attractiveness and to move closer to the "body perfect".

A survey of 3200 women in ten countries, sponsored by Dove, shows that the great majority wish the "media did a better job of portraying women of diverse physical attractiveness—age, shape and size (75%)" (Etcoff, Orbach, Scott, & D'Agostino, 2004, p. 43). Women older than 45 years reported that they would like to see women models of different ages, as well as diverse body weights and shapes. For younger women, models with diverse body shapes and weights were most important. Half of all women picked seeing "women of different body weights and shapes" as their top choice when asked about "better ways to depict women in the media". Dove's "Real Beauty" campaign, based on this report and hugely successful commercially, uses ordinary women with healthy body weights as advertising models. This has to be a step in the right direction, even if there is a contradiction between the messages that women are "naturally" beautiful just as they are, yet supposedly are nevertheless in need of a great number and diversity of beauty-enhancing products.

With respect to children, the negative effect of Barbie dolls on young girls highlights the need for dolls that embody a different, larger sociocultural body ideal. Unfortunately, we now have the even more disturbing Bratz dolls, marketed at girls age 6 onwards, which feature not only an unnaturally thin body, but also oversized heads with heavily made-up faces and bee-stung lips. This highlights the need to encourage dolls such as Emme, currently available only as a collector's item, to be mass-marketed to young girls in order to encourage more realistic, healthy body ideals for young girls. Health authorities, educators, and parents who are concerned about the increasingly young age of girls developing body dissatisfaction and disordered eating behaviours may want to question the body ideals relentlessly churned out by toy manufacturers.

CONSUMER CULTURE AS A "CAGE WITHIN"

The myths of the "body perfect" and the material "good life", often detrimental to individuals' identity and well-being, are central to contemporary consumer culture, but it is interesting to note that they are part and parcel of a wider array of myths, which are only just starting to be examined from a psychological perspective. The pursuit of a unique self through consumption and the exponential growth in consumer choice are two pertinent examples, which are discussed briefly before returning to the central concerns of the book.

Myths of consumer culture

As indicated in Chapter 1, uniqueness is an important identity motive (Vignoles et al., 2006), where people strive to be different from others, to stand out from the crowd. Consumers are encouraged to acquire and display material possessions in order to feel differentiated from others, and advertising promotes products and brands in such a way that their perceptions of uniqueness are enhanced. For example, consumer magazines have long featured instructional articles on "how to make your home say 'you'" and "what you can do to develop your personal style" (Kron, 1983, p. 67). Consumers are said to have a need for uniqueness that "is defined as an individual's pursuit of differentness relative to others that is achieved through the acquisition, utilization, and disposition of consumer goods for the purpose of developing and enhancing one's personal and social identity" (Tian et al., 2001, p. 50). Yet, this notion is mythical in at least two ways. First, the great majority of consumer goods are mass-produced and hence identical, although high-street chains limit the number of garments in a particular range precisely to avoid too many people seeing "their" dress or suit on somebody else walking past them in the road; the alternative option of custom-made, and hence unique, goods is available only to the affluent, rather than the ordinary, consumer. Thus, the idea that uniqueness can be achieved through mass-produced and mass-consumed goods is a paradox in and of itself. Second, the assumption that the identity motive for uniqueness is universal has to be questioned. Uniqueness may not be sought by everyone, although it is particularly important for European and American individuals of high SES, on whom the majority of self-concept research has been carried out. Collectivist cultures emphasise a self that is interdependent with others, rather than an independent, unique self (Markus & Kitayama, 1991), and recent evidence suggests that low-SES European Americans engage differently with symbolic and material culture, reflecting different notions of identity (Snibbe & Markus, 2005). College-educated, high-SES participants and their preferred cultural products (such as music CDs) emphasise the expression of uniqueness, control, and power, whereas less educated, low-SES respondents and their preferred products emphasise maintaining integrity, adjusting selves, and resisting influence. These findings are also consistent with the SES differences in the psychological functions of personal possessions reported in Chapter 2. Thus, the mythical nature of uniqueness through consumption is shown up by the fact that mass-produced consumer goods are ill-suited for the pursuit of being different from everybody else, and also because the very existence of this identity motive is culturally specific and historically relative (Baumeister, 1987), differing within mass consumer societies according to socio-economic status.

The choice of consumer goods now available in mass-consumer societies is incredible. Associated with this explosion in choice is another pervasive myth of consumer culture. Greater choice has usually been equated with many positive psychological outcomes (Snibbe & Markus, 2005). Therefore, the overabundance of products and brands has been celebrated as consumer empowerment, although probably more by companies and marketeers than individual consumers. Is the following scene in a café not familiar? Instead of simply ordering a coffee and getting it, there is now a bewildering array of choice, and a multitude of decisions to be made. We are asked: "How would you like your coffee today? Espresso, Americano, Filter, Cappuccino, Latte? Large, medium or small? Take out or drink here? With extra water? Decaffeinated? Fair Trade coffee? Ordinary or soya milk? And would you like to try one of our new coffee flavours—hazelnut, chocolate, or almond?" But is more choice always better? According to Schwartz (2004), the dramatic explosion in choice—from the mundane coffee in our example to the profound challenges of balancing career, family, and individual needs—has paradoxically become a problem instead of a solution. His research documents that too much choice can be detrimental to psychological and emotional well-being for those people who seek to maximise their consumer outcomes, rather than "satisfice", which means getting goods that simply fulfil their purpose adequately (Schwartz, Ward, Monterosso, Lyubomirsky, White, & Lehman, 2002). Thus, maximisers' attempts to find the best paradoxically lead to increased misery rather than to satisfaction. It has also been shown that too many options undermine the efficiency and quality of decision-making (Gigerenzer & Goldstein, 1996). Thus, the supposed paradise of overabundant choice is nothing but another consumer culture myth; instead, more is often less. Even if he intended a different meaning of the phrase, one is forcefully reminded of Orwell's (1949) dystopic society in *1984*, where "freedom is slavery".

Returning to the two consumer culture myths central to this book, if material goods are not likely to provide individuals with good tools for identity deficit repair and increased happiness, as documented here, the question arises: Why do we not abandon these consumer culture myths and stop buying never-ending quantities of consumer goods that do not fulfil our needs for identity and happiness? The reasons are clearly complex, but one concept is worth reviewing here because it offers some explanation for why people continue on the consumption bandwagon and because it helps to prepare the ground for an exploration of consumer culture as a "cage within". McCracken (1990) refers to the concept of *displaced ideal*. Personal ideals, such as happiness or attractiveness, are often removed from daily reality to a different place and time, such as an earlier golden age, a different society, a promising future, or—as highlighted in this book—to "ideal" people, such as celebrities or models. Material goods can serve as bridges to these displaced ideals. Before a person buys new consumer goods, there is the anticipation that they provide access to certain ideal circumstances that, at the time, still exist in the dim distance. For example, expensive "snazzy shades" are not just an ideal pair of sunglasses to wear but come with a whole set of aspirations, assumed relationships, and wished-for circumstances that go with having them: being "cool", popular, and successful; having a high income, a desirable partner, interesting and glamorous friends, a designer home, and an active social life. Once we actually buy such a coveted good, we only acquire a small, anticipatory part of the bridge, a tiny, concretised piece of the identity and way of life we really aspire to. Thus, the larger configuration of the ideal identity and lifestyle remains intact, even if buying the item turns out to be a disappointment. The ideal is not abandoned or judged unrealistic because of our disappointment. Instead, what follows is a successive series of transfers of ideals and hopes to other, increasingly more expensive, sets of goods and objects. Designer sunglasses give way to a super-expensive new outfit, which, in turn, gives way to multiple sets of new clothes, and so consumption goes on.

An appetite for consumption is, of course, considered vital for a thriving economy, and fuelling such an appetite is the purpose of advertising. This suggests that immense profits are to be made from people's misguided search for identity and happiness through consumption. In turn, this makes it highly unlikely that the idealised imagery in consumer culture will change any time soon. After all, if product sales failed to continue to rise, or even started to drop significantly, because a large enough number of people chose simpler, less consumer-oriented lifestyles, corporate interests would be seriously jeopardised. Indeed, the functioning of capitalism itself could be called into question.

Consumer culture as a cage

Consumer culture can become a "cage within". Once people have internalised its material "good life" and "body perfect" ideals as their own personal goals, they end up with a negative identity and negative emotions (because they almost invariably fall far short of these ideals), and with behaviours that damage their well-being, such as overspending, overshopping, or extreme body-shaping (because these ideals are unattainable or unhealthy). In this way, these ideals then function like bars in an internal cage, constantly reinforced by consumer culture, which prevent people from considering and pursuing alternative goals more likely to lead to happiness, fulfilling relationships, and a meaningful life. A brief summary of the psychological processes through which consumer culture ideals have a negative effect on our identity and well-being can be given in three main points (see Chapter 1 for more detail).

First, people have a need to evaluate themselves by comparing themselves to others and, given that the great majority of individuals fall far short of the "body perfect" and material "good life" typically embodied by idealised media models, social comparisons with such models leads many people to negative self-evaluation. However, individuals engage in these detrimental upward comparisons only, or mainly, if the comparison involves characteristics that are psychologically meaningful and important to them.

Second, this psychological significance depends on individuals' underlying value systems. Both the "body perfect" and material "good life" ideals are internalised by individuals, so that they form a personal value system that guides how they construe themselves, how they respond to consumer culture stimuli, and what ideals they pursue. Whether or not individuals, or groups of individuals, are vulnerable to detrimental consumer culture effects depends on the extent to which they have internalised ideal-body values or materialistic values as their own, personal goals.

The third argument, and the most central, concerns identity deficits and identity seeking. When individuals experience discrepancies, or gaps, between how they see themselves (actual identity) and how they would ideally like to be (ideal identity), they experience negative emotions. Thus, for those who have internalised consumer culture ideals, exposure to idealised models makes salient actual–ideal identity deficits, because their bodies and material standing are almost invariably inferior to those portrayed in advertising. Thus, consumer culture highlights identity deficits and contributes to their development in the first place. But it also offers a supposed remedy: consumers need only buy the promoted products to get closer to their ideal identity. Given that people use material symbols to compensate for perceived shortcomings in their identity, they engage in identity seeking through consumption. For instance, people might buy a "glamorous" outfit to feel more glamorous and confident, and this may work for some people, at least in the short-term. However, it is unlikely to provide a long-term solution for those who have chronic identity deficits of feeling unattractive.

Putting these points together, the central thesis of the consumer culture as a "cage within" emerges. Consumer culture is curtailing vulnerable people from within through value internalisation and construction of a negative identity, where people feel far away from their ideal and feel bad about this gap. Yet its pernicious effects go further because of the supposed, but illusory, solutions advertising dangles in front of people to manage and repair identity deficits and negative emotions. If they use consumption to strive for unhealthy and unrealistic material "good life" and "body perfect" ideals, this futile pursuit is likely to increase their identity deficits and negative emotions still further. In short, consumer culture is analysed as a "cage within" because the internalisation of these two ideals as personal value systems cannot but lead to negative identities and negative emotions, which, in turn, people then seek to remedy through consumption. Yet, as we have seen throughout the book, behaviours resulting from these pursuits are often unhealthy and damaging to well-being.

I would just like to state, for the sake of preventing any possibility of misunderstanding, that this book does not, of course, suggest that the acquisition and ownership of material goods should be demonised wholesale. Instead, it identifies a particular constellation of beliefs about the psychological benefits of material goods that, if they are endorsed by individuals as central aspirations and goals, are toxic for identity and well-being. Research that examines whether investing in experiences makes people happier than investing in possessions suggests that " 'the good life' . . . may be better lived by doing things than by having things . . . experiences make people happier because they are more open to positive reinterpretations, are a more meaningful part of one's identity, and contribute more to successful social relationships" (Van Boven & Gilovich, 2003, p. 1193). Both students and a nationally representative sample in the US thought of either a material purchase, defined as spending money with the primary intention of acquiring a material possession, and/or of an experiential purchase, defined as spending money with the primary intention of acquiring a life experience, such as concerts, sports activities, or travel. The overwhelming majority reported that experiential purchases contribute more to their happiness than material purchases, and an experiment confirms that thinking about experiential purchases puts people into a more positive mood than thinking about material purchases. Although there is no direct concern with different motives for pursuing material goods, this research does recognise that the same material good can constitute a mere consumer good or a vehicle for experiences. The implication is that, for instance, an expensive bike could be a material purchase (to obtain a tangible object), but it could also be an experiential purchase (to cycle 3000 miles across Europe for charity).

Similarly, it is feasible that obtaining money could be an overriding, utterly central life goal for a person who is spending most of his or her time and energy on this financial aspiration, but the identity and well-being implications are likely to differ dramatically depending on whether the primary aim is to show-off expensive possessions and boost a low sense of self-worth, or to procure funds to pay for life-saving medical treatment for a child or to alleviate people's suffering after a disaster, whether natural or human induced. Thus, the pursuit of money and goods does not necessarily have to be linked with the toxic motives of identity deficit repair and search for happiness. But when it is, then identity and well-being are in danger.

> Those choices that enable one to find ways of fulfilling one's potential, opening up latent talents, and becoming more autonomous in deciding one's own destiny – those choices can be argued to be empowering, but choices that restrict our capacity to either perceive or to act upon alternatives are disempowering.
>
> (Kavan, 2006, personal communication)

If one thought of consumer culture in terms of a set of scales, with benefits in one scale and drawbacks in the other, then certain identity positions appear to tip the scales more in one direction than the other.

Questions of vulnerability and generalisability

The internalisation of the "body perfect" and material "good life" ideals as personal values is identified here as major factors that make individuals vulnerable to negative consumer culture effects. Yet we find throughout this book that, regardless of individual differences, certain groups of people in mass-consumer societies are more adversely affected than others. In addition to this issue of vulnerability *within* mass-consumer societies, the question also arises to what extent the psychological processes identified in this book generalise *beyond* the well-developed mass-consumer cultures of Anglo-American and Western societies. These two issues are addressed in turn.

Chapter 1 emphasises multiple identities, and this book shows that identity construction through material goods and the pursuit of consumer culture ideals—for good or for ill—differs systematically, depending on how it intersects with other identity dimensions or social categories, such as gender, income level, or socio-economic background. The book is not intended to offer a systematic analysis of the workings of the social processes that give rise to these identity interconnections and intersections beyond the research presented, but one point that can be drawn out is that some of these appear to make a positive or a negative impact of consumer culture on identity more likely. Thus, female gender on the one hand, and low income and socio-economic background on the other emerge as identity "places" where the pursuit of the good life and the body perfect appear to give rise to particularly toxic impacts on identity, with lowered well-being as the likely consequence.

We saw that women endorse emotional buying motives more strongly than men, at least for buying in conventional shops and stores, which appear linked to the propensity to overspend, and that middle-aged, if not younger, women report stronger compulsive buying tendencies. However, I want to emphasise that these gender differences should not be misunderstood as an essentialist account of differences between male and female consumers. Rather, we are proposing that buying is likely to remain gendered only as long as women and men continue to internalise sociocultural norms and socially shared representations that frame shopping and buying as differentially linked to women's and men's social, personal, and gender identities. Such an interpretation is consistent with reports of no gender differences in compulsive buying in the recent large-scale US survey (Koran et al., 2006), as well as our own findings for younger consumers (see Chapter 5). What seems to be happening is that men are starting to be affected more strongly by compulsive buying, and so, just like our findings with respect to the impact of "body perfect" ideals on body image, men are also now adversely affected by consumer culture, and hence gender differences are being eroded.

In contrast to gender as a vulnerable social category, people on low income and of low socio-economic standing more generally emerge consistently as a group of individuals for whom the material "good life" ideal might have more toxic effects than for the relatively affluent. Although we did not find differences in compulsive buying tendencies according to income (see Chapter 5), for the new materialism we see that the pursuit of happiness through money and material goods has a significantly worse impact on subjective well-being in lower, compared to higher, income groups in both the UK and in Iceland (see Chapter 4). Low socio-economic standing may not make individuals more or less vulnerable to the impact of "body perfect" ideals, but—by definition—they are further away from the material "good life" ideal. This means greater discrepancies between their actual and ideal material standing, and hence more negative self-evaluation and emotions. Moreover, the pursuit of identity and happiness through material goods is bound to be even more unrealistic, and hence detrimental for their well-being. This argument is important, given the increasing wealth disparities in societies like the UK, but also in countries where consumer culture is relatively new and only wealthy elites are able to partake in it.

Indeed, most of the research reported in this book is from societies with a long-established mass-consumer culture, accompanied by a high degree of individualism and relative lack of community and social cohesion. In terms of cross-cultural differences, we saw that people from Hong Kong value possessions more for their collective identity functions (Chapter 2) and materialistic goals appear to have a less detrimental effect on the well-being of people in the former socialist Croatia, because they may not conflict so much with other-oriented goals (Chapter 4). However, it appears that the psychological processes of identity repair and identity seeking through the pursuit of consumer culture ideals are likely to generalise to the extent that countries adopt and adapt these ideals. One example is the introduction of US television to the island of Fiji, where girls quickly started to internalise the thin beauty ideal for women portrayed, overriding the indigenous full-figured beauty ideal for women (Chapter 6).

Globalisation of consumer culture increasingly reaches societies that we traditionally think of as developing countries. A prominent example is India, featured in an 84-page special of the *Observer Magazine* (2006), described as the "second-fastest growing economy in the world, poised to overtake all European nations by 2020 and even the United States by 2040" (p. 15), with Bollywood overtaking Hollywood as "the world's biggest film industry" (p. 41), and "saris [being] replaced by skinny jeans" (p. 74). Of course, poverty continues to be widespread in India, and is even exacerbated by the adaptation of the Western glitz style by a small elite, so that the "good life of the shopping malls and software companies, billboards advertising a 'modern lifestyle', the sense of well-being that elite Indians call 'feelgood', is an attitude cultivated against the grain of a larger reality in the country . . . a concerted effort by affluent Indians to dissociate themselves from the squalor, diversity and frustratingly unmodern nature of their country" (p. 18 and p. 15). Yet, against all this, we find an eruption of consumer culture, and proliferation of shopping malls in affluent suburbs. Siddharta Deb, currently writer-in-residence at the New School for Social Research in New York, observes:

> Urban, professional India signifies the triumphs of western capitalism in all its aspects, from business practices to consumer lifestyles. This India aims to be a superpower, to turn the present century into an Indian century in the same way that last century was an American one. The mother of all malls? Gurgaon [a suburb of Delhi] plan a Mall of India that will be bigger than the Mall of America in Minneapolis.
>
> (p. 16)

In terms of the psychological processes discussed in this book, I believe they most strongly apply to the consumer culture ideals of the material "good life" and the "body perfect", because they are predicated on the erroneous, but powerful, idea that identity and happiness result from the pursuit of these

ideals. For instance, women in a traditional culture who happen to be thinner than the fully-figured beauty ideal may also experience some discrepancy between their actual and ideal body, but they are probably are less likely to suffer psychological damage from that discrepancy, because the achievement of the cultural beauty ideal is not heralded as the hallmark of their individual identity and happiness. Yet, given the increasing globalisation of exactly these consumer culture ideals, I believe that the psychological processes that make consumer culture a "cage within" are starting to generalise to newly emerging mass-consumer societies.

SUMMING UP AND LOOKING AHEAD

The consumer culture as a "cage within" resonates with diverse critical analyses in the social sciences, including cultural studies, sociology, political studies, as well as earlier psychological writings. For instance, my view has some links to an early analysis by Fromm (1978), who describes two alternative basic modes of psychological functioning in current Western consumer society: a truly fulfilling, altruistic mode of "being" and as opposed to an alienating, self-centred mode of "having":

> In the having mode, there is no alive relationship between me and what I have. It and I have become things, and I have *it*, because I have the force to make it mine. But there is also a reverse relationship: *it has me*, because my sense of identity, i.e., of sanity, rests upon my having *it* (and as many things as possible). The having mode of existence is not established by an alive, productive process between subject and object: it makes *things* of both object and subject. The relationship is one of deadness, not aliveness.
>
> (pp. 82–83, emphases in original)

In contemporary consumer culture, the ideals of the "good life" and the "body perfect" are shifting to increasing extremes, which means that their internalisation and pursuit is increasingly unrealistic and leads to ill-health, both psychologically and physically. At the same time, they move individuals further and further away from fulfilling their psychological needs for intimacy with others, social interaction, meaningful activity, safety, relative simplicity, and autonomy. This "cage within" perspective has some resonance with conceptualisations of power within the fields of social theory, sociology, and political studies. For example, one interpretation of Foucault's analysis of power notes:

> Individuals are controlled through the power of the norm and this power is effective because it is relatively invisible. In modern society, the behaviour of individuals is regulated not through overt repression, but

through a set of standards and values associated with normality which are set into play by a network of ostensibly beneficent and scientific forms of knowledge.

(McNay, 1994, pp. 94–95)

If we include the technology of advertising among those forms of knowledge, then this analysis seems applicable to the subject matter of this book. Perhaps more significantly, in Lukes' elaboration (2005) of his original analysis of three-dimensional power, he describes the third dimension as "internalised illusions":

How are we to conceive of domination rendering those subject to it less free to live according to the dictates of their nature and judgment? . . . [Plausible] answers need to be spelt out by elaborating in detail its mechanisms, . . . such as the inculcation . . . of norms of fashion and myths of beauty, . . . domination can induce and sustain internal constraints upon self-determination – ways of undermining and distorting people's confidence in and sense of self and of misleading and subverting their judgment as to how best to advance their interests.

(pp. 121–122)

Without engaging in entrenched debates about "real" interests, two points in this quote are important for this book. First, Lukes highlights the importance of internalised constraints that undermine the fulfilment of people's needs, and this aspect of his analysis of power has connections with my analysis of consumer culture as a "cage within". Second, he calls for the need to elaborate in detail the mechanisms involved in the internalisation of beauty and fashion norms.

Here, I believe, the research in this book makes a novel contribution by identifying a set of psychological processes that link consumer culture ideals to people's identity and well-being, involving comparisons with idealised media models, identity seeking through material goods, and attempting to repair identity deficits and negative emotions through consumption. Moreover, these psychological processes are not only specified but are documented empirically in a rigorous and detailed research programme. Our findings for both adults and children are consistent with the proposal that beliefs about the psychological benefits of the material "good life" are unrealistic, and hence bad for well-being, although correlational nature cannot document causality. In contrast, an experimental design is particularly powerful because it does allow the identification of cause–effect relationships. This point is worth highlighting because the experimental approach is probably more familiar to psychologists than to scholars in media studies, communication, marketing science, and other social sciences. Thus, the studies that perhaps best exemplify and support the thesis of consumer culture as a "cage within" are our experiments documenting that exposure to idealised media models is an immediate cause of body dissatisfaction in adults and children.

In summary, the book offers a social psychological case study, if you will, of the impact of consumer culture. Yet it raises more questions than it can possibly endeavour to answer. This is a good thing, and the book casts its net widely, precisely because it wants to be an invitation to social scientists, including psychologists, to study further the impact of consumer culture on identity and well-being, as well as interventions aiming to prevent or reverse negative consumer culture effects. Addressing these issues in future research will be the task of many. Thus, the book wants to present a research agenda: simultaneities of uniqueness and fitting-in through consumer practices, identity construction and destruction through the symbolic and communicative meanings of material goods, and the entrapment and liberation of consumer choice all need to be examined longitudinally, as pathways that can lead to better or worse well-being outcomes. Other social scientists could and should pursue these issues at different levels of analysis.

As a social psychologist, I intend to pursue the research programme started in this book at the level of the individual. I am particularly interested in studying children's development over time because the psychological impact of consumer culture becomes particularly worrisome when we consider the increasing commercialisation of childhood:

> Corporations have infiltrated the core activities and institutions of childhood, with virtually no resistance from government or parents. Advertising is widespread in schools. Electronic media are replacing conventional play. We have become a nation that places a lower priority on teaching its children how to thrive socially, intellectually, even spiritually, than it does on training them to consume. The long-term consequences of this development are ominous.
>
> (Schor, 2004, p. 13)

The final comment to be made is that if this book can make a contribution towards making the bars of the consumer culture cage more visible, and encouraging others to join in this endeavour, then it is fulfilling its main aim. Helping future generations to escape as much as is possible from the "cage within" is a collective responsibility for us all.

References

Aaker, J. (1999). The malleable self: The role of self-expression in persuasion. *Journal of Marketing Research, 36*, 45–57.

Abrams, D., Rutland, A., & Cameron, L. (2003). The development of subjective group dynamics: Children's judgments of normative and deviant in-group and out-group individuals. *Child Development, 74*, 1–17.

Achenreiner, G. B. (1997). Materialistic values and susceptibility to influence in children. *Advances in Consumer Research, 24*, 82–88.

Achenreiner, G. B., & John, D. R. (2003). The meaning of brand names to children: A developmental investigation. *Journal of Consumer Psychology, 13*, 205–219.

Agliata, D., & Tantleff-Dunn, S. (2004). The impact of media exposure on males' body image. *Journal of Social and Clinical Psychology, 23*, 7–22.

Aloise-Young, P. A. (1993). The development of self-presentation: Self-promotion in 6- to 10-year-old children. *Social Cognition, 11*, 201–222.

American Psychiatric Association (APA) (2000). *Diagnostic and Statistical Manual for Mental Disorders, 4th Edition Text Revision (DSM-IV-TR)*. Washington, DC: APA.

Appadurai, A. (1986). *The social life of things: Commodities in cultural perspective.* Cambridge: Cambridge University Press.

Appadurai, A. (1990). Disjuncture and difference in the global cultural economy. In M. Featherstone (Ed.), *Theory, culture, society* (pp. 295–310). London: Sage.

Argyle, M. (2001). *The psychology of happiness* (2nd ed.). New York: Routledge.

Arlidge, J. (2000). Now bigger is the ideal figure. *Observer, June 25*, 15.

Arnould, E. J., & Thompson, C. J. (2005). Consumer Culture Theory (CCT): Twenty years of research. *Journal of Consumer Research, 31*, 868–882.

Babin, B. J., Darden, W. R., & Griffin, M. (1994). Work and/or fun: Measuring hedonic and utilitarian shopping value. *Journal of Consumer Research, 20*, 644–656.

Baird, A. L., & Grieve, F. G. (2006). Exposure to male models in advertisements leads to a decrease in men's body satisfaction. *North American Journal of Psychology, 8*, 115–121.

Bandura, A. (1986). *Social foundations of thought and action: A social cognitive theory.* Englewood Cliffs, NJ: Prentice Hall.

Bandura, A. (1989). Human agency in social cognitive theory. *American Psychologist, 44*, 1175–1184.

Banerjee, R. (2000). The development of an understanding of modesty. *British Journal of Developmental Psychology, 18*, 499–517.

Banerjee, R. (2002a). Individual differences in children's understanding of social evaluation concerns. *Infant and Child Development*, *11*, 237–252.

Banerjee, R. (2002b). Children's understanding of self-presentational behavior: Links with mental-state reasoning and the attribution of embarrassment. *Merrill-Palmer Quarterly*, *48*, 378–404.

Banerjee, R. (2002c). Audience effects on self-presentation in childhood. *Social Development*, *11*, 487–507.

Banerjee, R., & Dittmar, H. (in press). Individual differences in children's materialism: The role of peer relations. *Personality and Social Psychology Bulletin.*

Banerjee, R., & Lintern, V. (2000). Boys will be boys: The effect of social evaluation concerns on gender-typing. *Social Development*, *9*, 397–408.

Banerjee, R., & Yuill, N. (1999a). Children's understanding of self-presentational display rules: Associations with mental-state understanding. *British Journal of Developmental Psychology*, *17*, 111–124.

Banerjee, R., & Yuill, N. (1999b). Children's explanations for self-presentational behaviour. *European Journal of Social Psychology*, *29*, 105–111.

Bargh, J. A., Lombardi, W. J., & Higgins, E. T. (1988). Automaticity of chronically accessible constructs in person*situation effects on person perception: It's just a matter of time. *Journal of Personality and Social Psychology*, *55*, 4, 599–605.

Baudrillard, J. (1998). *The consumer society: Myths and structures*. London: Sage.

Baumeister, R. (1987). How the self became a problem: A psychological review of historical research. *Journal of Personality and Social Psychology*, *52*, 163–176.

Beaglehole, E. (1931). *Property: A study in social psychology*. London: Allen and Unwin.

Beggan, J. K. (1991). Using what you own to get what you need: The role of possessions in satisfying control motivation. In F. W. Rudmin (Ed.), *To have possessions: A handbook on ownership and property*. Special issue of the *Journal of Social Behavior and Personality*, *6*, 129–146.

Beggan, J. K. (1992). On the social nature of nonsocial perception: The mere ownership effect. *Journal of Personality and Social Psychology*, *62*, 229–237.

Belk, R. W. (1984). Three scales to measure constructs related to materialism: Reliability, validity, and relationships to measures of happiness. In T. C. Kinnear (Ed.), *Advances in Consumer Research, Vol. 11* (pp. 291–297). Provo, UT: Association for Consumer Research.

Belk, R. W. (1985). Materialism: Trait aspects of living in the material world. *Journal of Consumer Research*, *12*, 265–280.

Belk, R. W. (1987). Material values in the comics: A content analysis of comic books featuring themes of wealth. *Journal of Consumer Research*, *14*, 26–42.

Belk, R. W. (1988). Possessions and the extended self. *Journal of Consumer Research*, *15*, 139–168.

Belk, R. W. (1995). Collecting as luxury consumption: Effects on individuals and households. *Journal of Economic Psychology*, *16*, 477–490.

Belk, R. (2000). Are we what we own? In A. Benson (Ed.), *I shop therefore I am: Compulsive buying and the search for self* (pp. 76–104). New York: Jason Aronson.

Belk, R. W., & Pollay, R. W. (1985). Images of ourselves: The good life in twentieth century advertising. *Journal of Consumer Research*, *11*, 887–897.

Bell, B. T., Lawson, R., & Dittmar, H. (in press). The impact of music videos on adolescent girls' body dissatisfaction. *Body Image.*

Benight, C. C., Ironson, G., Klebe, K., Carver, C. A., Wynings, C., Burnett, K.,

Greenwood, D., Baum, A., & Schneiderman, N. (1999). Conservation of resources and coping self-efficacy predicting distress following a natural disaster: A causal model analysis where the environment meets the mind. *Anxiety, Stress and Coping: An International Journal, 12*, 107–126.

Bennett, M. (1990). Children's understanding of the mitigating function of disclaimers. *Journal of Social Psychology, 130*, 29–37.

Bennett, M., & Yeeles, C. (1990a). Children's understanding of the self-presentational strategies of ingratiation and self-promotion. *European Journal of Social Psychology, 20*, 455–461.

Bennett, M., & Yeeles, C. (1990b). Children's understanding of showing off. *Journal of Social Psychology, 130*, 591–596.

Benson, A. (Ed.) (2000). *I shop, therefore I am: Compulsive buying and the search for self.* New York: Aronson.

Benson, A. (2006). *Stopping overshopping: A comprehensive program to help eliminate compulsive buying.* New York: Stopping Overshopping LLC. Also online. Available at http://www.stoppingovershopping.com.

Bentler, P. M. (1995). *EQS: Structural equations program manual.* Encino, CA: Multivariate Software Inc.

Benzion, U., Rapoport, A., & Yagil, J. (1989). Discount rates inferred from decisions: An experimental study. *Management Science, 35*, 270–284.

Bergadaa, M., Faure, C., & Perrien, J. (1995). Enduring involvement with shopping. *Journal of Social Psychology, 135*, 17–25.

Berger, J., & Heath, C. (2007). Where consumers diverge from others: Identity signalling and product domains. *Journal of Consumer Research, 34.*

Berndt, T. J. (1979). Developmental changes in conformity to peers and parents. *Developmental Psychology, 15*, 608–616.

Black, D. W. (1996). Compulsive buying: A review. *Journal of Clinical Psychiatry, 57*, 50–54.

Black, D. W. (2006). Compulsive shopping. In E. Hollander & D. J. Stein (Eds.), *Clinical manual of impulse-control disorders* (pp. 203–228). Washington, DC: American Psychiatric Publishing.

Black, D. W., Gabel, J., Hansen, J., & Schlosser, S. (2000). A double-blind comparison of fluvoxamine versus placebo in the treatment of compulsive buying disorder. *Annals of Clinical Psychiatry, 12*, 205–211.

Black, D. W., Repertinger, S., Gaffney, G. R., & Gabel, J. (1998). Family history and psychiatric comorbidity in person with compulsive buying. *American Journal of Psychiatry, 155*, 960–963.

Blair, I. V., & Banaji, M. (1996). Automatic and controlled processes in stereotype priming. *Journal of Personality and Social Psychology, 70*, 1142–1163.

Blumberg, P. (1974). The rise and fall of the status symbols: Some thoughts on status in a post-industrial society. *Social Problems, 21*, 490–498.

Boldero, J., & Francis, J. (2000). The relation between self-discrepancies and emotion: The moderating roles of self-guide importance, location relevance, and social self-domain centrality. *Journal of Personality and Social Psychology, 78*, 38–52.

Bond, R., Dittmar, H., Singelis, T., Papadopoulou, D., & Chiu, M. (2002). Identity-related functions of material possessions in individualist and collectivist cultures. BPS Social Section Annual Conference, September 2002, Huddersfield, UK.

Borenkowski, D. L. G., Robinson, T. N., & Killen, J. D. (2000). Does the camera add

10 pounds? Media use, perceived importance of appearance, and weight concerns among teenage girls. *Journal of Adolescent Health*, *26*, 36–41.

Bourdieu, P. (1984). *Distinction: A social critique of the judgement of taste*. London: Routledge.

Bower, A. B., & Landreth, S. (2001). Is beauty best? Highly versus normally attractive models in advertising. *Journal of Advertising*, *30*, 1–12.

Bradburn, N. M. (1969). *The structure of psychological well-being*. Chicago, IL: Aldine Publishing.

Braun, O. L., & Wicklund, R. A. (1989). Psychological antecedents of conspicuous consumption, *Journal of Economic Psychology*, *10*, 161–187.

Brickman, P., Coates, D., & Janoff-Bulman, R. (1978). Lottery winners and accident victims: Is happiness relative? *Journal of Personality and Social Psychology*, *36*, 917–927.

Brislin, R. W. (1970). Back-translation for cross-cultural research. *Journal of Cross-Cultural Psychology*, *1*, 185–216.

British Medical Association (BMA) (2000). *Eating disorders, body image & the media*. London: BMA.

Brower, M., & Leon, W. (1999). *The consumer's guide to effective environmental choices: Practical advice from the Union of Concerned Scientists*. New York: Three Rivers Press.

Brown, A., & Dittmar, H. (2005). Think "thin" and feel bad: The role of appearance schema activation, attention level, and thin-ideal internalisation for young women's responses to ultra-thin media ideals. *Journal of Social and Clinical Psychology*, *24*, 1088–1113.

Brown, B. B., Clasen, D. R., & Eicher, S. A. (1986). Perceptions of peer pressure, peer conformity dispositions, and self-reported behavior among adolescents. *Developmental Psychology*, *22*, 521–530.

Brown, J. (2005). Money is best thing in the world, say primary children. *Independent*, December 19, 9.

Brown, R., & Hewstone, M. (2005). An integrative theory of intergroup contact. In M. P. Zanna (Ed.), *Advances in experimental social psychology* (Vol. 37, pp. 255–343). San Diego, CA: Elsevier–Academic Press.

Browne, G. J., Durrett, J. R., & Wetherbe, J. C. (2004). Consumer reactions towards clicks and bricks: Investigating buying behaviour online and at stores. *Behaviour & Information Technology*, *23*, 237–245.

Brownell, K. D. (1991). Dieting and the search for the perfect body: Where physiology and culture collide. *Behavior Therapy*, *11*, 1–12.

Burke, R. R. (1997). Do you see what I see? The future of virtual shopping. *Journal of the Academy of Marketing Sciences*, *25*, 352–360.

Burroughs, J. E., & Rindfleisch, A. (2002). Materialism and well-being: A conflicting values perspective. *Journal of Consumer Research*, *29*, 348–370.

Business Software Association (2002). Last accessed 18 August 2006 at http://www.bsa.org/usa/press/newsreleases//2002-11-12.1362.phtml

Bussey, K., & Bandura, A. (1999). Social cognitive theory of gender development and differentiation. *Psychological Review*, *106*, 676–713.

Caballero, M. A., Ramos, L., & Saltijeral, M. T. (2000). Posttraumatic stress dysfunction and other reactions of the victims of house burglary. *Salud Mental*, *23*, 8–17.

Caballero, M. J., & Solomon, P. J. (1984). Effects of model attractiveness on sales response. *Journal of Advertising*, *13*, 17–23.

Cafri, G., Thompson, J. K., Ricciardelli, L., McCabe, M., Smolak, L., & Yesalis, C. (2005). Pursuit of the muscular ideal: Physical and psychological consequences and putative risk factors. *Clinical Psychology Review, 25*, 215–239.

Campbell, C. (2000). Shopaholics, spendaholics, and the question of gender. In A. Benson (Ed.), *I shop, therefore I am: Compulsive buying and the search for self* (pp. 57–75). New York: Aronson.

Carlson, M. (2005). Money can't buy happiness? That's rich. *Los Angeles Times,* 20 January 2005. Last accessed 1 February 2005 at http://www.latimes.com/news/opinion/commentary/la-oe-carlson20jan20,1,3650784.column?coll=la-news-comment-opinions&ctrack=1&cset=true

Carver, C. S., & Baird, E. (1998). The American dream revisited: Is it what you want or why you want it that matters? *Psychological Science, 9*, 289–292.

Cash, T. F. (1990). *The Multidimensional Body-Self Relations Questionnaire.* Unpublished test manual. Norfolk, VA: Old Dominion University.

Cash, T. F., & Deagle, E. A. (1997). The nature and extent of body-image disturbances in anorexia nervosa and bulimia nervosa: A meta-analysis. *International Journal of Eating Disorders, 22*, 107–125.

Cash, T. F., Morrow, J. A., Hrabosky, J. I., & Perry, A. A. (2004). How has body image changed? A cross-sectional investigation of college women and men from 1983 to 2001. *Journal of Consulting and Clinical Psychology, 72*, 1081–1089.

Cash, T. F., & Pruzinsky, T. (Eds.) (2002). *Body image: A handbook of theory, research, and clinical practice.* New York: Guilford.

Catalano, E., & Sonnenberg, N. (1993). *Consuming passions: Help for compulsive shoppers.* Oakland, CA: New Harbinger.

Cattarin, J., & Thompson, J. K. (1994). A three year longitudinal study of body image and eating disturbance in adolescent females. *Eating Disorders: The Journal of Prevention and Treatment, 2*, 114–125.

CBC Newsworld (2006). No point using skinny models in ads, psychologist finds. Last accessed 28 December 2006 at http://www.cbc.ca/health/story/2006/11/15/thin-models.html

CBS News (2004). Becoming Barbie: Living dolls. Last accessed 5 December 2004 at http://www.cbsnews.com/stories/2004/07/29/48hours/main632909.shtml

Chang, L., & Arkin, R. M. (2002). Materialism as an attempt to cope with uncertainty. *Psychology and Marketing, 19*, 389–406.

Chernin, K. (1981). *The obsession: Reflections on the tyranny of slenderness.* New York: Harper & Row.

Childers, T. L., Carr, C. L., Peck, J., & Carson, S. (2001). Hedonic and utilitarian motivations for online retail shopping behavior. *Journal of Retailing, 77*, 511–535.

Christenson, G. A., Faber, R. J., de Zwaan, M., & Raymond, N. C. (1994). Compulsive buying: Descriptive characteristics and psychiatric co-morbidity. *Journal of Clinical Psychiatry, 55*, 5–11.

Christopher, A. N., & Schlenker, B. R. (2000). The impact of perceived material wealth and perceiver personality on first impressions. *Journal of Economic Psychology, 21*, 1–19.

Christopher, A. N., & Schlenker, B. R. (2004). Materialism and affect: The role of self-presentational concerns. *Journal of Social and Clinical Psychology, 23*, 260–272.

Ciarrochi, J., & Forgas, J. (2000). The pleasure of possessions: Affective influences and personality in the evaluation of consumer items. *European Journal of Social Psychology, 30*, 637–649.

Clark, N. (2004). Mirror, mirror on the wall ... are muscular men the best of all? *American Fitness*, *Jan–Feb*. Last accessed 8 March 2006 from FindArticles at http://www.lumiverse.com/p/articles/mi_m0675/is_1_22/ai_112408511

Clay, D., Vignoles, V., & Dittmar, H. (2005). Body-image and self-esteem among adolescent females: Testing the influence of sociocultural factors. *Journal for Research on Adolescence*, *15*, 451–477.

Coie, J. D., & Dodge, K. A. (1983). Continuities and changes in children's social status: A five-year longitudinal study. *Merrill Palmer Quarterly*, *29*, 261–282.

Coie, J. D., & Dodge, K. A. (1988). Multiple sources of data on social behavior and social status in the school: A cross-age comparison. *Child Development*, *59*, 815–829.

Collins, M. E. (1991). Body figure perceptions and preferences among preadolescent children. *International Journal of Eating Disorders*, *10*, 199–208.

Collins, R. L. (1996). For better or worse: The impact of upward social comparison on self-evaluations. *Psychological Bulletin*, *119*, 51–69.

ComScore Media Matrix (2002). November. Available at http://www.nua.ie/surveys/?f=VS&art_id=905358600&rel=true

Cram, F., & Paton, H. (1993). Personal possessions and self-identity: The experiences of elderly women in three residential settings. *Australian Journal on Ageing*, *12*, 19–24.

Cramer, P., & Steinwert, T. (1998). Thin is good, fat is bad: How early does it begin? *Journal of Applied Developmental Psychology*, *19*, 429–451.

Creditaction (2006). Debt facts and figures – compiled 4 May 2006. Last accessed 16 May 2006 at http://www.creditaction.org.uk/debtstats.htm

Cross, S. E., & Madson, L. (1997). Models of the self: Self-construals and gender. *Psychological Bulletin*, *122*, 3–37.

Csikszentmihalyi, M., & Csikszentmihalyi, I. S. (2006). *A life worth living: Contributions to positive psychology*. New York: Oxford University Press.

Csikszentmihalyi, M., & Rochberg-Halton, E. (1981). *The meaning of things: Domestic symbols and the self*. Cambridge: Cambridge University Press.

D'Astous, A. (1990). An inquiry into the compulsive side of "normal" consumers. *Journal of Consumer Policy*, *13*, 15–31.

D'Astous, A., Maltais, J., & Roberge, C. (1990). Compulsive buying tendencies of adolescent consumers. *Advances in Consumer Research*, *17*, 306–313.

Debenhams (2001). *Size guide*. [On-Line]. Available at http://www.debenhams.com

DeSarbo, W. S., & Edwards, E. A. (1996). Typologies of compulsive buying behavior: A constrained clusterwise regression approach. *Journal of Consumer Psychology*, *5*, 231–262.

Diener, E., & Biswas-Diener, R. (2002). Will money increase subjective well-being? A literature review and guide to needed research. *Social Indicators Research*, *57*, 119–169.

Diener, E., Diener, M., & Diener, C. (1995). Factors predicting the subjective well-being of nations. *Journal of Personality and Social Psychology*, *69*, 851–864.

Diener, E., Emmons, R. A., Larson, R. J., & Griffin, S. (1985). The satisfaction with life scale. *Journal of Personality Assessment*, *49*, 71–76.

Diener, E., & Fujita, F. (1995). Resources, personal strivings, and subjective well-being: A nomothetic and idiographic approach. *Journal of Personality and Social Psychology*, *68*, 926–935.

Diener, E., & Oishi, S. (2005). The nonobvious social psychology of happiness. *Psychological Inquiry*, *16*, 162–165.

Diener, E., Oishi, S., & Lucas, R. E. (2003). Personality, culture and subjective well-being: Emotional and cognitive evaluation of life. *Annual Review of Psychology*, *54*, 403–425.

Diener, E., & Seligman, M. E. P. (2005). Beyond money: Toward an economy of well-being. *Psychological Science in the Public Interest*, *5*, 1–31.

Diener, E., Suh, E. M., Lucas, R. E., & Smith, H. L. (1999). Subjective well-being: Three decades of progress. *Psychological Bulletin*, *125*, 276–302.

Dittmar, H. (1989). Gender identity-related meanings of personal possessions. *British Journal of Social Psychology*, *28*, 159–171.

Dittmar, H. (1991). Meanings of material possessions as reflections of identity: Gender and social-material position in society. In F. W. Rudmin (Ed.), *To have possessions: A handbook on ownership and property.* Special issue of *Journal of Social Behavior and Personality*, *6*, 165–186.

Dittmar, H. (1992a). *The social psychology of material possessions: To have is to be.* Hemel Hempstead: Harvester Wheatsheaf and New York: St. Martin's Press.

Dittmar, H. (1992b). Perceived material wealth and first impressions. *British Journal of Social Psychology*, *31*, 379–392.

Dittmar, H. (1994). Material possessions as stereotypes: Material images of different socio-economic groups. *Journal of Economic Psychology*, *15*, 561–585.

Dittmar, H. (2000). The role of self-image in excessive buying. In A. Benson (Ed.), *I shop, therefore I am: "Compulsive" buying and the search for self* (pp. 105–132). New York: Aronson.

Dittmar, H. (2001). Impulse buying in ordinary and "compulsive" consumers. In E. Weber, J. Baron, & G. Loomes (Eds.), *Conflicts and tradeoffs in decision making* (pp. 110–135). Cambridge Series on Judgment and Decision Making. New York: Cambridge University Press.

Dittmar, H. (2002). I shop therefore I am: Excessive buying and the self for self. In I. Garcia Ureta & E. Olabarri Fernandez (Eds.), *El consumo y la adiccion a las compras: Diferentes perspectivas* (Consumption and addictive buying: Different perspectives) (pp. 47–63). University of the Basque Country.

Dittmar, H. (2003). The psychology of buying and selling in the home. Report for the Office or Fair Trading, London. Online. Available at http://www.oft.gov.uk/NR/rdonlyres/2E00924F-1632-44B5-9EE7-5C1E81666647/0/716f.pdf [last accessed on 11 August 2006].

Dittmar, H. (2004a). Are you what you have? Consumer society and our sense of identity. *Psychologist*, *17*, 206–210.

Dittmar, H. (2004b). Understanding and diagnosing compulsive buying. In R. Coombs (Ed.), *Handbook of addictive disorders: A practical guide to diagnosis and treatment* (pp. 411–450). New York: Wiley.

Dittmar, H. (2005a). A new look at "compulsive buying": Self-discrepancies and materialistic values as predictors of compulsive buying tendency. *Journal of Social and Clinical Psychology*, *24*, 806–833.

Dittmar, H. (2005b). Compulsive buying behavior – a growing concern? An empirical exploration of the role of gender, age, and materialism. *British Journal of Psychology*, *96*, 467–491.

Dittmar, H. (2005c). Vulnerability factors and processes linking sociocultural pressures and body dissatisfaction: An introduction to the second special issue on body image. *Journal of Social and Clinical Psychology*, *24*, 1081–1087.

Dittmar, H. (in press). The costs of consumer culture and the "cage within": The impact of the material "good life" and "body perfect" ideals on individuals' identity and well-being. Commentary on Kasser, T., Cohn, S., Kanner, A. D., & Ryan, R. M. Some costs of American corporate capitalism: A psychological exploration of value and goal conflicts. *Psychological Inquiry*.

Dittmar, H., & Beattie, J. (1998). Impulsive and excessive buying behaviour. In P. Taylor-Gooby (Ed.), *Choice and public policy: The new welfare consumers* (pp. 123–144). London: Macmillan.

Dittmar, H., Beattie, J., & Friese, S. (1996). Objects, decision considerations and self-image in men's and women's impulse purchases. *Acta Psychologica* (special issue on Decision-making and Emotions), *93*, 187–206. [Also available at http://www.ukc.ac.uk/ESRC].

Dittmar, H., & Bond, R. (2007). I want it and I want it now: Self-discrepancies and materialistic values as predictors of ordinary and compulsive buyers' temporal discounting of different consumer goods. Manuscript in revision for publication.

Dittmar, H., & Drury, J. (2000). Self-image – is it in the bag? A qualitative comparison between ordinary and "excessive" consumers. *Journal of Economic Psychology*, *21*, 109–142.

Dittmar, H., & Halliwell, E. (2005). The role of self-beliefs in women's responses to idealised media images. Funded by the UK's Economic and Social Research Council's (ESRC) grant RES-000-22-0774. [A research report detailing the main findings can be downloaded at http://www.esrcsocietytoday.ac.uk/ESRCInfoCentre

Dittmar, H., Halliwell, E., & Ive, S. (2006). Does Barbie make girls want to be thin? The effect of experimental exposure to images of dolls on the body image of 5- to 8-year-old girls. *Developmental Psychology*, *42*, 283–292.

Dittmar, H., Halliwell, E., & Stirling, E. (in press). Understanding the impact of thin media models on women's body-focused affect: The roles of thin-ideal internalization and weight-related self-discrepancy activation in experimental exposure effects. *Journal of Social and Clinical Psychology*.

Dittmar, H., & Howard, S. (2004a). Professional hazards? The impact of model's body size on advertising effectiveness and women's body-focused anxiety in professions that do and do not emphasize the cultural ideal of thinness. *British Journal of Social Psychology*, *43*, 1–33.

Dittmar, H., & Howard, S. (2004b). Ideal-body internalization and social comparison tendency as moderators of thin media models' impact on women's body-focused anxiety. *Journal of Social and Clinical Psychology*, *23*, 768–791.

Dittmar, H., Long, K., & Bond, R. (2007). When a better self is only a button click away: Associations between materialistic values, emotional and identity-related buying motives, and compulsive buying tendency online. *Journal of Social and Clinical Psychology*, *26*, 334–361.

Dittmar, H., Long, K., & Meek, R. (2004). Buying on the internet: Gender differences in online and conventional buying motivations. *Sex Roles*, *50*, 423–444.

Dittmar, H., & Pepper, L. (1994). To have is to be: Materialism and person perception in working-class and middle-class British adolescents. *Journal of Economic Psychology*, *15*, 233–251.

Dittmar, H., Phillips, M., & Halliwell, E. (2007). When men think "muscular" and feel bad: Acute exposure to idealized media models as a cause of men's ideal-body self-discrepancies and body dissatisfaction. Manuscript in revision for publication.

Dixon, J. C., & Street, J. W. (1975). The distinction between self and not-self in children and adolescents. *Journal of Genetic Psychology*, *127*, 157–162.

Dodge, K. A., & Pettit, G. S. (2003). A biopsychosocial model of the development of chronic conduct problems in adolescence. *Developmental Psychology, 39*, 349–371.

Donahue, E. M., Robins, R. W., Roberts, B. W., & John, O. P. (1993). The divided self: Concurrent and longitudinal effects of psychological adjustment and social roles on self-concept differentiation. *Journal of Personality and Social Psychology, 64*, 834–846.

Donthu, N., & Garcia, A. (1999). The Internet shopper. *Journal of Advertising Research, 39*, 52–58.

Douglas, M., & Isherwood, B. (1979). *The world of goods: Towards an anthropology of consumption*. London: Allen Lane.

Doyle, K. O. (1992). The symbolic meaning of house and home. *American Behavioral Scientist, 35*, 790–802.

Driscoll, A. M., Mayer, R. N., & Belk, R. W. (1985). The young child's recognition of consumption symbols and their social implications. *Child Study Journal, 15*, 117–130.

Du Gay, P., Hall, S., Janes, L., Mackay, H., & Negus, K. (1997). *Doing cultural studies: The story of the Sony Walkman*. Vol. 1 in the series S. Hall (Ed.), *Culture, media and identities*. London: Sage.

Dweck, C. S., & Leggett, E. L. (1988). A social-cognitive approach to motivation and personality. *Psychological Review, 95*, 256–273.

Eating Disorder Association (2007). Available at http://www.edauk.com/

Elliott, A. (2005). *Not waving but drowning: Over-indebtedness by misjudgement*. London and New York: Centre for the Study of Financial Innovation (CSFI).

Elliott, R. (1994). Compulsive consumption: Function and fragmentation in postmodernity. *Journal of Consumer Policy, 17*, 159–179.

Erikson, E. (1980). *Identity and the life-cycle: A re-issue*. New York: Norton.

Ernst & Young (1999). The Second Annual Ernst & Young Internet Shopping Study. New York, NY: Ernst and Young LLP.

Erwin, P. (1993). *Friendship and peer relations in children*. Chichester: Wiley.

Etcoff, N., Orbach, S., Scott, J., & D'Agostino, H. (2004). The real truth about beauty: A global report. Last accessed 14 January 2007 at http://www.campaignfor realbeauty.com/uploadedfiles/dove_white_paper_final.pdf

Etzioni, A. (1988). *The moral dimension: Toward a new economics*. New York: Free Press.

Etzioni, A. (1998). Voluntary simplicity: Characterization, select psychological implications, and societal consequences. *Journal of Economic Psychology, 19*, 619–643.

Faber, R. J. (2004). Self-control and compulsive buying. In T. Kasser & A. D. Kanner (Eds.), *Psychology and consumer culture: The struggle for a good life in a materialistic world* (pp. 169–188). Washington, DC: American Psychological Association.

Faber, R. J., & Christenson, G. A. (1996). In the mood to buy: Differences in the mood states experienced by compulsive buyers and other consumers. *Psychology and Marketing, 13*, 803–820.

Faber, R. J., & O'Guinn, T. C. (1992). A clinical screener for compulsive buying. *Journal of Consumer Research, 19*, 459–469.

Fagot, B. I. (1977). Consequences of moderate cross-gender behaviour in preschool children. *Child Development, 48*, 902–907.

Faludi, S. (1991). *Backlash: The undeclared war against American women*. New York: Crown.

Featherstone, M. (1991). *Consumer culture and postmodernism*. London: Sage.

Feingold, A., & Mazzella, R. (1998). Gender differences in body image are increasing. *Psychological Science, 9,* 190–195.

Festinger, L. (1954). A theory of social comparison processes. *Human Relations, 7,* 117–140.

Finnegan, R. A., Hodges, E. V. E., & Perry, D. G. (1998). Victimization by peers: Associations with children's reports of mother–child interaction. *Journal of Personality and Social Psychology, 75,* 1076–1086.

Fischer, E., & Gainer, B. (1991). I shop therefore I am: The role of shopping in the social construction of women's identities. In G. A. Costa (Ed.), *Gender and consumer behavior* (pp. 350–357). Salt Lake City, UT: University of Utah Press.

Forston, M. T., & Stanton, A. L. (1992). Self-discrepancy theory as a framework for understanding bulimic symptomatology and associated distress. *Journal of Social and Clinical Psychology, 11,* 2, 103–118.

Fournier, S., & Richins, M. L. (1991). Some theoretical and popular notions concerning materialism. In F. Rudmin, *To have possessions: A handbook of property and ownership,* special issue of the *Journal of Personality and Social Behaviour, 6,* 403–414.

Fouts, G., & Burggraf, K. (1999). Television situation comedies: Female body images and verbal reinforcements. *Sex Roles, 40,* 473–481.

Fouts, G., & Burggraf, K. (2000). Television situation comedies: Female weight, male negative comments, and audience reactions. *Sex Roles, 42,* 925–935.

Fredrickson, B. L. (1998). What good are positive emotions? *Review of General Psychology, 2,* 300–319.

Fredrickson, B. L., & Roberts, T. (1997). Objectification theory: Toward understanding women's lived experiences and mental health risks. *Psychology of Women Quarterly, 21,* 173–206.

Frisby, D. (1984). *Georg Simmel.* London: Tavistock.

Frith, M. (2006). Role models? Backlash against fashion's thinnest. *Independent,* September 15.

Fromm, E. (1978). *To have or to be?* Harmondsworth: Penguin (originally published 1976).

Frost, R. O., Steketee, G., & Williams, L. (2002). Compulsive buying, compulsive hoarding, and obsessive-compulsive disorder. *Behavior Therapy, 33,* 201–214.

Furby, L. (1978a). Possessions: Toward a theory of their meaning and function throughout the life cycle. In P. B. Baltes (Ed.), *Life span development and behavior* (Vol. 1, pp. 297–336). New York: Academic Press.

Furby, L. (1978b). Possession in humans: An exploratory study of its meaning and motivation. *Social Behavior and Personality, 6,* 49–65.

Furby, L. (1980). The origins and early development of possessive behavior. *Political Psychology, 2,* 30–42.

Furby, L. (1991). Understanding the psychology of possessions and ownership: A personal memoir and an appraisal of our progress. In F. W. Rudmin (Ed.), *To have possessions: A handbook on ownership and property.* Special issue of the *Journal of Social Behavior and Personality, 6,* 457–463.

Furnham, A., & Calman, A. (1998). Eating disturbance, self-esteem, reasons for exercising and body weight dissatisfaction in adolescent males. *European Eating Disorders Review, 6,* 58–72.

Garcés Prieto, J. (2002). Experiencias de trabajo en la prevenciòn y tratamiento de la adicciòn al consumo. In I. García Ureta & E. Olibarri Fernández (Eds.), *El*

Consumo y la Adicción a las Compras: Diferentes Perspectivas (pp. 199–222). University of the Basque Country.

Garðarsdóttir, R. B. (2006). Materialism, income and money motives as influences on subjective well-being: A comparison between the UK and Iceland. D. Phil thesis, University of Sussex, UK.

Garðarsdóttir, R., Dittmar, H., & Aspinall, C. (2007). It's not the money, it's the quest for a happier self: Money motives impact the link between materialism and subjective well-being. Manuscript submitted for publication.

Ger, G., & Belk, R. W. (1996). Cross-cultural differences in materialism. *Journal of Economic Psychology, 17*, 55–77.

Giddens, A. (2001). *Sociology* (4th ed.). Cambridge: Polity Press.

Gifford-Smith, M. E., & Brownell, C. A. (2003). Childhood peer relationships: Social acceptance, friendships, and peer networks. *Journal of School Psychology, 41*, 235–284.

Gigerenzer, G., & Goldstein, D. G. (1996). Reasoning the fast and frugal way: Models of bounded rationality. *Psychological Review, 103*, 650–669.

Gillian, A. (2000). Skinny models "send unhealthy message". *Guardian*, May 31, 7.

Goffman, E. (1951). Symbols of class status. *British Journal of Sociology, 2*, 294–304.

Goffman, E. (1961). *Asylums*. New York: Anchor.

Goffman, E. (1968). The inmate world. In C. Gordon & K. J. Gergen (Eds.), *The self in social interaction: Vol. 1. Classic and contemporary perspectives* (pp. 267–274). New York: Wiley.

Goldberg, M. E., Gorn, G. J., Peracchio, L. A., & Bamossy, G. (2003). Understanding materialism among youth. *Journal of Consumer Psychology, 13*, 278–288.

Gordon, C. (1968). Self conceptions: Configurations and contents. In C. Gordon & K. J. Gergen (Eds.), *The self in social interaction: Vol 1. Classic and contemporary perspectives* (pp. 115–136). New York: Wiley.

Groesz, L. M., Levine, M. P., & Murnen, S. K. (2002). The effect of experimental presentation of thin media images on body dissatisfaction: A meta-analytic review. *International Journal of Eating Disorders, 31*, 1–16.

Grogan, S. (1999). *Body image: Understanding body dissatisfaction in men, women and children*. London: Routledge.

Grogan, S., Williams, Z., & Conner, M. (1996). The effects of viewing same-gender photographic models on body-esteem? *Psychology of Women Quarterly, 20*, 569–575.

Grouzet, F. M. E., Kasser, T., Ahuvia, A., Dols, J. M. F., Kim, J., Lau, S., Ryan, R. M., Saunders, S., Schmuck, P., & Sheldon, K. M. (2005). The structure of goal contents across 15 cultures. *Journal of Personality and Social Psychology, 89*, 800–816.

Gulerce, A. (1991). Transitional objects: A reconsideration of the phenomenon. In F. W. Rudmin (Ed.), *To have possessions: A handbook on ownership and property*. Special issue of the *Journal of Social Behavior and Personality, 6*, 187–208.

Halliwell, E. (2002). Sociocultural influences on body image concerns throughout adulthood. Unpublished doctoral thesis, University of Sussex, UK.

Halliwell, E., & Dittmar, H. (2003). A qualitative investigation of women's and men's body image concerns and their attitudes toward aging. *Sex Roles, 49*, 675–685.

Halliwell, E., & Dittmar, H. (2004). Does size matter? The impact of model's body size on advertising effectiveness and women's body-focused anxiety. *Journal of Social and Clinical Psychology, 23*, 105–132. Special issue on Media and Body Image.

Halliwell, E., & Dittmar, H. (2005). The role of self-improvement and self-evaluation motives in social comparisons with idealised female bodies in the media. *Body Image, 2*, 249–261.

Halliwell, E., & Dittmar, H. (2006). The role of appearance-related self-discrepancies for young adults' affect, body image, and emotional eating: A comparison of fixed-item and respondent-generated self-discrepancy measures. *Personality and Social Psychology Bulletin, 32*, 447–458.

Halliwell, E., Dittmar, H., & Howe, J. (2005). The impact of advertisements featuring ultra-thin or average-size models on women with a history of eating disorders. *Journal of Community & Applied Social Psychology, 15*, 406–413.

Halliwell, E., Dittmar, H., & Orsborn, A. (in press). The effects of exposure to muscular male models amongst men who use the gym and non-exercisers: The moderating role of exercising to increase muscle strength. *Body Image.*

Halman, L. (2001). *The European values study: A third wave.* Tilburg, Netherlands: EVS, WORC, Tilburg University.

Hamilton, K., & Waller, G. (1993). Media influences on body size estimation in anorexia and bulimia: An experimental study. *British Journal of Psychiatry, 162*, 837–840.

Hanley, A., & Wilhelm, M. S. (1992). Compulsive buying: An exploration into self-esteem and money attitudes. *Journal of Economic Psychology, 13*, 5–18.

Hargreaves, D., & Tiggemann, M. (2002). The effect of television commercials on mood and body dissatisfaction: The role of appearance-schema activation. *Journal of Social and Clinical Psychology, 21*, 287–308.

Harrison, K. (2001). Ourselves, our bodies: Thin-ideal media, self-discrepancies, and eating disorder symptomatology in adolescents. *Journal of Social and Clinical Psychology, 20*, 289–323.

Harter, S. (1999). *The construction of the self: A developmental perspective.* New York: Guilford.

Hassay, D. N., & Smith, M. C. (1996). Compulsive buying: An examination of the consumption motive. *Psychology and Marketing, 13*, 741–752.

Hatoum, I. J., & Belle, D. (2004). Mags and abs: Media consumption and bodily concerns in men. *Sex Roles, 51*, 397–407.

Hausmann, A. (2000). A multi-method investigation of consumer motivations in impulse buying behaviour. *Journal of Consumer Marketing, 17*, 403–419.

Hayo, B., & Seifert, W. (2003). Subjective economic well-being in Eastern Europe. *Journal of Economic Psychology, 24*, 329–348.

Heinberg, L. J., & Thompson, J. K. (1995). Body image and televised images of thinness and attractiveness: A controlled laboratory investigation. *Journal of Social and Clinical Psychology, 14*, 324–338.

Heinberg, L. J., Thompson, J. K., & Stormer, S. M. (1995). Development and validation of the sociocultural attitudes towards appearance questionnaire. *International Journal of Eating Disorders, 17*, 81–89.

Henderson-King, E., & Henderson-King, D. (1997). Media effects on women's body esteem: Social and individual difference factors. *Journal of Applied Social Psychology, 27*, 399–417.

Higgins, E. T. (1987). Self-discrepancy: A theory relating self to affect. *Psychological Review, 94*, 319–340.

Higgins, E. T. (1999). When do self-discrepancies have specific relations to emotions?

The second-generation question of Tangney, Niedenthal, Covert, and Barlow (1998). *Journal of Personality and Social Psychology*, *77*, 6, 1313–1317.

Higgins, E. T., Bond, R. N., Klein, R., & Strauman, T. (1986). Self-discrepancies and emotional vulnerability – how magnitude, accessibility, and type of discrepancy influence affect. *Journal of Personality and Social Psychology*, *51*, 1, 5–15.

Hite, C. F., & Hite, R. E. (1995). Reliance on brand by young children. *Journal of the Market Research Society*, *37*, 185–193.

Hobfoll, S. E. (1998). *The ecology of stress*. New York: Hemisphere.

Hochschild, A. (2003). *The commercialization of intimate life*. Berkeley, CA: University of California Press.

Hofstede, G. (1980). *Culture's consequences*. Beverly Hills, CA: Sage.

Hollander, E. (Ed.) (1993). *Obsessive-compulsive related disorders*. Washington, DC: American Psychiatric Press.

Huneke, M. E. (2005). The face of the un-consumer: An empirical examination of the practice of voluntary simplicity in the United States. *Psychology and Marketing*, *22*, 257–550.

Ikeuchi, H., Fujihara, T., & Dohi, I. (2000). Involuntary loss of the extended self: Survey results on the loss of important possessions by a great earthquake. *Japanese Journal of Social Psychology*, *16*, 27–38.

Inglehart, R. (2006). Political culture. In J. R. Baldwin, S. L. Faulkner, M. L. Hecht, L. Michael, & S. L. Lindsley (Eds.), *Redefining culture: Perspectives across the disciplines* (pp. 127–135). Mahwah, NJ: Lawrence Erlbaum Associates.

Interactive Media in Retail Group (2004). Women shoppers are taking over the internet. Last accessed 17 September 2004 at http://www.imrg.org/IMRG/press.nsf/

Internet Statistics Compendium (2006). Sample April 2006. Last accessed 29 June 2006 at http://www.e-consultancy.com/publications/internet-stats-compendium/

Irving, L. M. (1990). Mirror images: Effects of the standard of beauty on the self- and body-esteem of women exhibiting varying levels of bulimic symptoms. *Journal of Social and Clinical Psychology*, *9*, 230–242.

Irving, L. M., & Berel, S. R. (2001). Comparison of media-literacy programs to strengthen college women's resistance to media images. *Psychology of Women Quarterly*, *25*, 103–111.

James, W. (1981/1890). The consciousness of self. In *Principles of psychology: Vol. 1* (pp. 279–379). Cambridge, MA: Harvard University Press.

Janković, J. (2006). Materialistic values, value conflict and subjective well-being in a cross-cultural context. D. Phil thesis, University of Sussex, UK.

Janković, J., & Dittmar, H. (2006). The componential nature of materialistic values and subjective well-being: A comparison of students in Croatia, Germany and the UK. In A. Delle Fave (Ed.), *Dimensions of well-being: Research and intervention* (pp. 34–52). Milano: Franco Angeli.

Joshi, R., Herman, C. P., & Polivy, J. (2004). Self-enhancing effects of exposure to thin body images. *International Journal of Eating Disorders*, *35*, 333–341.

Journal of Industrial Economics (2001). Special issue on e-commerce. *49*, 415–558.

Jupiter MMXI (2000). WebMilestones Oct 1999–Sept 2001: Two years in the evolution of the internet in the UK. Available at http://uk.jupiter.mmxi.com/xp/uk/press/releases/

Kahle, L. R., & Homer, P. M. (1985). Physical attractiveness of the celebrity endorser: A social adaptation perspective. *Journal of Consumer Research*, *11*, 954–961.

Kahnemann, D., Krueger, A., Schkade, D., Schwarz, N., & Stone, A. (2004). A survey method for characterizing daily life experience: The day reconstruction method. *Science, 306*, 1776–1780.

Kalkbrenner, P. (2004). Advertising damages mental health. Portland Independent Media Centre. Last accessed 4 July 2006 at http://portland.indymedia.org/en/2004/06/290078.shtml

Kalodner, C. R. (1997). Media influences on male and female non-eating disordered college students: A significant issue. *Eating Disorders: The Journal of Treatment and Prevention, 5*, 47–57.

Kalymum, M. (1985). The prevalence of factors influencing decisions among elderly women concerning household possessions during relocation. *Journal of Housing for the Elderly, 3*, 81–99.

Kamptner, N. (1991). Personal possessions and their meanings: A life-span perspective. In F. W. Rudmin (Ed.), *To have possessions: A handbook on ownership and property*. Special issue of the *Journal of Social Behavior and Personality, 6*, 209–228.

Kasser, T. (2002). *The high price of materialism*. Cambridge, MA: MIT Press.

Kasser, T. (2005). Frugality, generosity, and materialism in children and adolescents. In K. A. Moore & L. H. Lippman (Eds.), *What do children need to flourish? Conceptualizing and measuring indicators of positive development* (pp. 357–373). New York: Springer.

Kasser, T., & Ahuvia, A. (2002). Materialistic values and well-being in business students. *European Journal of Social Psychology, 32*, 137–146.

Kasser, T., Cohn, S., Kanner, A. D., & Ryan, R. M. (in press). Some costs of American corporate capitalism: A psychological exploration of value and goal conflicts. *Psychological Inquiry*.

Kasser, T., & Kanner, A. D. (Eds.) (2004). *Psychology and consumer culture: The struggle for a good life in a materialistic world*. Washington, DC: American Psychiatric Association.

Kasser, T., & Ryan, R. M. (1993). A dark side of the American dream: Correlates of financial success as a central life aspiration. *Journal of Personality and Social Psychology, 65*, 410–422.

Kasser, T., & Ryan, R. M. (1996). Further examining the American dream: Differential correlates of intrinsic and extrinsic goals. *Personality and Social Psychology Bulletin, 22*, 280–287.

Kasser, T., Ryan, R. M., Couchman, C. E., & Sheldon, K. M. (2004). Materialistic values: Their causes and consequences. In T. Kasser & A. D. Kanner (Eds.), *Psychology and consumer culture: The struggle for a good life in a materialistic world* (pp. 11–28). Washington, DC: American Psychiatric Association.

Kasser, T., Ryan, R. M., Zax, M., & Sameroff, A. (1995). The relations of maternal and social environments to late adolescents' materialistic and prosocial values. *Developmental Psychology, 31*, 907–914.

Kasser, T., & Sheldon, K. M. (2000). Of wealth and death: Materialism, mortality salience, and consumption behavior. *Psychological Science, 11*, 352–355.

Kasser, T., & Sheldon, K. M. (2006). Material and time affluence as predictors of subjective well-being. Unpublished manuscript, Knox College, Galesburg.

Katz, J., & Farrow, S. (2000). Discrepant self-views and young women's sexual and emotional adjustment. *Sex Roles, 42*, 781–805.

Kay, K. (2006). Are size zero models too thin for the catwalk? *Daily Mail*, September 18.

Kilbourne, J. (1994). Still killing us softly: Advertising and the obsession with thinness. In P. Fallon, M. A. Katzman, & S. C. Wooley (Eds.), *Feminist perspectives on eating disorders* (pp. 395–418). New York: Aronson.

Kilbourne, J. (2006). Jesus is a brand of jeans. *New Internationalist, September*, 10–12.

Kilby, R. W. (1993). *The study of human values*. Lanham, MD: University of America Press.

Killen, J. D., Taylor, C. B., Hayward, C., Haydel, K. F., Wilson, D. M., & Hammer, L. (1996). Weight concerns influence the development of eating disorders: A 4-year prospective study. *Journal of Consulting and Clinical Psychology, 64*, 936–940.

Koran, L. M., Faber, R. J., Boujaoude, M. A., Large, M. D., & Serpe, R. T. (2006). Estimated prevalence of compulsive buying behavior in the United States. *American Journal of Psychiatry, 163*, 1806–1812.

Kron, J. (1983). *Home-psych.: The social psychology of home and decoration*. New York: Clarkson N. Potter.

Kuhn, M. H., & McPartland, T. S. (1954). An empirical investigation of self-attitudes. *American Sociological Review, 19*, 68–76.

Kuther, T. L., & McDonald, E. (2004). Early adolescents' experiences with, and views of, Barbie. *Adolescence, 39*, 39–51.

Kyrios, M., Frost, R. O., & Steketee, G. (2004). Cognitions in compulsive buying and acquisition. *Cognitive Therapy and Research, 28*, 241–258.

Labre, M. P. (2005). Burn fat, build muscle: A content analysis of men's health and men's fitness. *International Journal of Men's Health, 4*, 187–200.

La Greca, A. M., & Stone, W. L. (1993). Social Anxiety Scale for Children Revised: Factor structure and concurrent validity. *Journal of Clinical Child Psychology, 22*, 17–27.

Langlois, J. H., & Downs, A. C. (1980). Mothers, fathers, and peers as socialization agents of sex-typed play behaviors in young children. *Child Development, 51*, 1237–1247.

LaRose, R. (2001). On the negative effects of e-commerce: A sociocognitive exploration of unregulated on-line buying. *Journal of Computer-Mediated Communication, 6*. [On-line]. Available at http://www.ascusc.org/jcmc/vol6/issue3/larose.html

LaRose, R., & Eastin, M. S. (2002). Is online buying out of control? Electronic commerce and consumer self-regulation. *Journal of Broadcasting and Electronic Media, 46*, 549–564.

Laumann, E. O., & House, J. S. (1970). Living room styles and social attributes. The patterning of material artefacts in a modern urban community. *Sociology and Social Research, 45*, 321–342.

Lea, S. E. G., & Webley, P. (1995). Psychological factors in consumer debt: Money management, economic socialization, and credit use. *Journal of Economic Psychology, 16*, 681–701.

Lee, S., & Mysyk, M. (2004). The medicalization of compulsive buying. *Social Science & Medicine, 58*, 1709–1718.

Leit, R. A., Gray, J. J., & Pope, H. G. (2002). The media's representation of the ideal male body: A cause of muscle dysmorphia? *International Journal of Eating Disorders, 31*, 334–338.

Leit, R. A., Pope. H. G., & Gray, J. J. (2000). Cultural expectations of muscularity in men: The evolution of Playgirl centerfolds. *International Journal of Eating Disorders, 29*, 90–93.

Lejoyeux, M., Adés, J., Tassian, V., & Solomon, J. (1996). Phenomenology and psychopathology of uncontrolled buying. *American Journal of Psychiatry, 153*, 1524–1529.

Lejoyeux, M., Haberman, N., Solomon, J., & Adés, J. (1999). Comparison of buying behavior in depressed patients presenting with and without compulsive buying. *Comprehensive Psychiatry, 40*, 51–56.

Lejoyeux, M., Tassian, V., Solomon, J., & Adés, J. (1997). Study of compulsive buying in depressed patients. *Journal of Clinical Psychiatry, 58*, 169–173.

Levine, M. P., & Harrison, K. (2004). The role of mass media in the perpetuation and prevention of negative body image and disordered eating. In J. K. Thompson (Ed.), *Handbook of eating disorders and obesity* (pp. 695–717). New York: John Wiley.

Levine, M. P., & Piran, N. (2004). The role of body image in the prevention of eating disorders. *Body Image, 1*, 57–70.

Lindstrom, M. (2004). *Brandchild* (revised edition). London: Kogan Page.

Linn, S. (2004). *Consuming kids: The hostile takeover of childhood*. New York: New Press.

Loken, B., & Peck, J. (2005). The effects of instructional frame on female adolescents' evaluations of larger sized female models in print advertising. *Journal of Applied Social Psychology, 35*, 850–868.

Lorenzen, L. A., Grieve, F. G., & Thomas, A. (2004). Exposure to muscular male models decreases men's body satisfaction. *Sex Roles, 51*, 743–748.

Lowes, J., & Tiggemann, M. (2003). Body dissatisfaction, dieting awareness, and the impact of parental influence on young children. *British Journal of Health Psychology, 8*, 135–147.

Lukes, S. (2005). *Power: A radical view* (2nd ed.). New York: Palgrave Macmillan.

Lunt, P. K., & Livingstone, S. M. (1992). Shopping, spending, and pleasure. In *Mass consumption and personal identity* (pp. 86–100). Milton Keynes: Open University Press.

Lyons, B., & Henderson, K. (2000). An old problem in a new marketplace: Compulsive buying on the internet. *ANZMAC "Visionary Marketing for the 21st Century"*, 739–744.

Magee, A. (1994). Compulsive buying tendency as a predictor of attitudes and perceptions. *Advances in Consumer Research, 21*, 590–594.

Maloney, M. J., McGuire, J. B., & Daniels, S. R. (1988). Reliability testing of a children's version of the Eating Attitude Test. *Journal of the American Academy of Child and Adolescent Psychiatry, 27*, 541–543.

Malson, H. (1998). *The thin woman*. New York: Routledge.

March, J. G. (1978). Bounded rationality, ambiguity, and the engineering of choice. *Bell Journal of Economics, 9*, 587–608.

Markus, H., & Kitayama, S. (1991). Culture and the self: Implications for cognition, emotion, and motivation. *Psychological Review, 98*, 224–253.

Markus, H., & Nurius, P. (1986). Possible selves. *American Psychologist, 41*, 954–969.

Maslow, A. (1954). *Motivation and personality*. New York: Harper.

Mattel (2003). Corporation website. Last accessed 19 November 2003 at http://www.mattel.com/our_toys/ot_barb.asp

McCracken, A. (1987). Emotional impact of possession loss. *Journal of Gerontological Nursing, 13*, 14–19.

McCracken, G. (1990). *Culture and consumption*. Indianapolis, IN: Indiana University Press.

McElroy, S. L., Keck, P. E., Harrison, G., Pope, M. D., Smith, M. R., & Strakowski,

S. M. (1994). Compulsive buying: A report of 20 cases. *Journal of Clinical Psychiatry*, *55*, 242–248.

McNay, L. (1994). *Foucault: A critical introduction*. Cambridge: Polity.

Mead, G. H. (1913). The social self. *Journal of Philosophy*, *10*, 374–380.

Mead, G. H. (1934). *Mind, self, and society*. Chicago, IL: University of Chicago Press.

Mehta, R., & Belk, R. W. (1991). Artifacts, identity, and transition: Favorite possessions of Indians and Indian immigrants to the United States. *Journal of Consumer-Research*, *17*, 398–411.

Mendelsohn, A. (2003). Girls love the Emme doll. *The Orlando Sentinel*. Last accessed 23 October 2003 at http://www.azcentral.com/style/articles/0101emmedoll.html

Mendelson, B. K., Mendelson, M. J., & White, D. R. (2001). The Body-Esteem Scale for Adolescents and Adults. *Journal of Personality Assessment*, *76*, 90–106.

Mendelson, B. K., White, D. R., & Mendelson, M. J. (1996). Self-esteem and body esteem: Effects of gender, age and weight. *Journal of Applied Developmental Psychology*, *17*, 321–346.

Mick, D. G. (1996). Are studies of dark side variables confounded by socially desirable responding? The case of materialism. *Journal of Consumer Research*, *23*, 106–119.

Mick, D. G., & Bühl, D. (1992). A meaning-based model of advertising experiences. *Journal of Consumer Research*, *19*, 317–338.

Mills, J. S., Polivy, J., Herman, P., & Tiggemann, M. (2002). Effects of exposure to thin media images: Evidence of self-enhancement among restrained eaters. *Personality and Social Psychology Bulletin*, *29*, 1687–1699.

Mitchell, J. E., Burgard, M., Faber, R., Crosby, R. D., & de Zwaan, M. (2006). Cognitive behavioral therapy for compulsive buying disorder. *Behaviour Research and Therapy*, *44*, 1859–1865.

Morahan-Martin, J. (1998). Males, females and the internet. In J. Gackenbach (Ed.), *Psychology and the Internet* (pp. 169–195). London: Academic Press.

Morrison, T. G., Morrison, M. A., & Hopkins, C. (2003). Striving for bodily perfection? An exploration of the drive for muscularity in Canadian men. *Psychology of Men and Masculinity*, *4*, 111–120.

Murray, S. H., Touyz, S. W., & Beumont, P. J. V. (1996). Awareness and perceived influence of body ideals in the media: A comparison of eating disorder patients and the general community. *Eating Disorders: The Journal of Treatment and Prevention*, *4*, 1, 33–46.

Musher-Eizenman, D. R., Holub, S. C., Edwards-Leeper, L., Persson, A. V., & Goldstein, S. E. (2003). The narrow range of acceptable body types of preschoolers and their mothers. *Applied Developmental Psychology*, *24*, 259–272.

Myers, D. G. (2000). The funds, friends, and faith of happy people. *American Psychologist*, *55*, 56–67.

Myers, D. G., & Diener, E. (1995). Who is happy? *Psychological Science*, *6*, 10–19.

National Bureau of Statistics (2003). Republic of Croatia. Last accessed 31 March 2003 at http://www.dzs.hr

National Statistics Online (2003). The UK. Last accessed 31 March 2003 at http://www.statistics.gov.uk

Neuner, M., Raab, R., & Reisch, L. A. (2005). Compulsive buying in maturing consumer societies: An empirical re-inquiry. *Journal of Economic Psychology*, *26*, 509–522.

Newcomb, A. F., Bukowski, W. M., & Pattee, L. (1993). Children's peer relations: A meta-analytic review of popular, rejected, neglected, controversial, and average sociometric status. *Psychological Bulletin, 113*, 99–128.

Newsletter of the Federal Courts (2004). Bankruptcy judges warn young consumers about credit card debt. Last accessed 4 April 2005 at http://www.uscourts.gov/ttb/feb04ttb/bankruptcy/

Nickerson, C., Schwarz, N., Diener, E., & Kahneman, D. (2003). Zeroing in on the dark side of the American dream: A closer look at the negative consequences of the goal for financial success. *Psychological Science, 14*, 531–536.

Ninan, P. T., McElroy, S. L., Kane, C. P., Knight, B. T., Casuto, L. S., Rose, S. E., Marsteller, F. A., & Nemeroff, C. B. (2000). Placebo-controlled study of fluvoxamine in the treatment of patients with compulsive buying. *Journal of Clinical Psychopharmacology, 20*, 362–366.

Nisbett, R., & Wilson, T. (1977). The halo effect: Evidence for unconscious alteration of judgments. *Journal of Personality and Social Psychology, 35*, 250–256.

Norton, K. I., Olds, T. S., Olive, S., & Dank, S. (1996). Ken and Barbie at life size. *Sex Roles, 34*, 287–294.

Observer Magazine (2006). The new India: An 84-page special issue on the world's next superpower. 26 November 2006.

Office of National Statistics (2004). Percentage of adults who have used the internet in the 3 months prior to interview by purpose of access (Great Britain). Last accessed on 17 September 2004 at http://www.statistics.gov.uk/statbase/Expodata/Spreadsheets/D6932.xls

Ogilvie, D. M. (1987). The undesired self: A neglected variable in personality research. *Journal of Personality & Social Psychology, 52*, 379–385.

Ogilvie, D. M., & Clark, M. D. (1992). The best and worst of it: Age and sex differences in self-discrepancy research. In R. P. Lipka & T. M. Brinthaupt (Eds.), *Self-perspectives across the lifespan* (pp. 186–222). Albany, NY: State University of New York Press.

O'Guinn, T. C., & Faber, R. J. (1989). Compulsive buying: A phenomenological exploration. *Journal of Consumer Research, 16*, 147–157.

O'Guinn, T., & Shrum, L. (1997). The role of television in the construction of consumer reality. *Journal of Consumer Research, 23*, 278–294.

Oliver, K. K., & Thelen, M. H. (1996). Children's perceptions of peer influence on eating concerns. *Behavior Therapy, 27*, 25–39.

Olivero, N. (2000). Consumption in electronic environments: Understanding new consumer's behavior. In E. Hölzl (Ed.), *Fairness and cooperation* (pp. 323–328). Proceedings of IAREP/SABE. Wein: Wein Universitätsverlag.

Orwell, G. (1949). *Nineteen eighty-four*. London: Secker & Warburg.

Oyamot, C. M. (2004). Me, myself, and mine: The incorporation of possessions into the self. *Dissertation Abstracts International (Section-B), 65*, 2149.

Ozgul, S., Heubeck, B., Ward, J. & Wilkinson, R. (2003). Self-discrepancies: Measurement and relation to various affective states. *Australian Journal of Psychology, 55*, 56–62.

Parker, J. G., & Gottman, J. M. (1989). Social and emotional development in a relational context: Friendship interaction from early childhood to adolescence. In J. T. Berndt & G. W. Ladd (Eds.), *Peer relationships in child development* (pp. 95–131). Oxford: Wiley.

Passman, R. H. (1976). Arousal reducing properties of attachment objects: Testing the functional limits of the security blanket relative to the mother. *Developmental Psychology, 12*, 468–469.

Pedersen, E. L., & Markee, N. L. (1991). Fashion dolls: Representations of ideals of beauty. *Perceptual and Motor Skills, 73*, 93–94.

Pew Internet & American Life (2002). Women surpass men as e-shoppers during the holidays. Last accessed on 19 September 2003 at http://www.pewinternet.org/reports

Pew Internet & American Life (2004). Internet activities. Last accessed on 16 September 2004 at http://www.pewinternet.org/trends/Internet_Activities_4.23.04.htm

Pew Internet & American Life (2006). Internet penetration. Last accessed on 11 June 2006 at http://www.pewinternetorg/datatrends/?NumberID=18

Pierce, J. L., Kostova, T., & Dirks, K. T. (2003). The state of psychological ownership: Integrating and extending a century of research. *Review of General Psychology, 7*, 84–107.

Pinhas, L., Toner, B. B., Ali, A., Garfinkel, P. E., & Stuckless, N. (1999). The effects of the ideal of female beauty on mood and body satisfaction. *International Journal of Eating Disorders, 25*, 223–226.

Polivy, J., & Herman, C. P. (2002). Causes of eating disorders. *Annual Review of Psychology, 53*, 187–213.

Polivy, J., & Herman, C. P. (2004). Sociocultural idealization of thin female body shapes: An introduction to the special issue on body image and eating disorders. *Journal of Social & Clinical Psychology, 23*, 1–6.

Pope, H. G., Olivardia, R., Gruber, A., & Borowiecki, J. (1999). Evolving ideals of male body image as seen through action toys. *International Journal of Eating Disorders, 26*, 65–72.

Pope, H. G., Phillips, K. A., & Olivardia, R. (2000). *The Adonis complex: The secret crisis of male body obsession.* New York: Free Press.

Popkin, R. H., & Stroll, A. (1993). *Philosophy* (3rd ed.). Oxford: Made Simple.

Posavac, H. D., Posavac, S. S., & Posavac, E. J. (1998). Exposure to media images of female attractiveness and concern with body weight among young women. *Sex Roles, 38*, 187–201.

Posavac, H. D., Posavac, S. S., & Weigel, R. G. (2001). Reducing the impact of media images on women at risk for body image disturbance: Three targeted interventions. *Journal of Social and Clinical Psychology, 20*, 324–340.

Prelinger, E. (1959). Extension and structure of the self. *Journal of Psychology, 47*, 13–23.

Prentice, D. A. (1987). Psychological correspondence of possessions, attitudes, and values. *Journal of Personality and Social Psychology, 53*, 993–1003.

Prentice, D. A. (2004). Values and evaluations. In M. R. Banaji & J. T. Jost (Eds.), *Perspectivism in social psychology: The yin and yang of scientific progress* (pp. 69–81). Washington, DC: American Psychological Association.

Radin, F. (2002). Value hierachies and structures. In V. Ilišin & F. Radin (Eds.), *Youth and transition in Croatia.* Zagreb: Institute of Social Research.

Raudenbush, B., & Zellner, D. A. (1997). Nobody's satisfied: Effects of abnormal eating behaviors and actual perceived weight status on body image satisfaction in males and females. *Journal of Social and Clinical Psychology, 16*, 95–110.

Reed, D. L., Thompson, J. K., Brannick, M. T., & Sacco, W. P. (1991). Development and validation of the Physical Appearance State and Trait Anxiety Scale (PASTAS). *Journal of Anxiety Disorders, 5*, 323–332.

Ricciardelli, L. A., & McCabe, M. P. (2001). Children's body image concerns and eating disturbance: A review of the literature. *Clinical Psychology Review, 21*, 325–344.

Richins, M. L. (1991). Social comparison and the idealized images of advertising. *Journal of Consumer Research, 18*, 71–83.

Richins, M. L. (1994). Valuing things: The public and private meanings of material possessions. *Journal of Consumer Research, 21*, 504–521.

Richins, M. L. (2004). The material values scale: Measurement properties and development of a short form. *Journal of Consumer Research, 31*, 209–219.

Richins, M. L., & Dawson, S. (1992). Materialism as a consumer value: Measure development and validation. *Journal of Consumer Research, 19*, 303–316.

Ridgway, N. M., & Kukar-Kinney, M. (2005). "Hi, I'm a compulsive buyer": A content analysis of themes from testimonial telephone calls at QVC. *Advances in Consumer Research, 32*, 431–436.

Rindfleisch, A., Burroughs, J. E., & Denton, F. (1997). Family structure, materialism, and compulsive consumption. *Journal of Consumer Research, 23*, 312–325.

Rintala, M., & Mustajoki, P. (1992). Could mannequins menstruate? *British Medical Journal, 305*, 1575–1576.

Ritzer, G. (1995). *Expressing America: A critique of the global credit card society.* Thousand Oaks, CA: Pine Forge Press.

Roberts, J. A., & Jones, E. (2001). Money attitudes, credit card use, and compulsive buying among American college students. *Journal of Consumer Affairs, 35*, 213–240.

Roberts, J. A., Manolis, C., & Tanner, J. F. (2003). Family structure, materialism, and compulsive buying: A reinquiry and extension. *Journal of the Academic of Marketing Science, 31*, 300–311.

Roberts, J. A., & Tanner, J. F. (2000). Compulsive buying and risky behavior among adolescents. *Psychological Reports, 86*, 763–770.

Rochberg-Halton, E. (1984). Object relations, role models and cultivation of the self. *Environment and Behavior, 16*, 335–368.

Rogers, A. (1999). *Barbie culture.* Thousand Oaks, CA: Sage.

Rohlinger, D. A. (2002). Eroticizing men: Cultural influences on advertising and male objectification. *Sex Roles, 46*, 61–74.

Rokeach, M. (1973). *The nature of human values.* New York: Free Press.

Rook, D. W. (1987). The buying impulse. *Journal of Consumer Research, 14*, 189–199.

Rose, N. (1996). *Inventing our selves: Psychology, power, and personhood.* Cambridge: Cambridge University Press.

Rosenberg, M. (1965). *Society and the adolescent self-image.* Princeton, NJ: Princeton University Press.

Rowlinson, K. & Kempson, E. (1994). *Paying with plastic: A study of credit card debt.* London: Policy Studies Institute.

Ruble, D. (1983). The development of social comparison processes and their role in achievement-related self-socialization. In E. T. Higgins, D. N. Ruble, & W. W. Hartup (Eds.), *Social cognition and social development: A sociocultural perspective* (pp. 134–157). New York: Cambridge University Press.

Ryan, R. M., Chirkov, V. I., Little, T. D., Sheldon, K. M., Timoshina, E., & Deci, E. L. (1999). The American dream in Russia: Extrinsic aspirations and well-being in two cultures. *Personality and Social Psychology Bulletin, 25*, 1509–1524.

Ryan, R. M., & Deci, E. L. (2000). Self-determination theory and the facilitation of intrinsic motivation, social development, and well-being. *American Psychologist, 55*, 68–78.

Santor, D. A., Messervey, D., & Kusumakar, V. (2000). Measuring peer pressure, popularity, and conformity in adolescent boys and girls: Predicting school performance, sexual attitudes, and substance abuse. *Journal of Youth and Adolescence*, *29*, 163–182.

Schachter, S. (1951). Deviation, rejection, and communication. *Journal of Abnormal and Social Psychology*, *46*, 190–207.

Scherhorn, G. (1990). The compulsive trait in buying behaviour. *Journal of Consumer Policy*, *13*, 33–51.

Scherhorn, G., Reisch, L. A., & Raab, L. A. (1990). Compulsive buying in West Germany: An empirical investigation. *Journal of Consumer Policy*, *13*, 155–189.

Schlosser, S., Black, D. W., Repertinger, S., & Freet, D. (1994). Compulsive buying: Demography, phenomenology, and comorbidity in 46 subjects. *General Hospital Psychiatry*, *16*, 205–212.

Schor, J. B. (2004). *Born to buy: The commercialized child and the new consumer culture*. New York: Scribner.

Schultz-Kleine, S. S., Kleine, R. E., & Allen, C. T. (1995). How is a possession "me" or "not me"? Characterizing types and an antecedent of material possession. attachment. *Journal of Consumer Research*, *22*, 327–343.

Schwartz, B. (2004). *The paradox of choice: Why more is less*. New York: HarperCollins Publishers.

Schwartz, B., Ward, A., Monterosso, J., Lyubomirsky, S., White, K., & Lehman, D. R. (2002). Maximizing versus satisficing: Happiness is a matter of choice. *Journal of Personality and Social Psychology*, *83*, 1178–1198.

Schwartz, S. H. (1992). Universals in the content and structure of values: Theoretical advances and empirical tests in 20 countries. In M. P. Zanna (Ed.), *Advances in experimental social psychology* (Vol. 25, pp. 1–65). Orlando, FL: Academic Press.

Sedikides, C., & Brewer, M. (Eds.) (2001). *Individual self, relational self, collective self*. New York: Psychology Press.

Sedikides, C., Schopler, J., & Insko, C. A. (Eds.) (1998). *Intergroup cognition and intergroup behavior*. Mahwah, NJ: Lawrence Erlbaum Associates.

Seid, R. P. (1994). Too "close to the bone": The historical context for women's obsession with slenderness. In P. Fallon, M. A. Katzman, & S. C. Wooley (Eds.), *Feminist perspectives on eating disorders* (pp. 3–16). New York: Aronson.

Shaw, S. M., & Kemeny, L. (1989). Fitness promotion for adolescent girls: The impact and effectiveness of promotional material which emphasizes the slim ideal. *Adolescence*, *24*, 677–687.

Sheldon, S., Greenberg, J. L., & Pyzszynki, T. A. (2004). Lethal consumption: Death-denying materialism. In T. Kasser & A. D. Kanner (Eds.), *Psychology and consumer culture: The struggle for a good life in a materialistic world* (pp. 127–146). Washington, DC: American Psychological Association.

Sheldon, K. M., Ryan, R. M., Deci, E. L., & Kasser, T. (2004). The independent effects of goal contents and motives on well-being: it's both what you pursue and why you pursue it. *Personality and Social Psychology Bulletin*, *30*, 475–486.

Siever, M. D. (1994). Sexual orientation and gender as factors in socioculturally acquired vulnerability to body dissatisfaction and eating disorders. *Journal of Consulting and Clinical Psychology*, *62*, 252–260.

Sirgy, M. J. (1985). Using self-congruity and ideal congruity to predict purchase motivation. *Journal of Business Research*, *13*, 195–206.

Sirgy, M. J., Grewal, D., Mangleburg, T. F., Park, J., Chon, K. S., Claiborne, C. B.,

Johar, J. S., & Berkman, H. (1997). Assessing the predictive validity of two methods of measuring self-image congruence. *Journal of the Academy of Marketing Science*, *25*, 229–241.

Slater, D. (1997). *Consumer culture and modernity*. London: Polity.

Smith, P. B., Bond, M. H., & Kagitcibasi, C. (2006). *Understanding social psychology across cultures: Living and working in a changing world.* Thousand Oaks, CA: Sage.

Snibbe, A. C., & Markus, H. R. (2005). You can't always get what you want: Educational attainment, agency, and choice. *Journal of Personality and Social Psychology*, *68*, 703–720.

Snyder, M., & DeBono, K. G. (1985). Appeals to image and claims about quality: Understanding the psychology of advertising. *Journal of Personality and Social Psychology*, *49*, 586–597.

Social Trends (1994). Volume 25. Government Statistical Service Publications. London: Her Majesty's Stationery Office.

Social Trends (2004). Volume 35. Government Statistical Service Publications. London: Her Majesty's Stationery Office.

Solberg, E., Diener, E., & Robinson, M. D. (2004). Why are materialists less satisfied? In T. Kasser & A. D. Kanner (Eds.), *Psychology and consumer culture: The struggle for a good life in a materialistic world* (pp. 29–48). Washington, DC: American Psychological Association.

Solomon, M. R. (1985). *The psychology of fashion*. Lexington, MA: Lexington Books.

Solomon, M. R., Bamossy, G., & Askegaard, S. (2002). *Consumer behaviour: A European perspective* (2nd ed.). Harlow, UK: Pearson Education.

South Asian Psychological Network Association (2005). Tsunami Manual for Mental Health Advocates and Providers. Last accessed 19 December 2006 at http://www.oursapna.org/tsunami%20manual.htm

Spencer, M. (2006). Thin! How women got devoured by the cult of skinny. *Observer Woman*, August, 24–30.

Spitzer, B. L., Henderson, K. A., & Zivian, M. T. (1999). Gender differences in population versus media body sizes: A comparison over four decades. *Sex Roles*, *40*, 545–565.

Sproles, G. B. (1985). Behavioral science theories of fashion. In M. R. Solomon (Ed.), *The psychology of fashion* (pp. 55–70). Lexington, VA: D.C. Heath/Lexington Books.

Srivastava, A., Locke, E. A., & Bartol, K. M. (2001). Money and subjective well-being: It's not the money, it's the motives. *Journal of Personality and Social Psychology*, *80*, 959–971.

Stanford, J. N., & McCabe, M. P. (2002). Body image ideal among males and females: Sociocultural influences and focus on different body parts. *Journal of Health Psychology*, *7*, 675–684.

Stanjek, K. (1980). *Die Entwicklung des menschlichen Besitzverhaltens: Materialien aus der Bilduungsforschung*. Berlin: Max-Planck-Institut.

Stapel, D. A., & Tesser, A. (2001). Self-activation increases social comparison. *Journal of Personality and Social Psychology*, *81*, 742–750.

Statistics Iceland (2005). Last retrieved on 1 August 2005 at http://www.hagstofa.is??pageid=634&src=/temp/vinnumarkadur/laun.asp

Stein, B. (1985). The machine makes this man. *Wall Street Journal*, June 13, 30.

Steiner-Adair, C. (1994). The politics of prevention. In P. Fallon, M. A. Katzman,

& S. C. Wooley (Eds.), *Feminist perspectives on eating disorders* (pp. 381–394). New York: Aronson.

Stern, P. M. (1997). *Fat history: Bodies and beauty in the modern west.* New York: New York University Press.

Stice, E. (1994). A review of the evidence for a sociocultural model of bulimia nervosa and an exploration of the mechanisms of action. *Clinical Psychology Review, 14*, 633–661.

Stice, E., & Agras, W. S. (1998). Predicting the onset and remission of bulimic behaviors during adolescence: A longitudinal grouping analysis. *Behavior Therapy, 29*, 257–276.

Stice, E., Schupak-Neuberg, E., Shaw, H. E., & Stein, R. I. (1994). Relation of media exposure to eating disorder symptomatology: An examination of mediating mechanisms. *Journal of Abnormal Psychology, 103*, 836–840.

Stice, E., & Shaw, H. E. (2004). Eating disorder prevention programs: A meta-analytic review. *Psychological Bulletin, 130*, 206–227.

Stone, G. P. (1954). City shoppers and urban identification: Observations of the social psychology of city life. *American Journal of Sociology, 60*, 36–45.

Stormer, S. M., & Thompson, J. K. (1996). Explanations of body image disturbance: A test of maturational status, negative verbal commentary, social comparison, and sociocultural hypotheses. *International Journal of Eating Disorders, 19*, 193–202.

Strauman, T. J., & Glenberg, A. M. (1994). Self-concept and body image disturbance: Which self-beliefs predict body size overestimation? *Cognitive Therapy and Research, 18*, 105–125.

Strauman, T. J., & Higgins, E. T. (1987). Automatic activation of self-discrepancies and emotional syndromes – when cognitive structures influence affect. *Journal of Personality and Social Psychology, 53*, 6, 1004–1014.

Strauman, T. J., Vookles, J., Berenstein, V., Chaiken, S., & Higgins, E. T. (1991). Self-discrepancies and vulnerability to body dissatisfaction and disordered eating. *Journal of Personality and Social Psychology, 61*, 6, 946–956.

Strelan, P., & Hargreaves, D. (2005). Reasons for exercise and body esteem: Men's responses to self-objectification. *Sex Roles, 53*, 495–503.

Stunkard, A. J., Sorenson, T. I., & Schulsinger, F. (1983). Use of the Danish Adoption Register for the study of obesity and thinness. In S. Kety, L. P. Rowland, R. L. Sidman, & S. W. Matthysse (Eds.), *The genetics of neurological and psychiatric disorder* (pp. 115–120). New York: Raven Press.

Sutton-Smith, B. (1997). *The ambiguity of play.* Cambridge, MA: Harvard University Press.

Szymanski, M. L., & Cash, T. F. (1995). Body-image disturbances and self-discrepancy theory: Expansion of the Body-Image Ideals Questionnaire. *Journal of Social and Clinical Psychology, 14*, 143–146.

Tajfel, H. (Ed.) (1984). *The social dimension: Vols. 1 and 2.* Cambridge: Cambridge University Press.

Tangney, J. P., Niedenthal, P. M., Covert, M. V., & Barlow, D. H. (1998). Are shame and guilt related to distinct self-discrepancies? A test of Higgins's (1987) hypotheses. *Journal of Personality and Social Psychology, 75*, 1, 256–268.

Thompson, J. K. (Ed.) (2004). *Handbook of eating disorders and obesity.* Washington, DC: American Psychological Association Press.

Thompson, J. K., Heinberg, L. J., Altabe, M., & Tantleff-Dunn, S. (1999). *Exacting beauty: Theory, assessment, and treatment of body image disturbance.* Washington, DC: American Psychological Association.

Thompson, J. K., & Stice, E. (2001). Thin-ideal internalization: Mounting evidence for a new risk factor for body-image disturbance and eating pathology. *Current Directions in Psychological Science, 10,* 181–183.

Tian, K. T., Bearden, W. O., & Hunter, G. L. (2001). Consumers' need for uniqueness: Scale development and validation. *Journal of Consumer Research, 28,* 50–66.

Tiggemann, M. (2006). The role of media exposure in adolescent girls' body dissatisfaction and drive for thinness: Prospective results. *Journal of Social and Clinical Psychology, 25,* 523–541.

Tiggemann, M., & Pickering, A. S. (1996). Role of television in adolescent women's body dissatisfaction and drive for thinness. *International Journal of Eating Disorders, 20,* 199–203.

Trampe, D., Stapel, D. A., & Siero, F. W. (2007). On models and vases: Body dissatisfaction and social comparison effects. *Journal of Personality and Social Psychology, 92,* 106–118.

Turkel, A. R. (1998). All about Barbie: Distortions of a transitional object. *Journal of the American Academy of Psychoanalysis, 26,* 165–177.

UCLA Internet Report (2003). "Surveying the Digital Future" Year Three. Last accessed on 19 September 2003 at http://ccp.ucla.edu/pages/internet-report.asp

Underhill, P. (2004). *Call of the mall.* New York: Simon and Schuster.

Urberg, K. A. (1999). Introduction: Some thoughts about studying the influence of peers on children and adolescents. *Merrill Palmer Quarterly, 45,* 1–12.

Valence, G., d'Astous, A., & Fortier, L. (1988). Compulsive buying: Concept and measurement. *Journal of Consumer Policy, 11,* 419–433.

Van Boven, L., & Gilovich, T. (2003). To do or to have? That is the question. *Journal of Personality and Social Psychology, 85,* 1193–1202.

Van den Bogaard, J., & Wiegman, O. (1991). Property crime victimization: The effectiveness of police services for victims of residential burglary. In F. W. Rudmin (Ed.), *To have possessions: A handbook on ownership and property.* Special issue of the *Journal of Social Behavior and Personality, 6,* 329–362.

Van Strien, T., Frijiter, J. E. R., Bergers, G. P. A., & Defares, P. B. (1986). The Dutch Eating Behavior Questionnaire (DEBQ) for assessment of restrained, emotional, and external eating behavior. *International Journal of Eating Disorders, 5,* 295–315.

Veblen, T. (1899). *The theory of the leisure class.* New York: McMillan.

Verplanken, B., & Herabadi, A. (2001). Individual differences in impulse buying tendency: Feeling and no thinking. *European Journal of Personality, 15,* 72–83.

Vignoles, V. L., Regalia, C., Manzi, C., Golledge, J., & Scabini, E. (2006). Beyond self-esteem: The influence of multiple motives on identity construction. *Journal of Personality and Social Psychology, 90,* 308–333.

Wallendorf, M., & Arnould, E. J. (1988). My favourite things: A cross-cultural inquiry into object attachment, possessiveness and social linkage. *Journal of Consumer Research, 14,* 531–547.

Wapner, S., Demick. J., & Redondo, J. P. (1990). Cherished possessions and adaptation of older people to nursing homes. *International Journal of Aging and Human Development, 31,* 219–235.

Watling, D., & Banerjee, R. (in press a). Children's differentiation between ingratiation and self-promotion. *Social Development.*

Watling, D., & Banerjee, R. (in press b). Children's understanding of modesty in front of peer and adult audiences. *Infant and Child Development*.

Watson, D., Clark, L., & Tellegen, A. (1988). Development and validation of brief measures of positive and negative affect: The PANAS scales. *Journal of Personality and Social Psychology, 54*, 1063–1070.

Watson, J. J. (2003). The relationship of materialism to spending tendencies, saving, and debt. *Journal of Economic Psychology, 24*, 723–739.

Weilage, M., & Hope, D. A. (1999). Self-discrepancy in social phobia and dysthymia. *Cognitive Therapy and Research, 23*, 6, 637–650.

Wells, W. D. (Ed.) (1997). *Measuring advertising effectiveness*. Hillsdale, NJ: Lawrence Erlbaum Associates.

White, R. W. (1959). Motivation reconsidered: The concept of competence. *Psychological Review, 66*, 297–333.

Wicklund, R. A., & Gollwitzer, P. M. (1982). *Symbolic self-completion*. Hillsdale, NJ: Lawrence Erlbaum Associates.

Williams, G. C., Cox, E. M., Hedberg, V. A., & Deci, E. L. (2000). Extrinsic life goals and health-risk behaviors in adolescents. *Journal of Applied Social Psychology, 30*, 1756–1771.

Winnicott, D. W. (1953). Transitional objects and transitional phenomena: A study of the first not-me possession. *International Journal of Psycho-Analysis, 24*, 89–97.

Wirtz, P. W., & Harrell, A. V. (1987). Assaultive versus nonassaultive victimisation: A profile analysis of psychological response. *Journal of Interpersonal Violence, 2*, 264–277.

Wiseman, C. V., Gray, J. J., Mosimann, J. E., & Ahrens, A. H. (1992). Cultural expectations of thinness in women – an update. *International Journal of Eating Disorders, 11*, 85–89.

Wolf, N. (1991). *The beauty myth: How images of beauty are used against women*. New York: Morrow.

Wolfe, W. L., & Maisto, S. A. (2000). The effect of self-discrepancy and discrepancy salience on alcohol consumption. *Addictive Behaviors, 25*, 283–288.

Wong, N., Rindfleisch, A., & Burroughs, J. E. (2003). Do reverse-worded items confound measures of cross-cultural consumer research? The case of the material values scale. *Journal of Consumer Research, 30*, 72–91.

Wood, J. V. (1989). Theory and research concerning social comparisons of personal attributes. *Psychological Bulletin, 106*, 2, 231–248.

Woodfield, R. (2000). *Women, work and computing*. Cambridge: Cambridge University Press.

World Peace Book of Prayers for Hurricane Katrina Victims (2006). Last accessed 14 January 2007 at http://www.worldpeace.org/guest/katrina_book.html

Wright, N. D., Claiborne, C. B., & Sirgy, M. J. (1992). The effects of product symbolism on consumer self-concept. *Advances in Consumer Research, 19*, 311–318.

Wright, N. D., & Larsen, V. (1993). Materialism and life satisfaction: A meta-analysis. *Journal of Consumer Satisfaction, Dissatisfaction, and Complaining Behavior, 6*, 158–165.

Yamamiya, Y., Cash, T. F., Melnyk, S. E., Posavac, H. D., & Posavac, S. S. (2005). Women's exposure to thin-and-beautiful media images: Body image effects of media-ideal internalization and impact-reduction interventions. *Body Image, 2*, 74–80.

Young, C. (2000). Does the media dictate beauty standards? Last accessed 13 January 2007 at http://www.drkoop.com/fami. . .ns/features/body_standards.html

Zaninotto, P., Wardle, H., Stamatakis, E., Mindell, J., & Head, J. (2006). Forecasting obesity to 2010. Report for the UK Department of Health. Last accessed 30 August 2006 at http://www.dh.gov.uk/PublicationsAndStatistics/Publications/PublicationsStatistics/PublicationsStatisticsArticle/fs/en?CONTENT_ID=4138630&chk=XVZ/60

Zimbardo, P. (2007). *The Lucifer effect: Understanding how good people turn evil.* New York: Random House.

Zukin, S., & Maguire, J. S. (2004). Consumers and consumption. *Annual Review of Sociology, 30,* 173–197.

Notes

1 This paper also reports data from Greek students, which are excluded from the summary given here.
2 Discount rates were calculated, according to the standard formula (e.g. Benzion, Rapoport, & Yagil, 1989), as $r = (v_d/v_o)^{1/d} - 1$, where v_d is the amount of money that the respondent entered as a "compensation price" for having to wait, v_o is the magnitude of the immediate (voucher) money value, and d is the delay in days between the two.
3 There were no significant results with respect to family values, which are probably less relevant to students than to adults in later life.
4 For this study, due to length constraints, only the findings with respect to community values are reported, so that they can be compared to the student findings.
5 The average monthly income nationally for the occupational groups represented by the Icelandic sample was 286,617 kronur in the last quarter of the 2004 (Statistics Iceland, 2005). Based on an exchange rate of 1 GBP = 120 ISK, the average yearly income of the Islandic sample equates to £30,080.
6 Group differences can be tested statistically through imposing equality constraints concerning the strength of particular paths, and observing the effect of these constraints on model fit. A statistically significant difference in path strength is confirmed when the equality constraint produces a significant deterioration in model fit.
7 As a consequence, four items of the 15-item MVS were dropped; two that referred to buying rather than owning goods, and two that had low item-total correlations (see Dittmar, 2005a, for details).
8 These two studies had used a five-point response format; these mean scores were adjusted to the six-point response format used in Study 1 to make them comparable.
9 The analysis with younger adults was reported in Dittmar (2005b).
10 This article also examined emotional eating, and compared appearance-related self-discrepancies from a person's own standpoint with those from the standpoint of a romantic partner, i.e. individuals' beliefs about their partner would ideally like them to look like. Effects for emotional eating, related to bulimic symptoms, occurred only with respect to self-discrepancies from the romantic partner standpoint, and are therefore not reported here.
11 Sample sizes for the different analyses ranges from 140 to 319, depending on completion of coding at that stage.
12 Two independent raters coded all self-discrepancy statements into these 11 categories, and the initial agreement was 94%. Disagreements were resolved by discussion.
13 I am grateful to Monica Greco for this interesting observation, according to whom

the internal tension is between liberal-democratic governments as merely the facilitators of a "free" space wherein values "freely" compete and are "freely" chosen (the analogy with what happens in a market, as distinct from a polity, is not coincidental), while promoting particular values or forms of behaviour, such as telling people what to eat, how to live, and possibly what to believe.

Author index

Subject index